LORD ELG[...]
AND THE MAR[...]

WILLIAM ST. CLAIR is the author of *That Greece Might Still be Free*, awarded the Heinemann Prize by the Royal Society of Literature, and of other works about the age of Byron and Shelley on which he is a leading scholar. In 1981–2 he was Visiting Fellow at All Souls College, Oxford.

William St. Clair

LORD ELGIN
AND
THE MARBLES

Oxford   New York

OXFORD UNIVERSITY PRESS

1983

Oxford University Press, Walton Street, Oxford OX2 6DP

London Glasgow New York Toronto
Delhi Bombay Calcutta Madras Karachi
Kuala Lumpur Singapore Hong Kong Tokyo
Nairobi Dar es Salaam Cape Town
Melbourne Auckland
and associated companies in
Beirut Berlin Ibadan Mexico City Nicosia

Oxford is a trade mark of Oxford University Press

First published 1967 by Oxford University Press
First issued, with revisions, as an Oxford University Press
paperback 1983

British Library Cataloguing in Publication Data

St. Clair, William
Lord Elgin and the marbles.—(Oxford paperbacks)
1. Elgin marbles
I. Title
733'.3'09385   NB92
ISBN 0-19-285140-3

Printed in Great Britain by
Richard Clay (The Chaucer Press) Ltd.
Bungay, Suffolk

Preface

By far my greatest debt of gratitude is to Mrs. A. C. Longland of Abingdon who unreservedly made me a present of a collection of papers which belonged to her great-grand-uncle, Dr. Philip Hunt. These papers first aroused my interest in Lord Elgin's embassy. I am also particularly indebted to Lord Bruce who not only allowed me to examine the collections of papers about Lord Elgin at Broomhall but told me many interesting stories about his great-great-grandfather.

I owe thanks to the Council of the Royal Institute of British Architects for allowing me to quote from the manuscripts of Sir Robert Smirke; to the Trustees of the British Museum for permission to quote from the collections of Additional and Egerton Manuscripts; to the Trustees of the National Library of Scotland for permission to quote from their manuscript collection; to Lord Barrington and the Curator of the Ipswich and East Suffolk Record Office for permission to quote from the manuscripts of J. D. Carlyle; and to the Controller of Her Majesty's Stationery Office for use of Crown Copyright material in the Public Record Office and the Scottish Record Office.

I should like to thank Macmillan and Co. Ltd. and the Trustees of the Hardy Estate for permission to quote from *The Collected Poems of Thomas Hardy*; John Murray for permission to quote from *The Letters of Mary Nisbet, Lord Byron's Correspondence*, and *Byron, A Self-Portrait*; the Council of the Navy Records Society for permission to quote from *The Keith Papers*; and Odhams Books Ltd. for permission to quote from the *Dictionary of British Sculptors*.

For permission to reproduce illustrations I am indebted to the Trustees of the British Museum, the Victoria and Albert Museum, the Greater London Council and the Athenian newspaper *Tachydromos*.

Among the libraries which have helped me I should like to mention particularly the Gennadios Library at Athens, the Joint Library of the Hellenic and Roman Societies, and the Library of Lambeth Palace. I am indebted to several departments of the British Museum and especially to Mr. D. E. L. Haynes, the Keeper of Greek and Roman Antiquities. For advice and help on particular points I should like to record my gratitude to the late J. Christopher Herold, to Professor Leslie A. Marchand, Professor C. W. J. Eliot, Mr. David Charman, Frau Margrit Velte, Professor Michael Lewis and Dr. İlhan Özdil. Mrs. Anna Picken has given me valuable help in elucidating and translating documents in modern Greek.

W. L. St. C.

November 1966

Note to the New Edition

APART from the correcting of a number of misprints and minor factual errors, the text of the new edition is mainly a reprint of the first. I have however written a new and enlarged Epilogue which takes account of recent developments in the controversy. Some of the illustrations have also been changed, and I am glad to be able to include reproductions of an interesting water-colour of the Parthenon by Lusieri, and of a drawing by Ittar, another of Lord Elgin's artists, which shows an unusual display of tight-rope walking in Athens in 1800. I am grateful to the Trustees of the National Gallery of Scotland and to Mr. Rodney Searight for permission to reproduce these.

Nothing has occurred since the publication of the first edition to make me wish to alter the historical account, and although there are matters of style which I should have preferred to update (e.g. the use of latinized names for some of the monuments) it has not seemed essential to do so. The publication in the *Journal of Hellenic Studies*, 1972, of extracts from the manuscript diary of

William Gell further confirms the description of how Hunt stretched the terms of the firman given in Chapter 9; Leslie A. Marchand's edition of the *Letters and Journals of Lord Byron* brings together letters which were previously scattered in separate publications; and Frank Brommer's three books (*Die Skulpturen der Parthenon-Giebel*, Mainz, 1963; *Die Metopen des Parthenon*, Mainz, 1967; and *Der Parthenonfries*, Mainz, 1977) consolidate recent scholarship on the Parthenon sculptures.

June 1983   W. L. St. C.

Contents

Plates

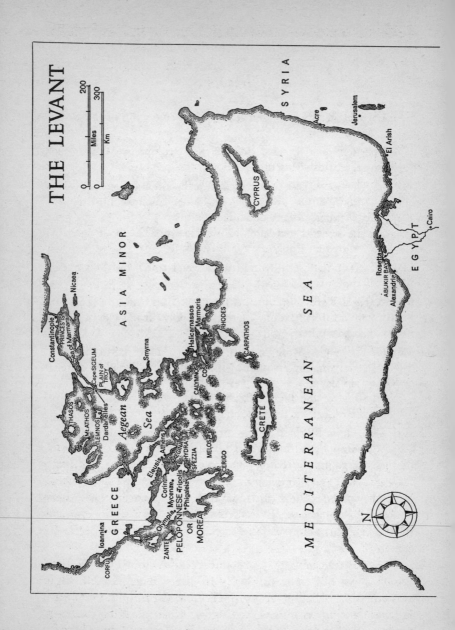

THE LEVANT

Chapter 1

An Embassy is Arranged

BRIGHTON in November is not everybody's idea of a holiday, but in November 1798 the Earl of Elgin had been advised to try warm sea bathing for the benefit of his health and to Brighton he had gone. While he was there he sent an unequivocal letter to the Foreign Secretary, Lord Grenville.

I regret extremely that the attention I am obliged to pay to the means recommended for the recovery of my health prevents my having the honour of waiting upon your Lordship and mentioning in a more satisfactory manner than by letter what I now beg leave to lay before you. . . . It has occurred to me as possible that it may be in your Lordship's intention to send to Constantinople an English representative equal in rank and situation to the Imperial and French Ministers at that Court. Should that supposition be founded I would venture to bring myself under your notice for that embassy. . . .

My health has, I confess, been one inducement with me for bringing forward the idea contained in this letter since I have much benefit to expect from a change of climate and a sea voyage.[1]

Lord Grenville thought Lord Elgin's idea an excellent one, discussed it with the King, and accepted it at once.[2] Within a few days[3] it was officially announced that Thomas Bruce, Seventh Earl of Elgin and Eleventh of Kincardine had been appointed Ambassador Extraordinary and Minister Plenipotentiary of His Britannic Majesty to the Sublime Porte of Selim III Sultan of Turkey.

The idea of going to Constantinople was not entirely Lord Elgin's own, but came originally from the King himself. Elgin was attending a ball given by the fleet at Weymouth in August. He was dancing with Princess Augusta when the King came up, made a joke, and led Elgin aside into a bow window. There he

explained that he thought the country should appoint an ambassador to Turkey and suggested that Elgin should apply for the post.⁴

Yet, unusual though the circumstances were of his appointment to Constantinople, Lord Elgin could certainly claim that he
had experience enough for such an office. Born into an ancient
and distinguished family, he had inherited the earldom while
still a boy and a splendid career had been open to him from the
first. After an extensive education in Britain and France he had
joined the army as an ensign in the Foot Guards. He passed
rapidly through the lower ranks and was soon in command of a
regiment which he himself had raised, the Elgin Highland
Fencibles. By the age of twenty-nine he held the rank of lieuten-
ant-colonel.⁵

Politics was the next profession he decided to try his hand at.
As a Scottish peer he did not have an automatic entry to the
House of Lords: he had to be elected as one of the sixteen representative peers. But this proved to be no problem. In 1790,
at the age of twenty-four, he applied to Henry Dundas who for
many years regulated all the parliamentary elections in Scotland.
Dundas was impressed and Elgin was duly elected.⁶ He took his
seat in the House of Lords and attended whenever his many other
duties allowed. He held the seat for the next seventeen years.

Elgin's diplomatic career started one year later when he was
twenty-five, almost by accident. The government was looking
for a man to go to Vienna at short notice to try to take advantage
of the accession of the new Emperor Leopold II. Dundas, impressed by the first speech that Elgin had made in the House of
Lords, offered him the job and Elgin accepted it eagerly. The very
same day Elgin was invited to dine with William Pitt, the Prime
Minister. After dinner, at which Elgin was the only guest, the
two men sat late discussing foreign affairs until at last Elgin felt
obliged to rise and go. On his way out Pitt said that the sooner
he left for Vienna the better, to which Elgin replied that he was
ready to go as soon as he had his written instructions. Pitt immediately sent for writing materials and drafted out instructions
there and then.⁷

Within twenty-four hours Elgin was on his way to Vienna as

Envoy Extraordinary from the British Government. He followed the new emperor on a tour of the Austrian territories in Italy exhorting him to transfer Austrian affections to Britain. Although he was largely unsuccessful he had established quite a diplomatic reputation by the time he returned to England in the summer of 1791.

The government then debated whether to employ him again, and Dundas wrote of him to Lord Grenville, the Foreign Secretary:

Although not very rich he is easy in his circumstances and would not with a view to emolument alone wish for employment. But if he can be creditably to himself employed in the public service it would give him pleasure to be so. He thinks himself perfectly safe in that respect in the hands of the present government. He will never urge you to anything nor will he ever bring forward any pretensions, but you will at any time find him ready to obey any call made upon the grounds I have stated.

As Dundas was writing this letter Elgin came into the room. Dundas read it over to him and Elgin, who was a good Tory, agreed that he had 'exactly delineated his sentiments'.[8] There was some discussion about which mission Elgin should be sent on. Berlin was suggested but Elgin did not fancy the place. He preferred Brussels as this would allow him to come back to England from time to time to pursue his political career in the House of Lords. To Brussels, therefore, he went as Envoy Extraordinary and he stayed there with frequent absences for two years. He acted as a kind of liaison officer with the Austrian armies which were trying to reconquer Belgium, and eventually left when the French invasion was clearly going to be successful.

It was not long before he had another important appointment. This time his dislike for Berlin was overruled: he was sent as British Minister Plenipotentiary to the Court of Prussia and stayed there for three years. At Berlin Elgin for the first time became thoroughly immersed in the intrigues of Europe, trying to bring Prussia into alliance with Great Britain. The more secret aspects of diplomacy in which he now found himself involved, came as rather a shock to him. He was surprised to learn that gathering intelligence was regarded as a normal part of his trade[9] and was horrified to discover that a British agent had been conducting separate negotiations with the Prussians without his knowledge.[10] Brought up in the days before the French Revolution when the nobility of Europe formed a close-knit club of like-minded men, Elgin's conception of his duties was already a little out of date. Nevertheless his straightforward approach to his task, although it impressed some as naïvety, brought him considerable success. He enjoyed greatly the pleasures and status of being an ambassador, although severe attacks of rheumatism already made visits to spas and watering places a frequent interruption to his social life in the capital. At Berlin Elgin's house provided lavish entertainment to numerous English visitors most of whom found him a congenial host and cultured companion, if a little cold.[11] One of his visitors was a young scholar and traveller called John Tweddell.[12] Tweddell became a great friend, but later Elgin was to wish that he had never existed.

When he heard that he was to go to Constantinople Elgin had every reason to expect that his career which had begun so brilliantly, was only just beginning. At the age of thirty-two he had already made his mark in the three professions open to a British nobleman, the army, politics, and diplomacy. Before setting about his preparations, he had another request to make to the Foreign Secretary. The Duke of Hamilton was very ill and said to be dying; when he was gone there would be a vacancy in the ranks of the Knights of the Thistle. Elgin, as soon as he heard the news, wrote to ask if he could be considered for the honour, but the Duke lingered on for another nine months and Grenville did not have to come to any decision.[13]

Elgin was still a bachelor. Since he had spent so much of his life abroad he had had few opportunities to find a wife. Perhaps his time at Berlin had shown him that bachelorhood was a disadvantage in an ambassador, although one of his visitors had complained that in the evenings Elgin's house was open to no one but 'a fair favourite, Madame Ferchenbeck'.[14] When he returned from Brighton to Broomhall, his magnificent new country house on the Fife side of the Firth of Forth, he did not take long to remedy the situation. Within a few weeks he had become engaged to marry a girl of good family from the other side of the Firth, Mary Nisbet of Dirleton.[15] She was twenty-one, a great beauty and a great heiress, then enjoying the delights of society life in Edinburgh. She seems to have hesitated a little before committing herself. Certainly it was a difficult decision to leave home and set out at once on a long journey in time of war to a largely barbaric land. But Elgin's qualifications were overwhelming and her family had no doubts. The rich Nisbets—their fortune was said to be £18,000 a year[16]—were happy to marry their daughter to a member of the nobility who was showing such promise. Elgin himself was so eager that he offered to give up his embassy,[17] but this sacrifice proved unnecessary and the marriage took place in March. Elgin wrote to the Foreign Secretary shortly before, asking him not to send him on the embassy too quickly as he wanted to get used to married life.[18]

The new Countess of Elgin was a rather silly girl, but full of good humour and intense interest in the exact details of everything and everyone around her. She was devoted to her parents and wrote them a series of cheerful gossipy letters about everything she did, confident, as an only child, that nothing she said about herself could fail to interest them. The parents promised to come and see her in Constantinople and this helped to make the departure from home more tolerable. Despite her good fortune, however, Lady Elgin remained just a little afraid of her grand husband. Eggy and Poll, as they called one another, seemed to be an ideal couple. They were undoubtedly in love and their affection continued to grow.[19] Yet, even from the beginning, the marriage had the suspicion of being one of convenience. The prospect of eventually adding the Nisbet estates to his own was of more importance to Elgin than he would perhaps have cared to admit. He was not a rich man and he was already in debt. He had pulled down the modest house in Fife which John Adam had built for his father and erected a bigger and more splendid country house, Broomhall, in its place. It was built by Thomas Harrison between 1796 and 1799 when Elgin was in Germany. To pay for this ambitious project and to help his diplomatic career Elgin had borrowed a large sum of money and was finding difficulty in meeting his bills.[20] With his marriage his money worries seemed to be over. Besides receiving at once a large marriage settlement, he could look forward in time to inheriting all the Nisbet fortune that was not bound by entail.

In the months that followed, Elgin began to select the staff to accompany him on his mission. For the embassy proper he decided to engage two private secretaries and a chaplain as well as numerous lesser servants and in all three he made an excellent choice. The first private secretary was William Richard Hamilton. He was twenty-two and this was the first step in a public career after his studies at Oxford and Cambridge. 'He has much good sense,' his sponsor wrote of him, 'and a great activity of mind; he is industrious and in the highest degree anxious to render himself useful. His manners are pleasing and his principles perfectly good so you may use him at once as your companion, your confidant, and your fag.'[21] Time was to bear out this judgement. The second private secretary was John Philip Morier, who was also twenty-two and in his first diplomatic post. He already knew something of the lands they were to visit and their languages since he had been born at Smyrna where his father was consul, and had lived there for some years before completing his education in England. He too was very well qualified for a successful public career.

The chaplain was the Reverend Philip Hunt, aged twenty-eight, a clergyman under the patronage of Lord Upper Ossory. He greeted his opportunity with enthusiasm, writing to his father:

As the Turks have now made a common cause with us to stop the progress of French desolation, it has been thought expedient by our court to send a *splendid* Embassy to Constantinople in order to enter into certain treaties for the mutual advantage of both countries. The Earl of Elgin is appointed Embassador Extraordinary etc. to the Porte, and by the interest of my worthy and excellent friend the Reverend Mr. Brand, Rector of Maulden, the situation of chaplain and private secretary to the Embassador will most probably be filled by me; . . . I have consulted Lord Ossory and my other friends here who all concur in describing it as a most brilliant opportunity of

improving my mind and laying the foundation of a splendid fortune . . .
I need only add that it is a situation to which the younger son of a
Nobleman might aspire; that it will be certainly attended with great
present advantages and most probably lead to an independent fortune.[22]

Hunt's hopes of acquiring an independent fortune and of raising
himself to the level of the younger son of a nobleman were soon
to be disappointed.

While he was making these preparations Elgin saw a good deal
of the architect, Thomas Harrison, who was still engaged on
putting the finishing touches to Broomhall. Harrison was an
architect in the Greek style who had made his reputation with his
design of Chester Castle. It was he who first put the idea to
Elgin which led eventually to the collection of the Elgin Marbles.
Harrison suggested that Elgin's embassy to Constantinople
presented a great opportunity of improving the knowledge of
Greek architecture in Great Britain. It was, he argued, now
admitted that the best models for classical architecture were in
Athens, and not at Rome where he and other architects in the
classical style had studied. Although the remains of the ancient
buildings in Athens were quite well known to architectural
students, and many of them had been drawn and published in
great detail, nevertheless, Harrison suggested, architects could
not be fired by mere books; what was needed were plaster casts
in the round of the actual objects.[23]

It was a sound suggestion with a modest aim, but Elgin took it
up with the enthusiasm of a crusader. Here was an opportunity,
he decided, of improving the whole level of artistic appreciation
in Great Britain. Architecture, sculpture, painting, even the design
of ordinary household goods, would all be improved. The
grandiloquence of his language is astonishing but he never
wavered from it. To make his embassy 'beneficial to the progress of the Fine Arts in Great Britain',[24] to bestow 'some benefit
on the progress of taste in England',[25] to improve 'the circumstances towards the advancement of literature and the arts',[26]
these were the sort of words he used, without apology, time and
again, to describe a plan to take some drawings and plaster casts
in Athens. There was no suggestion at all that the original

remains themselves should be removed. The almost universal acceptance in the late eighteenth century that the classical was the absolute standard of perfection in matters of taste can only partly explain this high ambition. Elgin's imagination worked on the grand scale.

A practical scheme was put to Lord Grenville that the government should equip the embassy with a professional artist and a number of men qualified to take plaster casts and make accurate architectural drawings. Elgin discussed the idea with Grenville, Pitt, and Dundas, but he was unable to transmit his enthusiasm. Their reaction was most discouraging. 'With respect to architectural pursuits,' Lord Grenville wrote, 'I really believe all has been done by travellers and the magnificent publications* of their discoveries that could reasonably be expected now, and I do not think that we could (at least from any funds at the disposal of the Foreign Department) defray with any propriety the expense of that encouragement which a person, qualified as you mention, would be entitled to expect for such an undertaking.'[27]

It was clear, therefore, that if anything was to be done in the artistic line it must be done at Elgin's own expense. He decided nevertheless to go ahead. The President of the Royal Academy, the venerable Benjamin West, was asked to advise, and for a few weeks Elgin's scheme was a favourite topic in and around the Academy.[28] Various eager young painters offered themselves, Thomas Girtin, Richard and Robert Smirke, William Daniell, but with none of them was Elgin able to arrange acceptable terms. Girtin later claimed that after hanging about Elgin's hall for many hours he was offered only £30 per annum—half as much as Elgin's valet—and that apart from his main task he was to assist Lady Elgin in 'decorating firescreens, work tables and other such elegancies'.[29] Then West suggested J. M. W. Turner, who was at that time only twenty-four and just beginning to make his name.

Turner was willing to go but his terms were too high. One of Elgin's conditions was that he should have the sole possession of every drawing and sketch that Turner should make and that

* Probably referring to Stuart and Revett. See below, p. 176.

Turner's leisure hours should be employed in giving drawing lessons to Lady Elgin. These were hard terms for a man who already considered giving lessons rather beneath him (he had been earning 5s. an hour) and whose main purpose in going would be to improve his own style by drawing from the classics. Turner demanded a salary of £400 per annum.[30] It was too much and the negotiation was abandoned. Elgin had missed his chance of engaging the greatest artist of the age. In describing this incident seventeen years later to the Select Committee on the Elgin Marbles, Elgin said: 'Turner . . . wished to retain a certain portion of his own labour for his own use; he moreover asked between seven and eight hundred pounds of salary, independently of his expenses being paid.'[31] No doubt Elgin's memory was at fault but one can hardly blame him. It must have been difficult in later years to imagine rejecting the great Turner for such a small sum. And it must have been equally difficult to imagine the great Turner, master of the sweeping landscape, deigning to reproduce for the benefit of architectural students the intricate niceties of Greek buildings.

Whether at £400 or £800 Turner was too expensive for Elgin. As Girtin's remarks show, he was thinking of something far less expensive. The reason for his apparent meanness was that he had been told by Sir Robert Ainslie, a former British ambassador at Constantinople, that his travelling painter, a German, had been paid only fifty guineas per annum and one of his conditions of service was that the whole of his works, drawings, pictures, and sketches should be Ainslie's sole property.[32] After these unfortunate negotiations with the Academy, therefore, Elgin decided that British artists were too expensive for him and postponed engaging someone until he should call at Italy on the way out.

Although the Government had been unsympathetic to Elgin's proposals to take artists and architects, they did agree to pay for a different kind of cultural speculation suggested by the Bishops of Durham and Lincoln. A story had long been current in Europe that the libraries of the East contained manuscripts of ancient authors unknown in the West. It was decided to attach to Elgin's embassy a scholar who would attempt to find them. To the classically educated statesmen of the time, the prospect of finding, say, the lost works of Livy was irresistible.

The man the bishops suggested for this task was Richard Porson, but, for some reason, the idea fell through. Porson, it is now recognized, was one of the greatest of classical scholars, and, as with Turner, it is tempting to guess at how his genius would have developed if he had gone to Constantinople. As he now exercised his Cambridge professorship mainly in a London cider cellar and combined drunkenness with a vile temper and disgusting personal habits, he is hardly likely to have been a success.[33]

In the end the man chosen was Joseph Dacre Carlyle, Professor of Arabic at Cambridge. Carlyle was a quiet scholarly man in holy orders who had spent most of his life at Cambridge. He had published several learned books on Arabic and had a taste for composing poetry.[34] To the public he was known, if at all, as the author of a proposal to convert the natives of Asia and Africa to Christianity by distributing to them a version of the Bible in Arabic, produced at the low price (for those days) of 12s. a copy.[35] He wished to pursue this scheme in the East.[36] Carlyle too had high hopes of making his fortune by his attachment to Elgin.[37]

Apart from the costs of paying for his staff which by the custom of the day he had to find for himself,[38] Elgin began to realize that his outlay on other things was greater than he expected. He was never slow at asking for favours and wrote again to Lord Grenville, in his usual unabashed way, to ask about his scale of allowances.

The arrangement rests entirely with you; I never did propose nor do I wish to propose anything on the subject. But I hope that the nature of my embassy, the assistance it is to hold out, at my expense, for researches of various kinds, the number of English officers naval as well as military who will naturally make my house their home, and the aid and support (always leading to much expense) which some Foreign Ministers in London assure me their governments expect from the English mission at Constantinople; these considerations, while they have guided me in the extent of my preparations, induce me to hope that your Lordship will put my embassy in point of appointments as well as in dignity on the footing of an extraordinary one.³⁹

After some negotiation Elgin's salary was fixed at £6,600 per annum plus certain expenses and Grenville steadfastly refused to grant him any more.⁴⁰ This was far less than Elgin had hoped for and, as things turned out, it was a pittance compared with the grandeur of his schemes.

Hunt, the chaplain, was the first to feel the effect. He arrived at London and found himself having to borrow from his family and friends. He wrote to his father:

I had fondly indulged the idea that from the instant my connection with Lord Elgin commenced, I should cease to be under the necessity of applying to you for money, but I have found a serious reverse, nor do I imagine I shall receive any part of my salary till after the conclusion of Our Embassy . . . I sincerely hope and I will use every exertion that the kindness of my friends may not be thrown away either by my indolence or ill conduct in a situation which certainly ought to lead to important improvement both for my instruction and emolument.

When Hunt set out he had only twelve guineas in his pocket.⁴¹

By August 1799, just nine months after the idea of the embassy was approved, the various members began to assemble at Portsmouth where the Admiralty had provided a warship, H.M.S. *Phaeton*, to take them to Constantinople. Elgin was already there when the news came through that the Duke of Hamilton had died. Although he had been made a Privy Councillor only a month before, Elgin was ever on the lookout for honours. He hastened to renew his application for the vacancy among the Knights of the Thistle that he had made when the Duke first fell ill. The *Phaeton* was held up by order of the Admiralty, he told Lord Grenville; there would just be time for the King to bestow the ribbon on him before she sailed. His request was not granted, the ribbon already having been promised.⁴² He put in another bid when the Duke of Queensberry fell ill the next year but was again unsuccessful.⁴³

The ship which the Admiralty had provided, H.M.S. *Phaeton*, was a frigate of thirty-eight guns under the command of Captain

Morris. She had only one deck, and as action could be expected on the voyage out, she could hardly be made comfortable. The party consisted of Lord and Lady Elgin, the secretaries Hamilton and Morier, the chaplain Hunt, McLean the physician, Carlyle the professor attached to the mission, Duff the courier, three personal maids for Lady Elgin, a few other female servants, and a number of Lady Elgin's dogs. The State room of the ship was divided into six compartments with green baize curtains. Lord and Lady Elgin had one each; the personal maids and other female servants had two; one was used as a mess; and the sixth was occupied by the five gentlemen (Duff was excluded). Hunt described the scene to his father:

In our little cabin twelve feet long, six broad and 6½ high were five beds, five gentlemen, 13 large trunks, 8 small do., 6 basons etc., 6 hats, 5 dressing gowns, 5 great coats and boat cloaks, 3 servants getting ready our shaving apparatus and a cabin boy brushing shoes; 5 foul cloathes bags, 4 portmanteaux, 2 pewter bottles, 2 lanterns, 2 umbrellas, a travelling library, brooms, supernumerary blankets, quilts, brushes, carpets etc. in most glorious confusion, and an Eighteen Pounder with its tremendous apparatus of carriage tackles, iron crow, balls and grape shot.[44]

Apart from the luggage carried aboard the *Phaeton*, Elgin had arranged for the heavier pieces to be sent on by merchantman. They included some carriages and pianos, numerous presents for the Turks, a complete set of ambassadorial gold and silver plate, and a great quantity of furniture. The merchantman also brought more servants, grooms, coachmen, and footmen.

By the beginning of September all was at last ready. Elgin had his last discussions with the Government and took his leave of the King. At one o'clock precisely on the 3rd Lord and Lady Elgin came aboard in the captain's barge to a salute of fifteen guns. The anchor was at once weighed and the embassy set sail.

Chapter 2

Great Events in the Levant

ELGIN'S instructions on the purpose of his embassy run to twenty-six pages, but, for the most part, they are both too wide-ranging and too limited to reveal the Government's intentions in appointing him. On the one hand he was to watch over the interests of His Majesty, promote trade, maintain British privileges and keep a watch for more, to protect all Christians 'particularly those of the reformed religion' and all the other generalities of the diplomat's rule book;* on the other hand Elgin was given certain specific objectives, to persuade the Turks to open the Black Sea to British trade, to obtain permission to cut timber there, to try to establish a British postal station at Suez and so on.[1] The main purpose of the embassy was, however, not stated: perhaps at the time it was too obvious. Elgin was to help in every way he could to expel the French from Egypt and the Eastern Mediterranean, and to keep the Ottoman Empire as friendly as possible to Great Britain. To explain the need for this we must go back to the beginning of 1798.

Early in that year the Directory, which was then the Government of France, appointed the successful young general, Napoleon Bonaparte, commander-in-chief of the 'Army of England', a force which had been assembled on the channel coast with the intention of invading Great Britain. Bonaparte made a quick tour of inspection of the staging areas and reported to the Government that the project was impossible. He suggested instead that the forces should be used to invade Egypt and his suggestion was at once adopted.

* In fact the Foreign Office used this part of the instructions as a draft for the instructions to another ambassador to Turkey nine years later.

In May a huge armada under Bonaparte's command set sail from Toulon, Genoa, and Ajaccio. It eluded the British warships in the Mediterranean and, without difficulty, captured Malta where the Knights of St. John of Jerusalem were still playing out the traditions of the crusades. Malta was proudly incorporated into the French Republic and a garrison was established. In the middle of June the armada set sail from Malta, again escaped the British warships which went hurrying past it on a foggy night, and arrived safely in Egypt six weeks later. Without much opposition the whole force was quickly disembarked.

Egypt at the time was nominally part of the Ottoman Empire, as indeed were most of the Balkans, the Middle East, and the North African coast. But any control which the Sultans at Constantinople had exercised over Egypt had long since vanished. The government, if government it could be called, was in the hands of the Mamelukes. These curious people had been originally mercenary soldiers brought from the Caucasus by the Sultans to help them keep down the Egyptians. First introduced to Egypt in the thirteenth century, they took over the government within a few years and remained in control for five centuries. They kept up their numbers and maintained their separateness by continuing to purchase young boys from the Caucasus for training as soldiers. The Mamelukes, still in 1798 numbering about 10,000, had spent their whole lives in military pursuits and were a formidable force.

The pretence of Turkish authority was, however, kept up most of the time. Whenever the Porte appointed a new Pasha of Egypt, he was met at Cairo by the Mameluke beys with impressive ceremony, and conducted to the citadel. There he lived in virtual imprisonment until his term of office was over, being used by whichever set of Mamelukes happened to control the citadel at the time as the legal authority for their excesses. The Turks had, of course, tried to re-establish their authority at various times but had always failed. Yet however much superior the Mamelukes were to any force the Turks could put against them, they were hardly a match for the French armed with modern European firearms and artillery. The Battle of the Pyramids (which took place a considerable distance from the pyramids) was a battle that French soldiers must dream of. They were decisively victorious with almost no casualties and the booty was enormous. Some days after the battle, the French made a conquerors' entry into Cairo with banners flying and bands playing. Bonaparte at once informed the French Government that their ancient dream had become a reality: Egypt was now a French possession.

The sudden French conquest of Egypt put the Turkish Government at Constantinople in a quandary. They certainly had no love for the Mamelukes and France was their oldest and safest ally. But they had no love for the principles of the French Revolution either and they were proud of being even the nominal rulers of Egypt. Ever since the sixteenth century France had been Turkey's staunchest friend and, as the Russians overran more and more of her vast empire in the north, she had taken comfort from having such a powerful ally. The latest war with Russia had been more disastrous than most and since then France's support had been lavish and practical. A strong French military mission was sent to Turkey to train up the Turkish forces into some kind of European military discipline; Turkish cadets were sent to the French military academy; French engineers built shore defences at the Dardanelles; and French constructors began to supervise the building of a modern Turkish fleet. The Comte de Choiseul-Gouffier who had been French Ambassador during this time had enjoyed a specially intimate relationship with the Ottoman Governments and, incidentally, as a token of gratitude, the Turks had allowed him to corner the antiquity market for France.

The audacity of the French policy towards the Porte is astonishing. The plan was this. At the very moment that Bonaparte was seizing Egypt, Talleyrand, the French Foreign Minister, would go to Constantinople and persuade the Turks that France was occupying Egypt in Turkey's own interest. If anyone could have put over this monstrous lie, Talleyrand was the man to do it. But Talleyrand had a genius for avoiding danger which was to keep him at the centre of power through the vicissitudes of the Revolutionary and Napoleonic periods and beyond. He had the sense to see that not even the Turks could be expected to swallow such a story and managed to delay his departure until it was safely too late.

While this procrastination was the salvation of Talleyrand, it put Ruffin, the French Chargé d'Affaires at Constantinople, in an acutely embarrassing position. When the French invasion fleet was well on its way across the Mediterranean, Ruffin was sent for by the Turkish Foreign Minister, and interrogated for three hours on what the purpose of the fleet was. Poor Ruffin, unlike the Turks, did not know anything about it: no one had bothered to tell him. All he could do was bumble out the usual diplomatic platitudes that, if there were such a fleet, it was certainly not intended against the Ottoman Empire with whom the French wished to maintain the friendliest of relations, etc. A week after this interview Ruffin discovered the truth. He was told by Talleyrand to persuade the Turks that the invasion of Egypt was not intended as an unfriendly act but as a service to help Turkey. Seldom has a diplomat been given a less convincing brief to speak to. Besides knowing in detail about the invasion plans, the Turks had also heard of the schemes circulating in France for the complete dismemberment of the Ottoman Empire. They knew too that Bonaparte had been interfering in their affairs by negotiating with other Pashas who paid as little heed to the government in Constantinople as the Mamelukes.

The Turks hesitated about what to do but they had little choice. On 6 August Ruffin was again summoned by the Turkish Minister. He was told he must remain within the walls of the French embassy, and if he had any communication to make to the Turkish Government he must call at night; all Frenchmen were to avoid showing themselves in public. 'When I took my leave from him,' said Ruffin in his report, 'I was given neither sherbet nor perfume nor handkerchief. The absence of the marks of honour confirmed my impression that I had not had a conference but a ministerial scolding.'² A month later, Ruffin was called yet again to the Turkish Foreign Minister. This time all the marks of honour were accorded and coffee was served. But this time the Turkish Minister was more strict. The Sublime Porte, he said, was pained to see an allied power seize without warning her most precious province, the navel of Islam. All diplomatic relations must be broken off at once. When coffee was finished the French minister was escorted by a military guard to the unsalubrious prison of the Seven Towers. A formal declaration of war followed a few days later. All Frenchmen in the parts of the Ottoman Empire over which the Porte exercised some control were arrested. They included a quiet antiquary living in Athens called Louis-François-Sébastien Fauvel who will appear later in the story.

The reason for the sudden stiffening of the Turkish attitude is not hard to find. On 1 August, even before Ruffin's scolding by the Turkish Minister, the British admiral Horatio Nelson had utterly destroyed the French fleet in one of the most brilliant naval battles of history. The Battle of the Nile (which was fought a considerable distance from the Nile) deprived the French army in Egypt of all means of returning home. Henceforth they were cooped up in Egypt and nothing the French Government could do was likely to rescue or reinforce them. To explain how the British managed thus to turn the tables so decisively on Bonaparte we must again go back to early 1798.

However ineffective the French 'Army of England' had appeared to Bonaparte, it had certainly not seemed so to the British Government. When Bonaparte was appointed commander-in-chief, fear approaching panic seized England. Measures were passed to erect barricades in the London streets with stores of hand grenades at each corner house; foreigners and suspected revolutionaries were interned in prison ships which could be immediately sunk at their moorings should the need arise; Habeas Corpus was suspended; the Volunteers drilled up and down the country; and Pitt the Prime Minister ordered a historical investigation into the preparations to meet the Spanish Armada to make sure nothing was overlooked. When the French force moved from the Channel to Toulon the panic relaxed somewhat, but the French continued to call it the 'Army of England' as a security precaution. The feeling among the British Government was that it was intended to invade Ireland. But they were quick to retaliate to the danger.

The British fleet had been withdrawn from the Mediterranean in 1796 and, to an outsider, it must have seemed extremely unlikely that ships could be spared to go there now when the British Isles themselves were threatened. No doubt Bonaparte counted on this. But the British Admiralty upheld the traditional naval principle that the first line of defence is the enemy's ports. Admiral St. Vincent, who was blockading Cadiz, was ordered to strain every nerve and incur considerable hazard by sending a squadron into the Mediterranean and he was advised to put it under the command of the promising officer Rear-Admiral Sir Horatio Nelson. St. Vincent had already come to the same conclusion even before his instructions from home arrived and Nelson had sailed. He was then thirty-nine, had been in the Navy since he was twelve and commanded ships since he was twenty. He had fought in every sea and had lost an eye and an arm in battle at different times. And, like Bonaparte, he considered that Almighty God had singled him out to be the instrument of His will.

When Nelson reached Toulon he found that Bonaparte had already gone. He at once set off in pursuit. There then followed a naval blind-man's-buff, with Nelson trying to guess where Bonaparte might be heading and rushing to try to cut him off. Nelson never did catch him before he reached Egypt although one night the fleets passed within a few miles of one another. Once ashore in Egypt Bonaparte thought he was safe. When Nelson suddenly attacked from the sea on 1 August, the French fleet was unprepared and it was completely destroyed. The whole balance of power in the Eastern Mediterranean was altered. With his usual skill Bonaparte persuaded the French government and the world that it was not his fault.

The Battle of the Nile and the subsequent Turkish declaration of war on France gave the British Government a wonderful opportunity of securing another ally and superseding France as the most favoured nation in the Ottoman Empire. They did not fail to take it. Hitherto Turkey had been regarded as a remote and unimportant country and Britain had not even bothered to maintain an official representative at Constantinople all the time. Instead they had been content to leave relations with Turkey in the hands of the Levant Company. The Levant Company was an English chartered company, which had been given exclusive rights in the British trade with the Eastern Mediterranean. It had been originally incorporated by Royal Charter in 1605 under the title of 'The Governor and Company of Merchants of England Trading to the Levant Seas' and since then it had been granted formidable privileges. It had the statutory right to appoint all British ambassadors, consuls and deputies in the Levant and to lay charges on its members—the 'Turkey merchants'—to support them. It had the right to impose fines, distrain goods, and send home under arrest anyone who offended against its monopoly. From time to time it ran its own fleet of warships. Although by Elgin's time the Levant trade had passed its peak, the company still supported consulates at Smyrna, Aleppo, Alexandria, Algiers and many smaller places, and it still maintained the fiction that it alone could appoint the ambassador to Turkey by formally electing the Government's nominee on the few occasions that the Government wished to interfere.[3] In 1799 the Government formally consulted the Levant company about Lord Elgin's appointment.[4]

The last British Ambassador to the Sublime Porte had been Robert Liston. He had left in 1794 and his private secretary, John Spencer Smith, an employee of the Levant Company, had been there ever since, first as chargé d'affaires and subsequently minister. Spencer Smith had satisfactorily conducted the affairs of the Levant Company and such diplomatic tasks as the Government gave him, when the French invasion of Egypt suddenly made his job one of the most important in the whole Foreign Service.

The Government decided to try to conclude an alliance with Turkey at once and Spencer Smith was told to start negotiations. But clearly his diplomatic task would be much easier if Britain could provide the Turks with some solid military help as well. This was quickly arranged. Brigadier General Koehler with seventy-six officers and men, mostly artillerymen and engineers, was sent from England to establish a British Military Mission and attempt the task of modernizing the Turkish forces on which the French had hitherto been employed. The Mission was accompanied by eighteen women and sixteen children.[5]

It was naval help, however, that Britain was best able to provide. Nelson had retired to Sicily (and the charms of Lady Hamilton) after the battle of the Nile and only a small squadron was left to blockade Egypt. The British Government had the excellent idea of sending out a dashing young naval captain to help the Turks. They chose Sir Sidney Smith who had the advantage of being the brother of John Spencer Smith.

Sir Sidney Smith was a sailor in the grand style, in the same mould as Nelson. He was then thirty-four and had been in the Navy since he was eleven; he had been promoted captain at the age of sixteen. He had fought in many battles in many seas during the American Revolutionary Wars but when peace came he had found the life of a naval officer too dull. During a war between Russia and Sweden he disobeyed Admiralty instructions and accepted an invitation from King Gustavus to be his naval adviser. He conducted the naval war personally from the King's yacht and was knighted for his services. On his return from Sweden, forgiven by the Admiralty, he was sent on a fact-finding tour of Turkey where his brother was minister. He spent several years exploring the harbours and tides of the whole coastline from the Black Sea to the Nile Delta and making himself thoroughly familiar with the Turkish Navy. When war between France and Britain broke out in 1793 Sir Sidney Smith was at Smyrna. He bought a ship at his own expense, collected a scratch crew of unemployed sailors, and sailed to join the British Mediterranean fleet. The French, with some justice, branded him as a pirate, but the Admiralty regularized his status and he took part in the burning of the port of Toulon. His next adventure was to be captured by the French as he was raiding their shipping near Le Havre and he was imprisoned in Paris. But before long he had escaped back to England.[6]

In deciding to send Sir Sidney Smith to help the Turks in 1798 the Government thought they had made a brilliant stroke. They reckoned, rightly, that his intimate knowledge of Turkey, his immense bravery, and extravagant flamboyance would appeal to the Turks and make up for lack of ships under his command. And they also reckoned, rightly, that the Turks might allow him to command their own fleet. But the Government was even cleverer, or as it turned out too clever. They decided to give Smith a diplomatic rank as well as a naval one. He was appointed 'Minister Plenipotentiary' jointly with his brother Spencer Smith to help his brother to arrange the treaty of alliance with Turkey. To give an active service officer a political as well as a military task is a hazardous proceeding at any time. To do so with a man who had made his reputation largely through dis-obedience was dangerous in the extreme. Nelson, for one, saw this immediately. He protested in the strongest possible language and threatened to resign and to take Sir William and Lady Hamilton home with him. But the Government insisted that the arrange-ment should stand. Nelson was soothed down despite a further disobedience of Smith in assuming, without authority, the rank of commodore. Sir Sidney Smith sailed through the Mediterranean with his one ship, the *Tigre*, and took up his station off the coast of Egypt to blockade the French. His success was so immediate and so tremendous that all was forgotten and forgiven.

Bonaparte, having conquered the whole of Egypt, led his army north against Syria. He captured Jaffa and one or two other towns, massacred their garrisons, and laid siege to Acre. Smith, with his usual gusto, flung himself into the battle. He landed men and guns from his ship and successfully resisted every attack that Bonaparte threw against the town. Bonaparte was compelled to give up the siege; he had suffered a major defeat and one which could not be concealed. The Egyptian expedition was now clearly doomed. Smith became a hero almost the rival of Nelson. The picture of Sir Sidney Smith standing with drawn sword in the breach at Acre seemed destined to become a romantic theme to compare with Wolfe at Quebec. The nation was in no mood to listen to criticisms: success in war is its own justification.

This then was the complicated situation into which Elgin had so eagerly thrust himself. Nelson was at Sicily with the Nea-politan court and the Hamiltons. General Koehler was somewhere in Turkey trying to help the Turkish army. One Smith brother, an employee of the Levant Company, was in charge of British affairs at Constantinople; the other, a national hero, was off the coast of Egypt holding both naval command and diplomatic rank. General Bonaparte and the French were in possession of Egypt but they had shown conclusively that they could not get out.

Chapter 3

The Voyage Out

W HEN the *Phaeton* left Portsmouth in September Lady Elgin was already two months pregnant, and it became clear before they had been long at sea that she was going to have an extremely uncomfortable voyage. She became sea-sick the second day out and nothing Dr. McLean could do succeeded in settling her stomach. It was decided, therefore, to stop for a few days at every suitable port of call to give her an occasional rest.[1] For everyone else the beginning of the voyage was remarkably pleasant. Captain Morris had obtained funds from the Government to entertain his distinguished guests and his table was always well supplied with fresh meat and good wine. He invited the ship's officers to dine in turn with the ambassador and his staff and the conversation was excellent.[2]*

Before long the strain of living in such a confined space produced some friction. Carlyle became Elgin's favourite and Hunt felt that he was not being treated as his rank entitled him.[3] He began to have second thoughts about the enterprise on which he had entered so eagerly, and wrote:

I began to ruminate on the novelty of my situation and I must own I felt somewhat of a depression of spirits, when I considered that I was entering into a new sphere of life in which talents might be required that I do not possess and attainments which I have neglected to acquire; in which I might not be so fortunate as to meet friends who would overlook my failings or interest themselves in my favour: in short that every moment was increasing my distance from my family and all my early connections and rendering personal communication with them impossible . . . that I might be weakening if not dissolving

---

* Captain Morris commanded a battleship H.M.S. *Colossus* at Trafalgar and eventually retired from the Navy as a Vice-Admiral. Among the lieutenants was Francis Beaufort, the famous hydrographer and inventor of the Beaufort scale.

attachments of those from whom I have received happiness and the most flattering marks of attention; and forming others which may be productive of little comfort or advantage.[4]

Morier, too, confided in his diary that he detected 'a great indifference on the part of Lord Elgin towards those most immediately dependent upon him'.[5] Already a certain coldness in Elgin's manner which was later to cost him the loyalty of many of his staff had begun to appear. His seriousness of disposition—partly caused no doubt by the pains of rheumatism from which he constantly suffered—contrasted sharply with the liveliness of his young wife. Another cause of misgivings among his entourage was that the Ambassador had now made it clear beyond all doubt that no one would be paid until the embassy was over. He stood by and allowed everyone on his party to pay their expenses and studiously avoided any mention of the subject of money.[6] However, the company accepted their bad luck, reconciled themselves to it, and put the subject of money out of their minds. Lisbon was reached without incident and after a few days rest Lady Elgin recovered her health.

A short distance out from Lisbon the *Phaeton* was joined in company by a fast American frigate. This caused Captain Morris great annoyance for the American consistently outpaced the *Phaeton*, but to the Elgins it was comforting to have another ship near by in case they were attacked. As they approached the Straits of Gibraltar the enemy could be expected and the ship was cleared for action.

On 20 September a sail was sighted and, instead of escaping in the other direction as might have been expected with so valuable a party on board, Captain Morris set off in pursuit. The chase lasted all day before the ship was overtaken and brought to with a shot across her bows. Unfortunately for the crew of the *Phaeton* who had high hopes of prize money, the ship turned out to be a neutral from Danzig and they had to let her go. The following day they chased another ship but she turned out to be another neutral—an American this time—and they had to let her go too.[7]

The next port of call was Gibraltar where the British garrison as at Lisbon were hosts and guides. St. Michael's Cave was specially lit for Lady Elgin to see, and several grand parties were held in honour of the Ambassador. The talk at Gibraltar was all about Nelson and Lady Hamilton and the Ambassador's party began to get excited at the prospect of meeting the great man when they reached Sicily. The rumour was circulating that Nelson was about to return to England with the King of Naples and the Hamiltons—perhaps a leak of Nelson's threat to resign in disgust at Sir Sidney Smith. But the general tenor of the stories was pretty near the truth. 'They say,' Lady Elgin wrote to her mother, 'there never was a man turned so *vain-glorious* (that's the phrase) in the world as Lord N. He is now completely managed by Lady Hamilton.'⁸

All too soon they had to leave Gibraltar, much to the misery of Lady Elgin. Neither calm nor storm agreed with her. She made an effort to attend the service on deck on the first Sunday at sea but it was no good. 'The calm I complained of so bitterly yesterday, was this morning succeeded by a brisk gale;' she wrote.

We have been going 8 and 9 notts an hour but the sea was very rough and the ship roled and poor Poll was exceedingly sick. However I contrived to dress myself very smart and attended the service on deck; it was almost too much for me and I was ill when I came down again; you never saw anything conducted with so much decency as it was, all the sailors nicely dressed and listening with the greatest attention.⁹

Lady Elgin was ill continuously for the next three days as the *Phaeton* made her way to Sicily, and lay in her cabin bathing her face in vinegar and expecting to die at any moment. At last, precisely a month after leaving Portsmouth, the *Phaeton* arrived safely, to everyone's great relief, at Palermo harbour. While, however, she was on her miserable voyage through the Western Mediterranean, another naval event, of greater importance, was occurring not far away.

After his repulse by Sir Sidney Smith at Acre, Bonaparte finally realized the hopelessness of the French position in Egypt and decided that he personally must escape before it was too late. He reported all his defeats as glorious victories to the French

Government and announced to the army in Egypt that he was
going on a tour of inspection. Instead of doing so, he waited
until a large part of the blockading British squadron was replen-
ishing in Cyprus and left Egypt secretly with four ships. He
sailed along the North African coast to avoid Sir Sidney Smith's
cruisers and then made a dash across the narrows to Corsica. On
30 September he must have passed within a few miles of the
Phaeton. A few days later Bonaparte sighted the French coast and
also a British fleet of twenty-two ships. The British admiral
mistook Bonaparte's squadron for some of his own ships and did
not give chase. As a result Bonaparte arrived safely at Fréjus
and, within a month, took over the government of France. Such
are the coincidences of history and such is the luck of great men.[10]

Of course the Elgins knew nothing of Bonaparte's flight when
they arrived at Palermo. They were much more interested in
meeting Nelson and the Hamiltons. As soon as the *Phaeton*
dropped anchor one of Lady Hamilton's servants came on board
to apologize for his mistress' absence because the Queen had sent
for her. But the next day the Elgins were settled in a magnificent
private palazzo near the Hamiltons' house, and were introduced
to the ménage.

Lady Elgin described the dinner party the first night ashore.

We dined with Sir William Hamilton and I had the satisfaction of
seeing her Ladyship and what is still more, heard her sing. I must
acknowledge she is pleasant, makes up amazingly, and did all she could
to make me accept of an apartment there, which I should have totally
to myself. However I did not in the least scruple to refuse her Ladyship.
She looked very handsome at dinner quite in an undress: my father
would say 'There is a fine Woman for you, good flesh and blood'.
She is indeed a Whapper! and I think her manner very vulgar. It is
really humiliating to see Lord Nelson, he seems quite dying and yet as
if he had no other thought than her. He told Elgin privately that he
had lived a year in the house with her, and that her beauty was nothing
in comparison to the goodness of her heart.[11]

Captain Morris was put to some embarrassment when he first
called at the Hamiltons' to see Nelson. He was met at the door by a
little old woman with a white bed gown and black petticoat.

Captain Morris took her for a servant, and rebuked her for inquisitiveness, before he was told that she was Lady Hamilton's mother. It was no doubt incidents like this that caused her to change her name from Duggins to Cadogan.

A few days later it was the birthday of the heir to the throne and the Court celebrated with a grand gala. In spite of the war and the loss of half of the kingdom to the enemy, they did not skimp. There was some difficulty about finding suitable clothes for Lady Elgin but she was prevailed upon to take part. She wrote:

It was out in a garden and everything completely Chinese, innumerable numbers of round tables very well served, and a vast quantity of attendants all dressed like Chinese; they say the fête cost £6000; the whole garden lit with coloured lamps, one of the avenues I dare say at least a mile long, quite full of lamps, it really outdid the Arabian Nights.[12]

Lady Elgin was to see more of the Arabian Nights in Turkey.

Sir William Hamilton is remembered nowadays chiefly as the husband of the famous Emma. But in his own day he had a great, and well-deserved, reputation as an antiquary. He had been Ambassador at Naples since 1764 and, ever since then, he had had a passion for collecting classical antiquities. Unlike almost all the collectors of the time his taste did not run to marbles or bronzes but to vases. At the time, the black and red Greek vases were still known as 'Etruscan'—because most had been found in Southern Italy—and were not highly thought of. Hamilton was one of the first to appreciate their true origin and recognize their worth and interest. By 1772 his collection consisted of 730 vases, several hundred antiquities of various other kinds and over 6,000 coins. But he discovered more and more that his passion for collecting was proving financially ruinous and he sold his whole collection to the British Museum. He had already described and engraved most of it in four large volumes which he published in Naples at his own expense, but his urge to collect was not so easily cured. Before long he had begun a second collection and he had the luck to achieve a collector's dream. For a few months he possessed one of the most celebrated of all classical antiquities, the Portland

Vase. He bought it at Rome for £1,000, but soon afterwards he was obliged to sell it and it passed into the possession of the Duchess of Portland. It is now in the British Museum. Fresh excavations in 1789 and 1790 brought many more vases on to the market in Naples and Hamilton was unable to resist. Again he discovered quickly that his hobby was beyond his means and he was forced to sell. His second collection, which was bigger than the first, was eventually sold in England, although a third of it was lost at sea on the voyage to England.[13]

In 1799, when Elgin met him, Sir William Hamilton was a broken man. Palermo was no substitute for his beloved Naples, and, for the first time for over thirty years, he had no collection of antiquities to amuse himself with. He was delighted to meet a man who shared to a large extent the same taste for antiquities. Hamilton's success as an archaeologist had been enormous—he had taught the world to appreciate a whole new field of classical art —but it was probably another of his successes that appealed to Elgin. Here was a man whose efforts had caused an obvious and substantial improvement in the arts of Great Britain. Copies of Hamilton's book had passed into the hands of Josiah Wedgwood the potter. The engravings inspired him with new ideas for designs on the ancient model and the account in the text set him experimenting to revive the ancient technique. Wedgwood's magnificent pottery immediately raised the whole level of the art and it has remained deservedly popular until the present day.[14] No doubt Elgin had hopes of doing for architecture and sculpture what Hamilton had done for pottery.

Elgin discussed with Hamilton his scheme for sending professional artists, architects and moulders to Athens which he had broached with so little success in England. Hamilton encouraged him to persist and provided him with practical advice and help. The first essential was to find the professional artist who would take charge of the whole enterprise. On Hamilton's recommendation Elgin engaged Giovanni Battista Lusieri, a well-known (at that time) Italian landscape painter who was then working at Taormina. Lusieri had enjoyed a successful private practice until the war with France obliged him to look for a permanent patron.

He had been engaged by the King as a court painter and had been commissioned to sketch the antiquities of Sicily. With Hamilton's help the King of Naples gave permission to release Lusieri from his engagement. His salary was to be £200 per annum, all found, and all his work was to be the sole property of Lord Elgin. The engagement was to last as long as Elgin's embassy.[15] In fact it lasted for over twenty years.

Elgin was delighted with his good fortune in finding Lusieri, 'the first painter in Italy',[16] and immediately made arrangements to look for the other men that he wanted. He decided to send William Richard Hamilton—his private secretary, not to be confused with the Ambassador—on a recruiting tour to Naples and Rome. Hamilton, therefore, was detached from the party.

The *Phaeton* stayed at Sicily for over a fortnight and everyone enjoyed himself in his own way. Elgin had long discussions with Nelson about the strategic situation, and with Hamilton about classical antiquities; Lady Elgin entered fully into the social life of the court; McLean and Morier climbed Mount Etna; and the scholars of the party explored the ruins of Taormina and investigated the phenomenon of Scylla and Charybdis. But again, unfortunately for poor Lady Elgin, the visit came to an end and the *Phaeton* set sail for the Aegean. Lady Elgin continued to be sick and the others to enjoy themselves. They called at several islands where they shot hares, partridges and turtles, and eventually arrived at Tenedos, the small island at the entrance to the Dardanelles where ships used to lie when the wind was unfavourable for the voyage upstream. They had to stay at Tenedos for a few days waiting for the wind to change and preparing for the last stretch of the journey. Once they entered the Dardanelles they knew they would be in the hands of the Turkish reception party.[17]

Meanwhile, when the *Phaeton* sailed from Sicily, William Richard Hamilton, Elgin's private secretary, and Lusieri his painter, were sent to Italy to try to recruit artists. They were also to try to find some musicians for an orchestra Elgin wanted at Constantinople. They went first to Naples and then to Rome. The French conquest of Italy had upset the artistic world as much as the political. The museums had been stripped and all the finest works of art sent to the Louvre. The antiquities most famous in the eighteenth century, the Laocoon, Apollo Belvedere, and Venus dei Medici, had been taken from Italy as well as a great many paintings. Artists were in great demand to help with the removals and were difficult to find. Besides, great numbers of artists had sided with the French during the Revolution and, as a result, Hamilton decided he would have to make inquiries about the political principles of potential candidates as well as their professional ability.

Before he left Elgin had drawn up a note of his requirements for Hamilton's guidance.

1. A man for casts
   A painter of figures
   To be under Lusieri. Their work to be entirely my property, and their labor at my disposal—to be if possible at the second table—a fixed salary—say about £50 per annum.
2. To procure materials for the Painters and casts.[18]

As usual Elgin had underestimated the difficulties and Hamilton was obliged to depart very considerably from his brief. The men he eventually recruited were a curiously mixed bunch, and they were more numerous and more expensive than Elgin had hoped.

As painter of figures, Hamilton engaged a savage-looking man from Central Asia called Theodor Iwanovitch. He was a Calmuck or Tartar and, according to Hamilton, was the only man of taste his nation ever produced. He had been captured by the Cossacks as a child and taken as a slave to the court at St. Petersburg. A member of the Russian Royal family gave him to his German mother-in-law while on a visit and he went to live at the court of Baden. There his talents as a painter were recognized and he was sent to Rome to study.[19] When Hamilton met him his reputation as an artist was already considerable. His salary was to be £100 per annum. He was known henceforward as 'Lord Elgin's Calmuck'.

The next men to be recruited were not on Elgin's list but, evidently, Hamilton had been asked to find an architectural draftsman to take measurements and make drawings of ancient buildings. Hamilton quickly discovered that one man alone could not be procured and he was obliged to engage two. One was an extremely deformed hunchback called Balestra and the other a young student called Ittar. Hamilton himself was a cripple and perhaps he had a natural sympathy with Balestra. He insisted to Elgin that Balestra's head and hand were not affected by his deformity. The salary for the two together was to be £125 per annum. Again with the man for making plaster moulds Hamilton found he had to recruit in pairs. Two men were engaged at a salary of £100 a year each, and Hamilton was fortunate to get them even at that price since there were only six moulders in all Rome: the rest were working in France.

The party of artists led by Hamilton and also some musicians whom he had recruited for Elgin's chamber orchestra arrived at Sicily in December after a good deal of difficulty in obtaining passports. But at Sicily they were stuck for four whole months owing to the impossibility of finding transport in wartime. The architects and moulders were set to work on the ruins of Agrigento and Syracuse and the results of their efforts during this period are among the Elgin collection.[20]

Eventually, after a much interrupted voyage, Hamilton and Lusieri presented the team to Elgin at Constantinople in May 1800. Elgin found them all acceptable and Lady Elgin was overjoyed.

Mr. Hamilton and his long-expected Caro of Vertioso (is that right?)* arrived yesterday. Only think, he has absolutely brought 6 musicians, 6 painters, and 2 formatori.† I will not say anything about them, but this I will say, that I think when my Dad hears the music he will be enraptured; I never heard anything equal to the first violin. He had the band at the Opera in Italy, and as for the painter—oh! Mother!!![21]

The artists and architects—all but Lusieri—were ordered to Athens at once to begin work. But such were the difficulties of transport that they did not arrive until August.

* Not quite. What she meant was 'Carro of Virtuosi'—cartload of artists.
† Lady Elgin's figures are wrong.

Chapter 4

Reception at Constantinople

WHEN the idea of Elgin's embassy had first been discussed in November 1798 its main purpose was clear. Sir Sidney Smith had been sent to help the Turks by sea; General Koehler to help by land; obviously Elgin would complete the trio on the diplomatic front by making a formal treaty of alliance. But in January 1799 Spencer Smith had announced from Constantinople that he and his brother, the joint British Ministers, had already managed to achieve this.[1] It was decided, therefore, that Elgin's mission should be to ratify the treaty and he was given a secondary object—to persuade the Turkish Government to open the Black Sea to British shipping and British trade. But here also Elgin was too late: while he was in Sicily, Spencer Smith had secured this concession as well.[2] It is hardly surprising, therefore, if the Smiths thought that Elgin's embassy was a little unnecessary.

As soon as he heard of the appointment of Elgin, Sir Sidney Smith wrote to Lord Grenville. He said the announcement had surprised everyone and paralysed the Turks with whom they were negotiating, by making them feel that all their work would have to be done again. Besides, the appointment of Elgin over the head of his brother Spencer was intolerable. Spencer could no more revert to second place than he himself could become a lieutenant in his ship the *Tigre*; he must be given a change of appointment —perhaps he could take over from Sir William Hamilton at the court of Naples.[3] Spencer Smith himself wrote in similar terms to Lord Grenville.[4] But Grenville would not agree—Spencer Smith must stay on as Secretary of Embassy but retaining his honorary rank of Minister Plenipotentiary.

Sir Sidney Smith's biographer tells a story of the reception of the news of Elgin's appointment at the Porte. It is perhaps a little too neat to be convincing.

When Sir Sidney Smith announced Lord Elgin's appointment to the Grand Vizier he was much grieved on his friend being displaced and asked 'But why should there be any change? we went on very well together; things went on very well.' Sir Sidney told him that the newly appointed ambassador was a great landed proprietor in Scotland, that he had great influence there, and that the English government were in the habit of conciliating such people by the appointment to high situations, as being the best things they had to bestow. The vizier then said 'Ah! then I understand that your government has also got its mountain chiefs to conciliate.' He then asked what he was called; what the name was. Sir Sidney told him the name in Arabic. 'Oh! but' said he, 'Elkin is very bad—it is evil genius—it is *the devil*. How could the English government send us such a person!'[5]

If the Turks were apprehensive about Elgin's arrival they certainly did not show it in their ceremony of welcome. At the Dardanelles lay the *Sultan Selim* of 132 guns, flagship of the Turkish fleet, built by the French, and on board was the Turkish admiral the Capitan Pasha. After an exchange of salutes with the *Phaeton*, the Elgins were received on board. They were astonished at their first sight of Turkish magnificence. The cabins were full of sofas, covered with yellow silk embroidered in gold, and the walls were decorated with swords and pistols, all embossed in gold. Dinner was served on fine Dresden china and coffee in diamond cups carried on a silver tray. The admiral showed his visitors over the ship which impressed even Captain Morris. He showed them his Japanese cabinets and candlesticks and two huge bowls of goldfish. Everything was covered with silk and cloth of gold. Then came the presents. The Elgins were given a model of the *Sultan Selim* made of diamonds with rubies and emeralds to represent the guns and flags, then some boxes of perfume, and rich Indian shawls. Finally twenty-five sheep and six oxen were driven on board the *Phaeton*, and new bread and fresh fruit were loaded into her in quantities far beyond anything the crew could be expected to consume.[6]

At the Dardanelles, much to his surprise, Elgin also met the

British Military Mission, which had been sent out with General Koehler, to help the Turks against the French. It was now engaged on the unwarlike task of repairing the shore defences that the French had built some years before. Poor General Koehler had had a very disappointing time. When he reached Constantinople the Grand Vizier was still assembling his army to march against the French in Egypt. Koehler immediately drew up a detailed strategic and tactical appreciation of the military situation, proposed an order of march for the Turkish army, and outlined the necessary command structure and division of the troops: with this plan he was sure it would not be long before Bonaparte was driven out of Egypt. He presented his plan to the Grand Vizier with a flourish and waited for his admiration. But Koehler had misjudged the Turkish character. The Grand Vizier thanked him politely, gave him all the honours of the court, and did nothing. Soon the Turkish army set off and despite all protests, Koehler and his mission were not even allowed to accompany it. Instead they were sent to the Dardanelles to the ignominious task on which Elgin found them.⁷

But although General Koehler was not to go down in history as the architect of victory over Bonaparte, to him does belong the small distinction of having collected the first of the Elgin Marbles. When the *Phaeton* had been held up by contrary winds at Tenedos the embassy party had gone on a day's expedition to the plain of Troy. Lady Elgin described it to her mother:

We took a basket of cold meat and eat our luncheon at 12 o'clock at a village called Sigamon; [Sigaeum]; from thence E. and I, Captain Morris, Major Fletcher (who came with letters from General Koehler to E.), Masterman,* Carlyle, Hunt, Morier, McLean and the Greek servant, mounted on asses. I could not get my own saddle so I was forced to ride on a Turkish one. We took guides and off we set to the supposed site of ancient Troy; we rode ten miles across the plain, saw camels grazing, and arrived at a romantic spot where they shewed us the ruins of the outside walls. And compleat ruins it is, for there are not two stones left one upon another, only it is visible there has been a great quantity of building. The Learned Men had taken Homer with

* One of Lady Elgin's maids.

them, and from examining the spot they agreed there was every appearance of its being the place. There being no twilight we were caught in the dark but only think of my riding 22 miles on a Turkish saddle too, without really being tired.[8]

Not a bad performance for a woman four months pregnant. On this picnic Elgin saw two famous monuments. Outside the village church at Yenicher were two seats; on the left was a sculptured relief of mothers and children; and on the right was a very ancient Greek inscription where the writing read from left to right and then right to left to prevent interpolation. Both these antiquities had been discovered about a hundred years before and had been coveted by many travellers since. Lady Mary Wortley Montagu could have had them for a small bribe in 1718 but the captain of her ship did not have the tackle to remove them. About the middle of the century another English traveller bid 400 Venetian sequins for them but the local inhabitants said they would destroy them rather than let them go, because once before they had sold a fragment and soon afterwards the village was infested with a dreadful plague. They began to beat the heads off the figures on the relief and succeeded with four out of five as can be seen today, and to deface the letters on the inscription.[9]

The French too had tried to obtain them. Louis XIV's Ambassador had offered a large sum [10] and so, recently, had the Comte de Choiseul-Gouffier.[11] But all without success. The reason why the local inhabitants were unwilling to let these antiquities go had nothing to do with any respect for their age or artistic merit. The Greek priests regarded them as an infallible remedy for various diseases. Hunt was given the explanation by the local priest when he visited Sigaeum sixteen months later:

To explain this [veneration for the antiquities] it may be necessary to mention that during the winter and spring a considerable part of the neighbouring plain is overflowed, thus afflicting the inhabitants with agues; and such is the state of superstition at present among the Greek Christians, that when any disease becomes chronic or beyond the reach of common remedies, it is attributed to daemoniacal possession. The Papas, or priest is then called in to exorcise the patient, which he generally does in the porch of the church, by reading long portions of Scripture over the sufferer; sometimes indeed the whole of the four gospels. In addition to this, at Yenicher, the custom was to roll the patient on the marble stone which contained the Sigean inscription, the characters of which never having been decyphered by any of their Διδάσκαλοι, were supposed to contain a powerful charm. This practice had, however, nearly obliterated the inscription.[12]

Elgin asked the Capitan Pasha if he could have these antiquities and his request was at once granted. A man who dispensed diamonds to his guest could hardly refuse a few pieces of old battered marbles which were valued only by the ignorant infidels. A party of soldiers from General Koehler's military mission went to Sigaeum armed with the written authority of the Capitan Pasha. Among the tears and protestations of the Greek priests they removed them to the Dardanelles.[13] They were loaded into the *Phaeton* and eventually found their way to Deptford. The story of the medicinal properties of these marbles was still being told at Yenicher twenty years later.[14]

About a week after leaving the Dardanelles the *Phaeton* arrived at Constantinople over two months after she had set sail from Portsmouth. Lord and Lady Elgin came ashore and were taken in golden chairs to the British Palace. Soon afterwards a Turkish officer arrived, accompanied by ninety servants, bringing flowers, fruit and sweets, to present the government's compliments on Elgin's arrival. When the flowers and fruit had been piled in the hall, the officer brought in eight trays with fine pieces of Berlin china, each cup filled with different sorts of sweets and covered with a different coloured handkerchief.

A few days later another officer arrived with a similar gift from another Turkish dignitary but he only brought thirty servants. So the first fortnight passed with a succession of calls by important Turks all with some gift. But the giving was not all in one direction. Elgin had come well prepared to respond in kind. One officer who called was given a gold watch and chain set in diamonds, another a pair of English pistols, and another a ring set in diamonds. Everyone, including every servant, was given something.

These were only the preliminaries. The main ceremonies were

Elgin's two presentations, to the Grand Vizier, and to the Sultan himself. The Turks at that time, as now, liked to keep their women at a distance, and certainly did not admit them to their ceremonial. But Lady Elgin was determined not to be left out. Fortunately the Grand Vizier himself was away with the army in Syria and the more liberal Caimacan Pasha, who was taking his place at Constantinople, agreed to let her come. But there was one condition—she must come dressed as a man so as not to offend his more scrupulous friends. Lady Elgin was put down on the list as 'Lord Bruce, a young nobleman'.*

The audience with the Caimacan Pasha was fixed for Thursday 21 November with a grand ball to follow. Lady Elgin wrote to her mother the night before:

Is my dear Mother's expectation raised to the highest pitch? and is she dying to know what sort of pelisse† *Lord Bruce* is in possession of? Know then, that when I had taken leave of you last night,‡ I went to bed but not to sleep; for my brain was filled with Grand Turks, Viziers, Pashas, Pelisses—and then my ball came in for a share to occupy my thoughts. As for Eggy, he slept like a Top! tho' in the evening he had been modest, and affected to be annoyed at having a speech to make and particularly allarmed at *my* hearing him.[15]

But the morning of the 21st was wet and windy and the audience was postponed. Much to Lady Elgin's consternation a great quantity of chickens, turkeys, and pastry prepared for the ball had to be thrown away.

The audience took place a few days later. A large number of horses and boats were hired and several hundred soldiers and servants to form the ambassadorial procession. They crossed by boat to the Seraglio and were received by the Caimacan Pasha. Elgin had ordered three brocade bags to be made, one to contain his credentials to the Grand Vizier, one for his credentials to the Sultan, and one for the instrument of ratification of the Treaty of Alliance. After short formal speeches of friendship on both sides

* Lord Bruce is the family name of the eldest son of the Earl of Elgin. A Lord Bruce was born only five months after the audience.
† A rich fur coat which the Turks bestowed on important guests as a sign of welcome and high favour.
‡ By letter of course.

the bags were handed over. Then Elgin, 'Lord Bruce' and the other members of Elgin's party were invested with pelisses and introduced to the dignitaries and officials of the court. When this was over Elgin was given a further present—of a horse with gold trappings—and the ambassadorial party went in procession back to the British Palace.

The audience with the Sultan took place three days later. This time the foreign embassies at Constantinople were stripped for the day to provide the horses, carriages, boats, grooms, chamberlains, stewards, and soldiers that were required. Some 2,000 janissaries led the procession. The ceremony began before dawn and lasted nearly all day. The Turks insisted on keeping the ambassador's party waiting at a number of places to show their contempt for foreigners. It waited at the gate of the city, again outside the Seraglio, again outside the inner gate of the Seraglio, and finally for several hours outside the Sultan's chamber itself. Lord Elgin was also occasionally pushed roughly off the road by the janissaries. The Turks made quite clear, however, that these apparent insults were entirely a matter of etiquette. Yet more pelisses were bestowed and the whole party was given a meal of twenty-six courses, served on silver platters.

At last, with their shoulders and necks held by guards, Lord Elgin, 'Lord Bruce' and eleven others were led through rows of white eunuchs into the audience chamber, the room which Carlyle described as 'the abode of misery, and more frequently perhaps than any other place upon earth, the scene of guilt and horror'.[16] It was a small, dark room furnished solely with jewelled decorations. Even the windows looked out only into aviaries. The throne on which the Grand Signor sat was, Lady Elgin wrote,

like a good honest English bed; the counterpane on which the Monster sat was embroidered all over with immense large pearls. By him was an inkstand of one mass of large Diamonds, on his other side lay his saber studded all over with *thumping* Brilliants. In his turban he wore the famous Aigrette,* his robe was of yellow satin with black sable, and in

---

* A jewel from the Sultan's head-dress given as a mark of the highest honour. Nelson was given one after the Battle of the Nile.

a window there were two turbans covered with diamonds. You can conceive nothing in the Arabian Nights equal to that room.[17]

The short formal speeches were again delivered on both sides, although with some difficulty because Turkish etiquette forbade the Sultan to cast his eyes on a foreigner or speak to him directly. Then came the procession home and another ball.

Again Elgin followed the custom of distributing presents. To the Sultan he presented a huge chandelier, a large musical table clock, a gold enamel box, a bezoar stone and 350 Turkish yards of satin, brocade, velvet, and damask. To the Grand Vizier (in absentia) he gave a diamond box and two pieces of ermine worth 1,500 guineas; to the Caimacan Pasha, a diamond box worth 500 guineas; to the Reis Effendi, diamonds and sables worth 1,250 guineas; to another dignitary, diamonds and furs worth 1,000 guineas; to another, a diamond box and ring worth 500 guineas; and so on to all the Turks that he met. He gave clocks, watches, pistols, and furs, but above all he gave pieces of cloth, silk, tabby, satin, brocade, velvet, and damask. Altogether he distributed about 1,300 yards* of various materials and several hundred members of the court received gifts of one kind or another.[18]

Shortly after the two receptions Elgin submitted a claim to the Foreign Office for expenses incurred in his first fortnight. It totalled about £7,000 and it did not include the cost of about half the material and many of the other gifts which he had brought with him from England. In Elgin's instructions on taking up the post of Ambassador Extraordinary to Turkey occurs the following sentence: 'At your audience with the Grand Vizier you are to insist on being treated with the same ceremonies and respect that are or have been shewn to the ambassadors of any other crowned heads.'[19] No one could complain that in this respect at least Elgin had not done his best.

* The Turkish yard was only twenty-seven inches, but even so.

Chapter 5

The Smith Brothers

Now that the initiation ceremony was over, Elgin settled down to begin work. Very quickly he discovered that the British Embassy at Constantinople did not run in the same way as British Embassies elsewhere. The brothers Smith, Spencer and Sir Sidney, were not professional diplomats well versed in official procedures. They had not taken at all kindly to their supersession and in fact continued to behave exactly as if Elgin had never been appointed Ambassador at all.

Spencer Smith, it will be remembered, had been British Minister since Sir Robert Liston left Constantinople in 1795. When Elgin was appointed he was demoted to Secretary of Embassy but, to ease the transition, he was allowed to retain the honorary title of 'Minister Plenipotentiary'. In addition he was charged with looking after the affairs of the Levant Company, by whom, of course, he had originally been appointed. The idea was that Elgin should take over all the diplomatic business leaving Smith in charge of all questions of trade which were the chief concern of the Levant Company.

With other personalities the arrangement might have worked, but it became clear within days that Elgin and Spencer Smith were never going to agree. Spencer Smith had gone native after his long stay in the East. He had violent likes and dislikes, could not separate private life and official business, and loved intrigue of all kinds. It was perhaps because he behaved as unpredictably as a Turkish official that he was able to achieve his two diplomatic successes, the Treaty of Alliance and the promise to open the Black Sea to British trade. His deviousness rasped sharply on Elgin whose experience at Berlin had given him a horror of intrigue and a determination to be undisputed master of his embassy.

Spencer Smith began by declaring that he would help Elgin in every way he could[1] but, whatever his intentions, he frustrated him from the start. Elgin discovered only by degrees how his subordinate was behaving. First he was surprised that there were so few official papers, and, on inquiry, found that Smith had kept some from him. Next he discovered that Smith continued to deal direct with the Turkish Government every day without telling him what he was discussing. Then he heard that Smith had ordered British officials in the Levant not to correspond with the Ambassador. Then he heard from the Turkish government itself that Smith had made a complaint to them that Elgin was exceeding his powers in discussing tariffs. Then the Turks began to give Elgin information in confidence on condition that he did not tell Spencer Smith.

As each of these irregularities came to light Elgin gave Spencer Smith increasingly severe scoldings and several times read over to him the exact terms of his appointment. Each time Spencer Smith promised to do better in future, but the conclusion is inescapable that he was trying deliberately to sabotage Elgin's efforts and restore the old monopoly of the Levant Company in diplomatic matters. Less than a month after Elgin's arrival there occurred an incident which Elgin regarded as the last straw. The Swedish and Danish Ministers and several other foreign representatives protested to him strongly that the British Consul at Aleppo had illegally seized some of their mail. Elgin at once asked Spencer Smith to show him the papers on the subject. After several days' delay Smith sent him a packet of papers accompanied by a note saying it contained all the information about one side of the question; when Elgin had read them he would send him the papers on the other side.[2]

Elgin's initial relations with Sir Sidney Smith were hardly more cordial. He knew Smith well and had a great personal admiration for him. As soon as he arrived he sent Smith a long friendly letter announcing the start of his embassy.[3] But it was no good: the Smiths were not men to listen to hints. The first thing that alerted Elgin was to see a letter signed by Sidney Smith as 'Minister Plenipotentiary' although he knew perfectly well that his diplomatic commission had ended with Elgin's arrival,[4] if not before. Then Elgin heard from the Turks what lay behind it.

After the escape of Bonaparte the command of the French forces in Egypt devolved on General Kléber. He was a severely practical man and realized as well as Bonaparte that the French position in Egypt was, in the long run, untenable. He therefore immediately made overtures about the possibility of peace terms. Sir Sidney Smith, cruising in his ship the *Tigre* off the coast of Egypt, saw a chance to bring about a peace settlement. He invited representatives of the French on board to discuss a possible evacuation of Egypt. Whether he had the legal power to do this is extremely doubtful; governments do not usually entrust questions of peace and war to naval captains however successful. By the time of Elgin's arrival Smith had even led the French to believe that he was negotiating on behalf of both the Turkish and the British Empires. The Turks, not unnaturally, were very annoyed and protested in the strongest terms to Elgin. After the success at Acre the Grand Vizier had taken the field with a huge army and had hopes of expelling the French by force of arms: by him alone could such questions be decided. Elgin was put in a thoroughly humiliating position. He sent his private secretary, Morier, to be his official link with the Grand Vizier's army and gave Sir Sidney Smith a sharp reprimand for exceeding his powers. He did not however—and this was his biggest mistake— forbid the negotiations explicitly, and to the Turks he could only apologize for the insubordination.[5]

To complete his discomfiture Elgin had to deal with the ineptitude of General Koehler. Elgin had insisted as soon as he arrived that the British Military Mission should come back from repairing the Dardanelles forts and be employed on more active service. General Koehler had returned to Constantinople but his manner had made him very unpopular with the Turks. He styled himself 'General Officer Commanding His Majesty's Land Forces in the Ottoman Dominions' although his force of seventy-six men was already depleted by disease, and, as Elgin said, 'he claimed to himself the respect paid to a Buonaparte and a Suvarov'.

Elgin reported all his difficulties in his official despatches to Lord Grenville. But after only six weeks of frustration he decided that his position was intolerable. He wrote privately to Grenville asking him to remove Spencer Smith and reprimand Sidney Smith. 'Seeing Englishmen in authority in Turkey,' he wrote, 'takes away all delight in reading Don Quixote.'[6]

All this bickering and petty jealousy was clearly brought home to Lord Grenville not only by the letters of complaint from Elgin but from letters protesting their own sides of the story from Spencer Smith, Sir Sidney Smith and General Koehler. At first he did not pay much attention. As Foreign Secretary of a country at war he had a great many more important things to think about. It was unfortunate that he did not take more interest, for it was mainly uncertainty about the exact status of the various officers in the Levant that led to the fiasco of the Convention of El Arish. This was one of the most disastrous muddles of the whole war.

At the end of January Sir Sidney Smith's negotiations with the French about terms to evacuate Egypt suddenly achieved success. At the Syrian town of El Arish, where the Grand Vizier was encamped with the Turkish army, he concluded, without reference to his superiors, the Convention of El Arish. Under the terms of this convention the French were to leave Egypt, neither victors nor conquered; they were to be conveyed back to France in British ships on condition that they did not fight against Turkey or Great Britain in the current war; Egypt was to be restored to the Turks. General Kléber ratified the convention on behalf of the French within a few days. On 16 February, Elgin wrote to Lord Grenville: 'I have infinite satisfaction in informing your lordship that on 24th ult. a capitulation was signed in the Grand Vizier's camp at El Arish, in consequence of which the French are to evacuate Egypt within the space of three months.'[7] The success of Sir Sidney Smith's negotiations had led Elgin to overlook the fact that Smith had entered into them without proper authority. Elgin also wrote at once to Nelson asking him to provide ships to help evacuate the French.[8] Soon afterwards he began to issue passports for the safe conduct of the French in Egypt back to France.

On 24 February, however, Elgin received an official despatch from Lord Grenville dated 13 December—that is over a month before the Convention of El Arish was signed. This despatch instructed Elgin in the strongest possible language that no arrangement was to be entered into with the French except on condition that they surrendered themselves as prisoners of war. The parole system, Grenville wrote, had been broken so often by the French that in future it would be forbidden. The despatch also declared that precisely similar instructions had been sent to Lord Keith, the naval commander-in-chief in the Mediterranean, for passing on to Sir Sidney Smith. This despatch rendered the Convention of El Arish null and void and invalidated the passports that Elgin had begun to issue: the whole agreement to clear Egypt of the French had been illegal from the start.

As soon as he received the fatal despatch Elgin rushed off to the Porte to tell the Turks what had happened and to try to arrange a graceful withdrawal from the Convention. But, as luck would have it, it was the feast of Bairam and the Turks insisted that no business could be conducted until it was over. And so another vital fortnight passed before Elgin saw the Caimacan Pasha.[9] When at last Elgin was given an audience and had explained what had happened the reaction of the Turks can be guessed. Sir Sidney Smith, they said, was a 'Minister Plenipotentiary'; far from doubting his powers he had taken the initiative in promoting the negotiations. Poor Elgin could only confess that Smith had acted without instructions and that he was unable to control him.[10]

Then the Turks made a suggestion which was well within the rule book of Eastern warfare but horrifying to a British nobleman brought up in the gentlemanly days before the French Revolution. They proposed that the arrangements for carrying out the Convention of El Arish should go ahead, but that when the French were safely aboard British ships on their way home, the convention should be disowned and the French seized as prisoners of war. Elgin, whose respect for the code of honour of international relations was exceptional even for his own times, was indignant at the suggestion and refused even to discuss it.[11] But somehow a hint of it appeared in the papers of his private secretary Morier which later fell into the hands of the French.[12]

On 28 March, to complete the muddle, Lord Grenville wrote again to Elgin. The British Government, he said, had just heard of the Convention of El Arish; although it was quite contrary to the policy laid down in the despatch of 13 December, they had decided to accept it after all.[13]

It was too late. Events in Egypt had taken their inexorable course. Soon after the ratification, the Grand Vizier with his large rabble of an army had marched into Egypt to take over Cairo from the French in accordance with the Convention. He was almost at Cairo when Lord Keith, the British Commander-in-Chief, received his copy of the British Government's instructions of 13 December. Being a blunt man, and having had no instructions to the contrary from Elgin, he acted at once. On 18 March he wrote simply to Kléber that he could not now assent to any terms other than unconditional surrender. Kléber's reaction was equally straightforward. Within forty-eight hours he countermanded all orders about evacuation, and notified the Grand Vizier that the armistice was at an end. On 20 March he suddenly attacked the Turkish army at Heliopolis, defeated them utterly, and drove them right out of Egypt. Small parties of the Grand Vizier's army found their way back to Jaffa but large numbers of them were killed, taken prisoner, or died of thirst in the desert. The French were again in full possession of Egypt.

The muddle over the Convention of El Arish prolonged the war in Egypt for another fifteen months. Many thousands of French, British, Turks, and of course Egyptians were to be killed in the subsequent fighting and thousands more died of disease. After all that, the terms on which the French did eventually leave Egypt were almost exactly those which had been agreed at El Arish in the first place.

For Elgin himself the results of the fiasco at El Arish were not as bad as one might have expected. When a disaster of such dimensions occurs it is not usually enough to be personally innocent: the innocent fall with the guilty. Elgin, however, seems to have successfully persuaded the British Government that he had done all he could and that he was not responsible. He came out of the incident with his reputation largely unscathed. But there was one man who did not exonerate Elgin so lightly. Napoleon Bonaparte became convinced that the Convention and its subsequent disavowal was an elaborate plot engineered by Elgin. He was sure that Elgin wanted to deceive the French and seize them on their passage to France: there was even a story that the French were to be massacred as soon as they came into British power.[14] Bonaparte formed a strong personal hatred for Elgin whom he later described as 'one of the greatest enemies of the nation'.[15] He convinced himself that it was Elgin who caused the ill-treatment of the French prisoners in Constantinople[16] and began to blame him for all the reverses of his Egyptian policy.[17] It is even said that he believed that Elgin sent the information that led to the destruction of his fleet at the battle of the Nile—an event that occurred no less than fifteen months before Elgin arrived at Constantinople.[18] In some circumstances it can be rather flattering to be hated by a great man. It was just Elgin's luck that he should later fall into the hands of the man who misjudged him so violently.

But life at Constantinople was not all frantic diplomacy. There were the grand fêtes, the parties, the balls, the concerts, and the whist, perpetual whist. Spencer Smith later wrote a book on the game.[19] The missions of the foreign powers entertained one another in turn in their sumptuous palaces and vied with one another in their magnificence. Lady Elgin constantly complained of having to entertain large parties of 'hottentots', but she seems to have enjoyed it well enough. Only on Sundays were there no parties: alone of the missions the Elgins insisted that there should be no card-playing or dancing on that day. But Lady Elgin was not a person to be contented with the social round: she decided to branch out a bit. She struck up a friendship with the sister of the Capitan Pasha and began to pay her frequent visits. When the Capitan Pasha was at home this lady kept house for him; when he was away she served her turn in the Sultan's harem. Lady Elgin went both to the Capitan's and to the harem. On one occasion Elgin found her dressed in Turkish costume with the other ladies when he called to see the Capitan on business. And she began to teach the ladies of the harem the delights of Scottish country dancing. Very soon Lady Elgin was a great favourite of the Turks and the object of great jealousy among the other foreign ladies at Constantinople.

In April the Elgin's first child was born, and being a boy received the family title of Lord Bruce. Shortly afterwards Lady Elgin's mother and father, Mr. and Mrs. Nisbet, arrived from Scotland to stay with their daughter for a holiday. As they had promised at the time of her marriage they had made the long and dangerous journey only four months after their daughter left. They were to stay at Constantinople and in Greece for nearly a year before returning home. Needless to say Lady Elgin was overjoyed.

Elgin himself—despite the El Arish episode—became more and more popular with the Turks. Further presents were heaped upon him—horses, jewellery, furs, fabrics, and a 200-ton yacht for his private use if he wanted to explore the Greek Islands. The Capitan Pasha set a new precedent in Turkish etiquette by himself calling at the British Palace and the other Turks began to abandon the attitude of arrogance towards the British which the Turkish court had previously insisted upon as a matter of routine. As an Ambassador Elgin was extremely successful. The price was high. Elgin's days were long and tiring. He worked hard, tolerating with good grace the lengthy ceremoniousness of Turkish business, and fighting helplessly against Smith and the Levant Company merchants. For weeks on end he struggled at his business leaving Lady Elgin very much on her own. His health did not stand the strain. Contrary to his expectation the climate of Constantinople did not help his rheumatism but made it worse. He also suffered severely—as did Lady Elgin—from the fever which regularly swept the city. Worst of all he contracted a severe skin disease of the face and an extremely painful tic.[20] Gradually the disease ate into his face until he lost the whole of the lower part of his nose.[21] He was monstrously disfigured for the rest of his life.

Relations with the Smith brothers did not improve. Sir Sidney Smith's arrogance had not been chastened by the experience of

El Arish. He continued to see himself as the one man who could bring about a settlement with France. He subscribed to the naïve but attractive theory that the French were being held down by the tyrant Bonaparte and only needed a signal to throw off their chains and re-establish the *ancien régime*. He was soon surrounded by a circle of flattering émigré royalists. Now Lord Keith, the naval Commander-in-Chief, kept a close watch on him and General Koehler was sent to the Grand Vizier's army partly to act as a counterweight. Elgin's private secretary, Morier, went to and fro between Constantinople and Syria keeping Elgin informed of what Sir Sidney was up to.

Spencer Smith was harder to deal with. Lord Grenville had been unwilling to have him removed as this would have meant the end of his career and he persuaded Elgin to give him another chance. But he need not have bothered. Smith just could not get used to being in second place and the long tale of disobedience, intrigue, and spite was soon repeated. In March there was a complete breakdown. Elgin refused to see Smith altogether and would not even correspond with him. He wrote again and again to Grenville asking for Smith to be removed and the arrangement with the Levant Company to be terminated. In May speaking terms were resumed as a result of a stiff letter from Grenville to Smith, but the rapprochement did not last long. There were virtually two independent British Missions at Constantinople and the British community in the Levant sided with one or the other according to taste.[22]

At last the situation at Constantinople became so notorious and Elgin pressed so hard that in October it was discussed by the British Cabinet. The first words of common sense on the whole matter came from Dundas. 'Either Lord Elgin or the Smiths should come away,' he wrote to Grenville, 'for the public service never can go on with any effect or even safety in the hands of such jarring and discordant instruments.'[23]

It was decided to leave Sir Sidney Smith but to ask the Levant Company to recall Spencer Smith and hand over responsibility for their affairs to Elgin. At long last, in January 1801, to Elgin's intense relief, Spencer Smith received his order of dismissal.

He was replaced, at Elgin's request, by 'a very pleasant lively man and a most capital whist player' called Alexander Straton.[24] On his way home Spencer Smith made a tour of Levant Company establishments and paid a visit to his brother's naval squadron. Everywhere he went he proclaimed that he had been done down by the wicked Earl of Elgin and spread as much slander about him as he could.[25] Shortly after his return to England he entered Parliament. Elgin had made his second enemy, not perhaps to be compared with Napoleon Bonaparte but dangerous nevertheless. Smith departed from the scene with bad grace and time did not blunt his bitterness.

Chapter 6

Work Begins at Athens

IN August 1800 Lord Elgin's artists at last arrived in Athens to begin the work that was to improve the arts in Great Britain. They paid their respects (with the usual presents) to the Turkish authorities and established themselves in the town. The British Consul Logotheti took them under his protection.

Athens was then a shabby, miserable little town. It was inhabited by a motley population from all parts of the Ottoman Empire who all lived on the north and east slopes of the Acropolis. About half were Greeks, a quarter Turks, and the rest Albanians, Jews, Negroes, and others. There were probably no more than thirteen hundred houses in all.[1] Round the town was a wall only ten feet high that had been built twenty years before to keep out roving bands of bandits and to make the taxation of the enclosed inhabitants easier to collect.[2] The Acropolis was nominally a military fortress but its few guns were dismounted and purely for show. The garrison lived with their families in huts on the Acropolis so badly built that they crumbled whenever there was heavy rain.[3] Athens was the forty-third city of European Turkey.[4]

For most of the period of Turkish rule Athens had been the property of one of the numerous lesser dignitaries of the Ottoman court, the Chief of the Black Eunuchs, and its revenues had gone to support the Imperial harem at Constantinople. In 1760, however, it lost this privileged position and was henceforth auctioned by the Sultan to the highest bidder who then had the right to put the proceeds of taxation into his own pocket.[5] Thirty-five years of unbelievable extortion had followed but by 1800 normal Turkish standards of administration had been re-established. Athens was ruled by two officials, the Voivode or

Governor, and the Disdar, military governor of the Acropolis. Their rule, though shaming, was no longer tyrannous. All the races mixed freely and the Voivode even had a Greek wife. The garrison of Turkish soldiers on the Acropolis were somewhat arrogant and bullying, but then they were rarely paid and were untroubled by military duties.

Among the mean houses of Athens there stood out, in violent contrast, the remains of its magnificent ancient buildings and these—as now—were its only claim to distinction. There were not many of them. On the Acropolis were the ruins of three buildings of the greatest age of Greece, the Parthenon, the Erechtheum and the Propylaea, and, in the lower town, another of the same period, the Theseum. Besides these four were the remains of several smaller and less interesting monuments of later centuries, the Tower of the Winds, the Monument of Lysicrates, and the Monument of Philopappos, and some pillars of a gigantic temple to Olympian Zeus. There were other signs of the greater days, but, for the most part, they were well hidden.

As the ancient buildings were the only substantial structures in the whole of Athens, every one that had any roof left was still in use. The Erechtheum was a gunpowder magazine, the Theseum was a church, the Tower of the Winds was the headquarters of the Whirling Dervishes, and the Monument of Lysicrates was a storeroom for a French Capuchin Convent. The Turks living on the Acropolis built their houses, vegetable gardens, and fortifications round about the ruins or made use of them as it suited their purpose. Inside the Parthenon was a small mosque, and the spaces between the pillars of the Propylaea were half bricked up to provide a kind of castellation for the guns. Everywhere it was obvious that for years the ruins had been a main source of building materials. Slabs of crisp-cut marble were built into the rude modern walls, and, here and there, pieces of sculpture could be seen among the fortifications. Many of the houses in the town had an ancient fragment set above their door as a charm.

The temples of Athens which Lord Elgin's artists had come to study were not only the most complete of the buildings surviving from classical Greece, they were the best. In them the art of classical architecture had reached its highest point. They were unsurpassed.

First and foremost, above all others was the Parthenon, or Temple of Athena. It was built between 447 and 432 B.C. on the Acropolis of Athens, the rocky hill that rises in the middle of the Attic plain, and which had been from the earliest times both the fortress and the religious centre of the people of Athens. The previous temple had been destroyed in the Persian invasion of 480 and the Acropolis had lain desolate for a generation. But in that generation Athens had not only recovered from the war but had put herself at the head of a rich and powerful league of Greek states. In these few years Greek literature, philosophy, architecture, politics, in fact the whole of Greek civilization suddenly burst into flower.

About the middle of the century the Athenian statesman Pericles began a huge programme of public works intended to give Athens the magnificence of a great imperial city. The sculptor Phidias was commissioned to create a colossal gold and ivory statue of the city's patron goddess Athena and the architect Ictinus to build a fitting temple to house it. The Parthenon was the result. It was built throughout in the finest-grained white marble in the Doric order of Greek architecture. The natural simplicity of this style was brought out and enhanced by extreme precision of workmanship and subtlety of proportion. Innumerable delicate refinements were included in the design to offset the optical illusions which a mathematically correct temple would have created. In the perfection of the art, the art itself was concealed.

It was not only in its architecture that the Parthenon was supreme. Each of the pediments was filled with a group of sculptured figures, carved in the round, which represented a story from Athens's mythology—the birth of Athena in one side and the contest of Athena and Poseidon for the land of Attica in the other. Around the outside of the temple every second panel, or metope, was carved in high relief with scenes from the wars of gods and giants and lapiths and centaurs. Perhaps most striking of all, round the whole temple was a frieze in low relief depicting the Panathenaea, the great religious ceremony that took place every four years on the Acropolis.

All these were of a perfection hitherto unattained in architectural sculpture (and perhaps never since) and were executed under the superintendence of Phidias himself. Plutarch, writing five hundred years later of the glories of Periclean Athens, observed 'every work of the time of Pericles had from the moment of its creation the beauty of an old master, but yet it retains its freshness and newness to this day. There is a certain novelty that seems to bloom upon them which keeps their beauty untouched by time, as if they had perpetual breath of life, and an unageing soul mingled in their composition.'6 Whether or not the Parthenon was the finest building ever erected is a debatable question. However, from the day it was built many competent judges have thought so, and the view still has a strong following today.

The other classical buildings of Athens, though not on the grand scale of the Parthenon, were also exquisite examples of Greek architecture. At the entrance to the Acropolis Pericles commissioned the Propylaea, a large marble ceremonial gateway with several porches and chambers in a mixture of Doric and Ionic styles. The road up to the Acropolis was narrow and steep. It zigzagged up the hill and then led straight through the Propylaea to the open ground of the Acropolis. It seems to have been designed so that the visitor to the Acropolis would see the Parthenon to its best advantage as soon as he passed through. The Propylaea, though undecorated with sculpture, contained, like the Parthenon, all the grandeur and refinement of which Greek Doric was capable. It was built between 437 and 432 but financial stringency caused by war put an end to the building before it was complete.

Also on the Acropolis was an Ionic Temple, the Erechtheum, built between 421 and 405. It was sited on the lowest ground of the Acropolis so that the lightness of the Ionic style made a foil to show off the grandeur of the nearby Parthenon. It too was in marble and included all the decorative detail and sculptured embellishments that suit the Ionic order so well. On either side of the main sanctuary were two porches, one of which was supported not by columns but by women in heavy drapery the folds of which resemble the fluting of the Parthenon columns opposite. According to an old story, these ladies with the weight of a whole porch on their proud unbending heads commemorated the ignominy of the people of Carya, the only city of the Peloponnese that had sided with the Persians. They were thus called Caryatids.

Finally on the Acropolis, tucked away in a corner bastion, was the dainty little temple of the Athena Nike. This miniature Ionic building, lavishly decorated with sculpture, was built at about the same time to commemorate the victory over the Persians. In the lower town was yet another temple of the classical period—the Temple of Hephaestos, commonly called the Theseum. It was of marble, in the Doric order, and was begun in 449. Like the Parthenon it was decorated with sculpture in the pediments and metopes and had a sculptured frieze at each end of the building. It too was an extremely fine building, but in its situation in the low ground of Athens it was completely dominated by the temples on the Acropolis.

These superb buildings, the product of a single generation of outstanding genius, had had an eventful history since the fifth century B.C. It is surprising that they survived at all. For nearly a thousand years they stood as perfect as the day they were built. The Romans and the Byzantines stripped Athens of her statues and the city was even subjected to a sack by Alaric the Goth, but the buildings themselves were left untouched. The first blow was struck sometime after the fifth century A.D. when Christianity was adopted as the official religion. Great damage was done to the east end of the Parthenon to make room for an apse and holes were knocked in the sides so that windows could be let in. The Erechtheum and Theseum suffered too: the interiors of both were torn out as they were converted into churches. The damage caused by this crude conversion was bad enough but worse soon followed. A large number of the decorative sculptures were deliberately defaced in some outburst of religious iconoclasm.

It was a thousand years later before any further major damage was done. Byzantines and Franks, Catalans and Navarrese,

Florentines and Venetians, came and went but miraculously the buildings survived. Even the conquest of the infidel Turks in the fifteenth century made little difference. They converted the Parthenon into a mosque by building a minaret on top of it and turned the Erechtheum into the seraglio and harem of the Military Governor. Then in the seventeenth century, when the Turks were being hard pressed by the Venetians, the fatal destruction took place. In 1645 the Propylaea, which was being used as a gunpowder magazine, was struck by lightning and exploded. Henceforth it was a ruin. Then in 1686 the little temple of Athena Nike was deliberately thrown down by the Turks to clear the bastion for an artillery position. Finally on 26 September 1687 the Parthenon itself was struck.

The Venetians under a general called Morosini succeeded in laying siege to the Acropolis. The Parthenon, which had now taken the place of the Propylaea as the gunpowder magazine, received a direct hit from one of the Venetian cannon and the whole building exploded. The roof was blown off; a huge gap was torn in the long colonnades on either side; and much of the sculpture was utterly destroyed. The Erechtheum too was badly damaged by the blast. Not content with this achievement Morosini proceeded to further excesses. When the garrison surrendered and he took possession of the Acropolis he decided to take home to Venice as a trophy of his conquest the large group of sculptures from the western pediment which had survived the explosion. But when his engineers were lowering the massive statues their cables broke and the whole group was shattered. The following year Morosini was compelled to withdraw from Athens, leaving the Acropolis a heap of marble rubble.*

The fragments of the temples and sculptures that had been destroyed provided ready-to-hand building materials for the Turks and, being of very fine marble, they were eminently suitable for burning into lime. The Turks made liberal use of them. As can be seen by any visitor to Asia Minor even today,

* A head from one of the pedimental figures, now in Paris, was taken back to Venice as a trophy by Morosini's secretary. Two heads from a metope, now in Copenhagen, were taken by another officer of his army.

the Turks are totally indifferent to ruins, especially ruins left by other peoples. If a building can be used, even if only for a goat-pen, it is allowed to remain or is adapted; if it is in the way, or if the material is considered useful, it is knocked down or plundered without a qualm; but if it merely exists, getting in nobody's way, they seldom remove it merely to clear the space—they leave it to crumble.

Many of the ancient buildings of Greece, unfortunately, contributed to Turkish building projects. In Athens alone at least three perished during the eighteenth century. An ancient bridge over the Ilissus and an aqueduct of Hadrian were reduced to their foundations and a well-preserved Ionic temple of the classical period disappeared in its entirety. Elsewhere in Greece the story was the same. Successive travellers bear witness to the constant attrition. The surviving columns at Sunium and Corinth became fewer and fewer; the last remains above ground of the Temple of Zeus at Olympia disappeared; in Asia Minor in at least two places the Turks built lime kilns within the columns of a temple so as to be near their materials.

The Parthenon, however, seems to have been regarded as exceptional even by the Turks. Although it suffered its share of accidental damage and the Turks made no positive efforts to preserve it, they did attempt—though in the most feeble way—to prevent the damage from becoming worse. First of all, no one was ever given official permission to remove sculptures still on the building. This was absolute and not even the most un-scrupulous Voivode or Disdar dared break it. Even the permission later given to Lord Elgin is an extremely doubtful exception. But besides conserving the sculptures on the building, it also seems to have been Turkish policy to forbid the removal even of the detached pieces which were to be found lying around on the Acropolis. Unfortunately during the eighteenth century a danger developed which the Turkish authorities were unable to control.

More and more travellers from Western Europe began to find their way to Greece. For the most part they were rich and it was their interest in the classics that took them so far from 'civilized' Europe. These travellers were prepared to pay handsomely for pieces of original sculpture and the Turks were unable to resist. Voivode after Voivode and Disdar after Disdar were successfully bribed to allow sculptured fragments to be taken away, although the pretence that this was illegal was carefully maintained.

There thus began a steady export to all parts of Europe of the fragments found on the Acropolis. What is worse the Turks realized that small, easily transportable fragments found a ready market and began deliberately to break off choice pieces from the buildings. Occasionally—and this can be clearly seen in the sculptures that still survive—they even deliberately defaced them to emphasize their contempt and to raise the offers of their mortified customers. The more stupid of them (but they seem to have been fairly numerous), mystified at how the foreigners could attach such value to broken pieces of marble, concluded that gold must be hidden in them and joined hopefully in the destruction. The travellers, avid for even the smallest piece by the hand of Phidias to show off to their friends at home, were able to convince themselves that their unscrupulous souvenir-hunting was really rescuing ancient art from Turkish barbarism.

Unfortunately the pieces that were thus saved from the Turks were, all too often, lost to the world. On their return the souvenir hunters frequently lost interest in their acquisitions, or their heirs dispersed or destroyed their collections. All means of tracing them quickly disappeared. Apart from pieces removed in 1687 small fragments of the Parthenon sculptures have subsequently come to light in Palermo, Padua, Paris, Würzburg, and Karlsruhe—no doubt brought from Athens in the eighteenth century. Three pieces found their way to the cellar of the Vatican Museum. A large slab of the frieze obtained somehow in 1744 was in the possession of the Royal Academy in London. Other fragments lay in English country houses—Chatsworth and Marbury Hall each had their precious morsel. The Society of Dilettanti had another. A part of the frieze was dug up in a garden in Essex in 1902— how it got there is not known. Three fine pieces known to have been obtained by the traveller Chandler in 1765 have disappeared.[7] What others, one wonders, are still to be discovered and how many more are lost for ever?[8]

During the last twenty years of the eighteenth century a slight brake was put on the dispersal—but not by the Turks. The antiquity market at Athens was successfully cornered by one man, a Frenchman called Louis-François-Sébastien Fauvel. As he plays a very important part in the later story it may be as well to introduce him fully at this stage.[9]

Fauvel was by profession a painter and, as such, he had accompanied the young French nobleman, the Comte de Choiseul-Gouffier on a Hellenic tour in 1780. When Choiseul-Gouffier was appointed French Ambassador to the Porte three years later, he again took Fauvel with him and established him at Athens as his full-time antiquarian agent.* He obtained permission from the Porte for him to draw and take casts. In fact, in this respect, Choiseul-Gouffier's motive in sending Fauvel to Athens was almost exactly the same as Elgin's now was with Lusieri. Choiseul-Gouffier, however, had his eyes on more than drawings and casts: he set Fauvel to collect for him as many original antiquities as he could. His instructions were clear enough: '*Enlevez tout ce que vous pourrez,*' he wrote. '*Ne négligez aucune occasion de piller dans Athènes et dans son territoire tout ce qu'il y a de pillable. N'épargnez ni les morts ni les vivants.*'[10] Choiseul-Gouffier had the good luck to be French Ambassador at the time when French influence at Turkey was at its height and there was little that the Turks refused him. A sizeable collection of sculptures was collected at Athens and elsewhere in Greece and shipped back to France. The British Ambassador of the time—a nice touch this in view of his successor's activities—protested vigorously and ineffectively to the Porte against the export even of the casts.

Choiseul-Gouffier's greatest ambition was to obtain some of the sculpture from the Parthenon but here the Turks drew the line. In spite of constant requests they refused categorically to

---

* On the Monument of Philopappos at Athens one can still read
'AUGUSTE DE CHOISEUL GOUFFIER
FOUCHEROT
FAUVEL
1776 ET 1781'
Foucherot was Choiseul Gouffier's draftsman. He had accompanied Choiseul-Gouffier on an earlier Hellenic tour in 1776.

give him permission to remove any from the building. He did, however, have some success. By judicious bribing of the Disdar Fauvel obtained at different times a fine slab of the frieze and a metope that were dug up among the ruins. These two pieces were despatched to France and arrived safely a few years later. In 1788 Fauvel bought another metope that had fallen from the building during a storm and had broken into three pieces.[11]

But Choiseul-Gouffier was never to enjoy the collection of marbles and casts from the Parthenon that he had built up with great pain. He was a nobleman of one of the great families of France and when the Revolution came he remained loyal to the Royalist cause. The French Government disowned him as a traitor and he was compelled to go into exile in Russia. The antiquities that had reached France, including the two pieces from the Parthenon, were declared national property. The casts were for the most part destroyed. The metope that had come down in the storm was left behind at Athens.

Despite his patron's downfall, Fauvel stayed on at Athens. He took possession of the antiquities that still remained there, including the metope, as recompense for arrears of his pay, and accepted money from the French Government to keep them for the national collection. He also began to build up a collection of his own. With such an old campaigner on the spot the casual travellers found it more difficult to buy fragments: anything that came up for sale went straight to Fauvel's store-room. For example, in 1795, the English traveller J. B. S. Morritt of Rokeby made a secret agreement with the Disdar to buy a metope and part of the frieze, but before they could be got away, Fauvel heard about the scheme and threatened to denounce the Disdar.[12] In 1798, however, his fortunes took a plunge. When Turkey declared war on France after Bonaparte's invasion of Egypt all the French subjects in the Ottoman Empire were arrested and put into prison. Fauvel was no exception and, although later set free, he was again out of the way when Lord Elgin's artists arrived in Athens. His antiquities were sequestrated.

When Lusieri and Elgin's other artists arrived, they knew

nothing of the lively trade in sculpture fragments that had supple-
mented the incomes of successive Disdars for so many years.
They had not come to compete in this market. Their purpose was
quite clear—they were to draw and mould and measure. Elgin
was certainly interested in acquiring original sculptures, but the
artists were given this very much as a secondary task—they were
merely to keep their eyes open for any pieces that could be
obtained.

The first priority was to set to work on drawing and moulding
the Parthenon but at once they ran into difficulties. The Disdar
refused to allow the artists on to the Acropolis on the grounds that
when they climbed the buildings they would overlook the
Turkish homes and spy on their women. This was a sad blow but
the Disdar was adamant and nothing could be done. It was clear
that they would need that favourite instrument of Turkish
government, a firman. A firman was a letter from the Ottoman
Government in Constantinople, usually the Grand Vizier himself,
addressed to one of its officials asking for a favour to be conferred
on an individual. Such a document was not as one might suppose:
in fact, in the disordered state of the Turkish Empire, it was often
little more than permission to make the best bargain one could
with the local authorities. But it was something and, if supported
by a large sum of money, it usually did the trick. Elgin seems to
have succeeded in obtaining a firman on this occasion requesting
the Disdar to allow his artists on the Acropolis, but for some
reason it was not accepted.

While they were waiting, the artists decided to set to work
on the chief monuments outside the Acropolis, the Theseum and
the Monument of Lysicrates. As these were both church properties permission was easily given. But again there were snags. They
discovered that in all Athens they could not obtain timber for
scaffolding or even ropes for lifting their materials. Timber was
sent for from the island of Hydra, but for the ropes and other
tackle they had a windfall. Fauvel, when working for the Comte
de Choiseul-Gouffier had brought from Toulon some excellent
equipment including a large cart big enough to transport heavy
materials. Since Fauvel was now in jail the Turks were happy to

give all these things to the agents of the British Ambassador. The cart was to be a source of contention for fourteen years.*

At long last work began and very good work it was. The drawings of Theodor the Calmuck and of the architects are now in the British Museum. They are elegant, well-finished, and remarkable for their extreme attention to detail. Those of the Calmuck especially are considerable works of art. Not only did he draw the sculptures accurately in the state of decay in which he found them but also, with astonishing imagination and good judgement, he made lively restorations on paper of how they must have looked in their original condition. Unfortunately, the Calmuck was extremely lazy and had an uncommon relish for strong liquor. Lusieri could only make him work by a judicious administration of brandy.

For Lusieri's drawings we unfortunately have to rely for our knowledge on contemporary accounts since most of his Athenian drawings were destroyed. They too seem to have been very good. Lusieri specialized in large panoramas, seven or eight feet long,† with the outlines of every detail of the landscape delineated in pencil and then coloured in water-colours. He had several views in preparation at the same time so that he could work comfortably on one of them, whichever way the wind was blowing. His meagre figure sitting drawing under an umbrella became one of the familiar sights of Athens. The detail of his drawing was so intricate that many people thought he used a telescope and it seems quite probable that he did. Unfortunately he was an extremely slow worker and often he had to rub out part of a view he was working on because the growth of trees and the alteration of buildings had made it out of date before the rest of the picture was complete. Besides being very slow at his drawing Lusieri was very much inclined to leave his drawings half finished or uncoloured. He excused himself by saying that if he once began colouring he would be so fascinated that he would not have patience to return to the dry details of outline.[13] But

* A water-colour of the Erechtheum painted by Robert Smirke in 1803 (and now in the Library of the Royal Institute of British Architects, London) shows this cart prominently in the foreground.

† One which he drew of Constantinople was eighteen feet long.

these faults were in the right direction. There is no doubt that for Elgin's purpose of obtaining an exact record of the buildings of Athens he had found the right men.

In February 1801—that is six months after their arrival in Athens—Elgin's artists were allowed on to the Acropolis for the first time. They did not have a firman but they obtained permission in the usual Turkish way. They paid. Every day they entered the fortress they paid the equivalent of £5 to the Disdar. Elgin reckoned it was worth the price and Lusieri, the Calmuck, and the architects went up daily to make their drawings. So they continued happily for several months.

Then suddenly there was a change. The time had come for the first of the mouldings of the Parthenon sculpture to be taken. The scaffolding was all erected and the moulders were ready to begin work. At that very moment the Disdar announced that all access to the Acropolis for all the artists was forbidden. Bribes were of no avail. The Disdar was quite immovable. Nothing less than a firman from the Porte would persuade him. He had been told by the Porte that a French force was again gathering at Toulon and all military installations were to be closed to foreigners. The Turks, after their experience of the Egyptian expedition of Bonaparte, believed that the Toulon force was directed against some other part of the Ottoman Empire. The artists therefore returned sadly to their work in the lower town and wrote to Elgin begging him to obtain a firman.

Chapter 7

In Search of Ancient Manuscripts

ACCORDING to one very popular interpretation of history, the Renaissance in Western Europe in the fifteenth century is directly attributable to the capture of Constantinople by the Turks in 1453. According to this interpretation the scholars who had kept the light of classical culture burning through all the vicissitudes of the decline of the Roman Empire fled from their last refuge to Italy clutching the precious manuscripts that contained the essence of Greek civilization; the arrival of these scholars and their manuscripts in the West caused a rebirth of interest in the classics and led to the glories of Renaissance and Modern Civilization.

True or false, the surprising fact about this theory was that very few of the works of classical authors which were so avidly searched for during the Renaissance and later came from the East: the great majority were discovered in the libraries of Italy and Western Europe where they had lain neglected during much of the Middle Ages. For centuries, scholars in the West had felt sure that if they could only search the libraries of Constantinople and the parts of the Ottoman Empire which were formerly part of the Eastern Roman Empire they would discover the lost works of many more classical authors. Ancient authors still extant spoke of a vast body of Greek and Latin literature and it was evident that only a tiny proportion had survived in the West. The three great tragedians, Aeschylus, Sophocles and Euripides, for example, were known to have written over three hundred plays but only thirty-three still existed. Livy wrote a history of Rome in one hundred and forty-two books: only thirty-five had been handed down. And to Western scholars even a fragment of an unknown work was a great treasure.

On the face of it there was good reason to suppose that manuscripts of the classics might still be found. The Turks had, for the most part, allowed the Christian communities to remain unmolested and many monasteries and the Greek Patriarchate itself had an unbroken tradition going back to the time of the early Christian emperors. Greek was still spoken, in some cases recognizably classical, and the Greeks of Constantinople considered themselves the heirs of the old imperial aristocracy.

The greatest hope, in most scholars' minds, was that there were manuscripts in the Seraglio at Constantinople. The Seraglio had been the palace of the Byzantine emperors before the Turkish conquest and the Turks in their usual way had merely taken it over and adapted it. It contained a great many things from before the conquest: perhaps there was a remnant of the imperial library? But the Seraglio was absolutely closed to all Christians and even to most Moslems on all but the most extraordinary occasions. It was impossible to say what was there and what was not.

Two years before Elgin's embassy set out, a book on Constantinople by James Dallaway, a former chaplain to the Levant Company at Constantinople, was published in London. It was almost certainly this book which revived interest in the subject of the Seraglio Library in the minds of the English bishops. 'By comparing the accounts of different relators,' wrote Dallaway, 'it is evident that many manuscripts both Greek and Latin as well as oriental are kept [in the Seraglio] in confused heaps without arrangement or catalogue.' Dallaway also asserted as a fact that the Turks preserved with due veneration no less than one hundred and twenty manuscripts in folio, chiefly New Testament and commentaries, which had belonged to the Emperor Constantine himself.[1]

It was to look for classical manuscripts—and if possible to obtain access to the Seraglio Library—that Professor Carlyle had been attached to Lord Elgin's mission. The Bishops of Lincoln and Durham had persuaded the Government to allow this addition even although they refused Elgin's own more ambitious proposals. As a professor of Arabic, Carlyle also wanted to acquire oriental manuscripts, and, as a clergyman, he was interested in manuscripts of the Bible. And he still maintained some interest in his schemes for converting the Moslems by giving them copies of the Bible in Arabic.

When the embassy arrived at Constantinople Carlyle at once began his efforts to obtain admittance to the Seraglio Library. Elgin put in a request for a firman to the Porte, but he might have reckoned on Turkish procrastination. The Turks professed eagerness to be helpful, but weeks passed and no firman was forthcoming. In January plague broke out in the neighbourhood of the Seraglio and this was the signal for all foreigners to retire within their palaces. Access to the Seraglio became out of the question until the last traces of the plague had gone. Carlyle spent the first weeks, therefore, in exploring the oriental literature of the public libraries at Constantinople of which there were about a dozen. He searched the bazaars for oriental manuscripts and bought a great number.

He also made the acquaintance of the Patriarch of Constantinople. The Patriarch lived in great splendour completely in the Turkish style (inevitably Carlyle compares his palace to the Arabian Nights) and received him with great friendliness. He wrote him letters of introduction to his ecclesiastical colleagues in the Ottoman Empire and promised to be as helpful as he could. Carlyle discussed with him the plans to distribute the Bible in Arabic but he was not very encouraged. The Patriarch had heard nothing of a first consignment of 5,000 volumes that had been sent from England many months before. The Patriarch of Jerusalem, who also lived in Constantinople, received Carlyle with equal friendliness. He, too, had heard nothing of the consignment of Bibles that had been sent to Alexandria and after this disappointment Carlyle seems to have abandoned this part of his plan.

At the end of December Carlyle, by Elgin's influence, was given permission to look for manuscripts in the Church of St. Sophia. The great church of Justinian had been converted into a mosque after the Turkish conquest and infidels were now only occasionally admitted. There was hope that somewhere in the vast building there might be the remains of a library. Carlyle and Hunt had been allowed to visit at the time of Elgin's reception as an Ambassador and the superintendent had pointed out to them a compartment secured with a very heavy lock which, he said, had formerly been a chapel. According to the superintendent, a priest and a boy had been in the chapel at the time of the capture of Constantinople celebrating mass; the door had been shut tight by an earthquake and had not been opened since. After some negotiation Carlyle and Hunt were allowed into this chamber. They went to St. Sophia in great secrecy to avoid being seen by the Turks and the rusty lock was forced. But there were no manuscripts and no skeletons of priests: the chamber was completely empty. All they found of any interest were some very badly defaced wall paintings and mosaics.[2]

In January Elgin persuaded the Turks to allow General Koehler to go from Constantinople to join the Grand Vizier's army in Syria. Elgin had been determined all along that the British Military Mission should be employed on more active service than repairing the Dardanelles forts but he had now another reason. He wanted General Koehler to act as a brake on Sir Sidney Smith's disobedience, and he gave him authority, if necessary, to order Smith back on board his ship. Spencer Smith, out of loyalty to his brother, had encouraged the Turks in their opposition to letting General Koehler go. To make sure, therefore, that General Koehler's departure was not delayed at the last moment on some pretext it was arranged that he should leave Constantinople secretly and suddenly with only a few of his staff and make the journey as far as possible by land: the rest of the mission would follow later by the much easier sea route.[3]

Carlyle, realizing that his hopes of entering the Seraglio Library in the near future were remote, asked if he could join the party and visit the monasteries of the Holy Land on the way. This was an ambitious plan for a middle-aged clergyman, but Carlyle insisted, and it was accepted.

Travelling in Turkey in 1800 was no easy business and much of the area they were to pass through was almost unknown to Europeans. But in the next two years nearly all of Elgin's party did a great deal of travelling in dangerous areas, and Carlyle was one of the most adventurous of them all. After their first round of journeys Carlyle and Hunt drew up some notes for use as hints to their successors. They give a pretty clear idea of what conditions were like.

Preparations for a tour from Constantinople. Unless you mean to visit the interior parts of the country the adoption of the Oriental dress is not necessary: but if you do, the Tartarian or Polish dress will be found the most convenient. In this case a defence for the eyes will be wanted; and the best is made with a piece of paste board cut into the shape of a crescent, covered with green silk and bound round the front of the cap by means of a silk ribband.

The best European dress consists of a white hat with a broad brim, a light-coloured broadcloth greatcoat, silk and cotton mixed waistcoat, trowsers or loose pantaloons of Manchester or Nankeen and strong roomy half boots. A large Venetian mantle or German cloak would prove a useful and salutary companion at night. A portable bed frame would conduce much to comfort in a country so full of vermin, particularly if furnished with a Moskito curtain, but if so much baggage be thought too cumbersome, a small hair Mattrass, and a carpet to spread it on, cannot well be dispensed with.

Three dozen of clean shirts must be taken for there are very few places where our mode of washing linen is understood. The bedding and the rest of the baggage ought to be divided into such portions as are fit for conveyance on horseback. An English saddle (made very hollow in the back) should be taken with you, or at least a Turkish saddle accommodated as much as possible to our mode of riding. It is necessary to provide yourself with kitchen utensils, a portable furnace, and (in your voyages) with a quantity of charcoal, also with table linen, plates etc. An Armenian or Greek servant must be hired for cooking your victuals.

On the mode of conveyance by land. Horses are to be hired in most places of the continent but if the country is very rocky and mountainous it would be advisable to chuse mules. In the Isles of the Archipelago in general you must be contented with Asses . . . The usual rate of going is about 3 geographical miles per hour. The horse hire varies from two to three piastres a day for each beast including all expenses.* There is usually a man to every two horses who accompanies

---

* The rate of exchange in 1800 made 1 Turkish piastre equivalent to 1s. 7d. sterling. There were 40 paras to a piastre.

them on foot and receives a backshish or gratuity of 20 paras a day.

Your guides, if their horses are hired by the day will devise various pretexts for detaining you on the road such as the distance of good night quarters etc. They will also endeavour to prevail on you not to visit many interesting spots either because they fear the roads will cripple their horses or because they know the price of barley there is high. You must be on your guard against all such interested manœuvres.

In general it is best to avoid associating with you in these tours officious Greeks or Franks* of the Towns whose only object at best is to live well for a few days and take a pleasant ride at your expense, and who, of course, will endeavour to detain you as long as possible on the road, especially at such places as afford good eating and drinking.

The best night quarters are in the Greek monasteries which are to be found almost everywhere. On your departure pay the full value of the provisions which you have consumed and leave a few piastres as a present to the church. In default of a monastery, a peasant's cottage neatly swept out is infinitely preferable to a Turkish Konak—for in the former you will be well protected from the night air and feel no material inconvenience but from fleas: in the latter you will be exposed to the wind on all sides and devoured by bugs. . . .

Immediately upon your arrival at a new place visit the chief thereof, whether Turk or Greek, and present your firman. He becomes then responsible for your safety and good treatment but would otherwise be piqued at your neglect. A Turkish guard is always an incumbrance and attended with considerable expense but is frequently expedient by way of protection from insult or from robbery. In the first case a single attendant is sufficient but in the second the force necessary for your protection varies with the danger from two to twenty men. . . .

Your firman will have more or less authority in proportion as the province or district has more or less dependence on the Porte: for in some provinces that dependence is very slight indeed and in a few virtually null. It is here you must have recourse to the other means of protection such as presents. . . .

Useful Hints. Avoid having the air of examining Turkish fortresses. If you should be questioned about the motives of your tour, you may reply that it is the custom of your country, and that you have read much of Greece in ancient books, of which you may exhibit a proof that will serve to amuse. The most current notion is that you are in

In Turkey the word 'Frank' is still sometimes used to denote any Western European.

search of hidden treasure, it being impossible for them to conceive that you travel merely to examine the mouldering ruins of ancient towns and temples . . .

The national character differs extremely in the various parts of the Empire. In the first place a great line of distinction must be drawn between the European and Asiatic Turks. The former corrupted by too much power and by their intercourse with the Greeks are perfidious, and proud. The latter are more simple in their manners and trustworthy. Among the Greeks the Islanders of the Archipelago and in general the inhabitants of large towns are a very selfish insidious and perfidious people . . .

Presents of money are always expected by the attendants of the persons whom you visit whether Greeks or Turks and these in fact constitute their wages. But it is best to distribute this yourself instead of employing a deputy. At every house you are treated after the fashion of the country with pipes and coffee and the attendants when you retire expect their fee at the door.

When you travel thro' a country suspected to harbour the plague you will, of course, ask questions at every village about its existence; but it never happens that you can hear the real truth so much is the interest of every place affected by the reputation of harbouring the disorder. If you ask directly whether the plague exists there and receive a positive denial of it, the answer is by no means to be relied on; but if you ask whether there is any sickness in the village and receive for answer that there is a feverish complaint but which they assure you is not the plague, you have then very strong reasons for suspecting it. In which case suffer no intercourse with the villagers but what is accompanied with every precaution, and by no means suffer your servants to stroll into the bazar for brandy or on any pretence whatever.[4]

The party set off in January 1800. Apart from Carlyle, it consisted of General Koehler, two of his officers, a military draftsman, and thirty attendants. All were dressed as Turks and were well armed. The plan was to strike straight across Asia Minor from north-west to south-east. No European had been that way for about a hundred years and the journey took them through the territory of many warlike pashas. Some turned out to be hospitable, others unfriendly depending largely on their current relations with the Porte.

All the members of the expedition were interested in classical antiquities and they made many diversions to look at ancient remains. They copied numerous inscriptions and the draftsman drew the more interesting buildings. They also tried to make a rough map of their route, noting anything of geographical interest, and attempting to identify ancient cities from the names of the modern villages. The journey took about a month, at first on horseback, latterly on camels. Carlyle kept a detailed diary of the journey and he also indulged his taste for writing verses. His poetic manner—which affected his prose as much as his verse—made him rather a joke with the soldiers but they seem to have liked him well enough. The following passage, written among the ruins of Nicaea, the place where the great council of the church formulated the Nicene creed, is a typical example of his style.

Just as the sun appeared we emerged from the dell in which we had been for some time travelling; when as sweet a scene opened upon us as can be conceived. In front was the lake of Nicaea bending through its green valley. Immediately between us and the lake rose up a woody hill, which, by intercepting the centre of the prospect seemed to divide the expanse of water before us into two separate reaches. Along the opposite side of the lake ran a range of dark mountains, scarce yet, except on their most prominent parts, illuminated by the sun—the snowy summits of Olympus empurpled by the reflection of the morning clouds, terminated the view. To the left the minarets of Nicaea were seen peeping out of the water at the extremity of the lake. To the right the lake stretched itself till it was lost amongst the windings of the mountains.

It is not possible to form an idea of a more complete scene of desolation than Nicaea now exhibits:—streets without a passenger, houses without an inhabitant, and ruins of every age, fill the precincts of this once celebrated city. The deserted mosque, whose minaret we ascended in order to obtain a general notion of the plan of the place bore evident marks of having been erected from the remains of a Christian church and many of these upon a closer inspection shewed clearly that they had formerly belonged to a Pagan temple:—our Mohammedan mosque was falling to decay and like its predecessors in splendour must soon become a heap of rubbish—what a *generation* of ruin was here![5]

Carlyle was also inspired to some verses of which the following is a sample. He was a true precursor of Byron.

> Nicaea hail! rcnown'd for fierce debate,
>   For synods bustling o'er yon silent spot.
> For zealous ardour—for polemic hate—
>   For truth preserv'd, and charity forgot.

> Full oft, th'historic record as I've scann'd
>   Has fancy's touch those solemn scenes pourtray'd,
> Bid thy proud domes display the mitred band,
>   Thy streets unfold the long-drawn cavalcade.

> Those scenes are past—thy streets no longer shew
>   Their busy throngs—yet is there breast so cold
> As calm can trace, without one trilling glow,
>   What thought has pictur'd and what fame has told?

> Those scenes are fled—those domes are swept away—
>   Succeeding domes now totter to their fall,
> And mouldering mosques on moulder'd fanes decay
>   While desolation bends to grasp them all.[6]

From Asia Minor Carlyle crossed to Cyprus and there he met Sir Sidney Smith. Smith told him that the Convention of El Arish had just been signed and Carlyle decided to alter his plans. He decided to leave General Koehler, and cross to Alexandria to have a look at Egypt now that—as he thought—peace was restored. When his ship was off Alexandria, however, he and Sir Sidney Smith heard of the disowning of the Convention by the British Government and the subsequent battles in which over 10,000 Turks were killed.

Customs were different in those days and Carlyle was determined not to be done out of his trip to Egypt. Despite the renewal of the war he went ashore under a flag of truce with an officer of Sir Sidney Smith's staff and met the French generals. They gave him a handsome dinner and showed him the sights of Alexandria. He was introduced to some of the scholars and scientists who had accompanied the expedition and also (laid on specially for his benefit) saw some of the best French troops on parade.

From Alexandria Carlyle made a journey to Jerusalem and visited the ancient monastery of St. Saba. Only a fortnight before he was there some Bedouin bandits had attacked the monastery, set fire to part of it, and killed a large number of the monks. But Carlyle was not daunted. The Governor of Jerusalem furnished him with an escort of the very same bandits to protect him from their friends.

Carlyle was then permitted to examine the library but there was little of interest. He wrote to the Bishop of Lincoln:

Except twenty-nine copies of the Gospels and one of the Epistles, this celebrated library does not contain anything valuable. . . . I was permitted by the Superior to bring along with me six of what I judged the oldest Mss. viz. two copies of the Gospels, one of the Epistles, two books of Homilies and apostolic letters, which I took for the sake of the quotations, and a copy of the Sophist Libanius, the only work like a classic author that I met with. I hope the Patriarch will allow me to convey them to England.[7]

From Jerusalem Carlyle went to the Grand Vizier's Headquarters which were now established at Jaffa and then made his way back through the Greek Islands to Constantinople.

Back at Constantinople Carlyle renewed his efforts to gain admittance to the Seraglio Library. The Turks, as usual, hummed and hawed, and the stories about ancient manuscripts became more and more confusing. The Turks began to say that there was no library in the Seraglio at all; then that there were two; then they suggested that Carlyle might look in a building near St. Sophia that they said had been shut ever since the Turkish conquest. Carlyle himself met a Frenchman who declared that his brother had personally seen Greek and Latin manuscripts in the Seraglio. Elgin and Carlyle pressed on with their requests more and more eagerly.

While he was awaiting the results of the protracted negotiations, Carlyle, with Hunt's assistance, explored every Greek monastery in Constantinople and in the nearby Princes Islands. He also examined thoroughly the library of the Patriarch. In none of them did he discover a single fragment of any unknown classical author: the libraries consisted almost entirely of religious works of one kind or another. The monks attached little value to manuscripts, much preferring printed editions, and Carlyle was able to buy a number of those he thought the most interesting. The Patriarch of Jerusalem also allowed him to borrow some from his library to be sent to England to be collated. Altogether he collected about twenty-eight manuscripts mostly mediaeval.

At last after many months delay Carlyle began to make progress in his attempt to enter the Seraglio. He obtained an introduction to the people who really could help him. One was the Capitan Pasha who was fast becoming a firm friend of the Elgins: the other was Youssuf Aga, the steward of the Sultan's mother. The Capitan Pasha had been a slave in the Seraglio brought originally from Georgia; he had been a childhood friend of the Sultan and, when he came to the throne, had emerged after thirty years in the Seraglio to take command of the Turkish Fleet. Youssuf Aga, a Cretan, had started life as a ship's writer; he became a favourite first of the Pasha of Anatolia and then of the Sultan's mother; despite his humble title, he too was one of the most powerful men in the Ottoman Empire. After a liberal distribution of presents and a good deal of ceremony Carlyle was given a letter of introduction from Youssuf Aga to the governor of the Seraglio. He was escorted to the library on a day in November 1800, almost a year after his arrival at Constantinople.

Unlike all the other libraries he had visited, the Seraglio Library was carefully looked after. The books were arranged with titles showing in padlocked cases in a small cruciform building near the Seraglio Mosque. Carlyle was permitted to look at every one. But the result was bitterly disappointing. This is his report to the Bishop of Lincoln.

The whole number of Mss in the Library amounts to 1294 much the greatest part of which are Arabic; these are however most of the best Persian and Turkish writers but alas, not one volume in Greek, Hebrew or Latin! . . . Such, my Lord is the famous Library of the Seraglio! respecting which so many falsehoods have been advanced; but which, I am now very clear both from the manner in which it is secured, the declarations of the Turks, and the contradictory accounts of the Franks, was never before subjected to the examination of a Christian.[8]

Now that he had examined the Seraglio Library Carlyle's main mission in the East had been accomplished. He had wanted (since the Black Sea was now open to British ships) to make a journey along the north coast of Asia Minor to Trebizond examining the monasteries on the way, but the long delay in negotiating with the Turks made that impossible. He decided to go home.

He had, however, one last hope. In the rocky promontory of Mount Athos there were twenty-four monasteries that had survived the Turkish occupation as a virtually independent community: perhaps in the Holy Mountain he might yet find an ancient manuscript. He decided, therefore, to visit Athos on his way back and, if possible, to examine other monasteries of mainland Greece. He had been very lonely on his previous expedition and he persuaded Elgin to allow Hunt to accompany him on this journey.

Armed with numerous firmans and letters of introduction the two travellers set off in March 1801. They stopped at the Dardanelles on their way to examine the plain of Troy and make their contribution to the controversy that was then raging in academic circles about the exact location of ancient Troy. Hunt visited the church from where the first of the Elgin collection of marbles had been removed by General Koehler's soldiers in 1799 and also, with the help of the local pasha, obtained a number of other statues and inscriptions on behalf of Lord Elgin. Carlyle continued his meticulous journal and composed poems appropriate to the romantic spots they visited. But on the plain of Troy he and Hunt met some competition. Another party of English travellers were engaged on exploring it at the same time. This is a suitable moment to introduce another character in the story, the Reverend Edward Daniel Clarke.

Clarke was a Cambridge don, a mineralogist. In company with one of his pupils, J. M. Cripps, he was making one of the grandest of all grand tours. He had crossed Europe by means of Scandinavia, Russia, and the Crimea and was intending to visit Asia Minor, Syria, the Holy land, Egypt, and Greece. Clarke was a man of quite astonishing energy and thoroughness. The account of his travels which he published later in six large volumes is encyclopaedic.[9] He noted down absolutely everything that took his fancy on the theory that even isolated scraps of information might be useful to somebody. Apart from descriptions of scenery, and of the people, he included current prices in the markets, lists of plants, observations on geology, and the temperature each day at every place he visited compared with London. Besides employing a professional painter, he made numerous rather amateurish sketches, some of them little more than silhouettes, and copied every inscription he found even if it consisted of only a few fragmentary letters. At each place he dutifully compared his impressions with the descriptions of former travellers from ancient times onwards. And everywhere he was on the look out to buy statues, inscriptions, manuscripts, coins, and other antiquities.

A fierce argument broke out between the two pairs of travellers about the site of ancient Troy and they parted in great disgust with one another. But unlike most quarrels, instead of subsiding with the passage of time, it became more and more intense.[10] At first Clarke's enmity was directed entirely against Carlyle—a simple rivalry between two Cambridge dons; it did not extend to Elgin who in fact treated him with great friendship, opened his home to him, obtained privileges for him from the Porte, and even presented his pupil Cripps with a collection of Egyptian antiquities. But after a few months Clarke became embittered with Elgin too and with all his works. He openly joined the faction that had supported Spencer Smith at Constantinople and, as will be seen later, there was no limit to the slanders he was prepared to tell. By a curious irony Lusieri was accompanying Clarke in the Troad for a few days before the quarrel broke out and gave him a few of his sketches. Later he gave him a few more. As it turned out these are (with one exception) the only drawings of Lusieri's that survived Elgin's embassy and by the terms of the contract they ought to have belonged to Elgin. Instead they helped to embellish Clarke's own book.[11]

After leaving Clarke, Carlyle and Hunt spent about three weeks in the Troad, Homer in hand, tracing on the ground the scenes of the Iliad. They came to the conclusion that Homer was often wrong but, as Hunt wrote modestly in his diary, 'It would be an invidious task to attempt destroying any of the enthusiasm that is felt in reading some of the immortal works of the ancient writers by shewing in what instances they have deviated from geographical precision in their allusions to local scenery.'[12] They then crossed to Tenedos and Lemnos and, after very nearly perishing in a severe storm, arrived by sea at Athos.[13]

The first monastery they visited was Batopaidi and it turned out to be more like a fortress than a religious retreat. It was surrounded by high walls interspaced with towers, and cannon lay in the embrasures. The outer gate was doubly plated with iron, and there were three more gates to be negotiated before they could enter. At each stage they saw more cannon mounted on carriages, ready to be brought forward to the defence.

Despite their warlike appearance the monks, of whom there were about two hundred and fifty, received the travellers with great kindness. They showed them over the twenty-seven churches attached to the convent and their farms and vineyards. They would have paid more attention to their guests but it was Easter and the peninsula was crowded with thousands of pilgrims. These pilgrims were of all Balkan races, Albanians, Bulgarians, and Wallachians, and for the most part were professional bandits. They brought their arms with them and shot off their muskets perpetually in celebration. Whenever these bands of robbers made a successful raid or act of piracy, they came to Athos, received absolution, and handed over part of their spoils. At Easter all the 'pilgrims' arrived together and arranged for masses to be said for themselves during the coming year. The economy of Mount Athos was largely dependent on their contributions.

Once they had settled in to their strange surroundings Carlyle and Hunt asked to be allowed to see the library. For a few days all they could get were evasive answers. At last Carlyle, becoming impatient, invoked his letter from the Patriarch and insisted that he should be shown the library. The visitors were thereupon taken to a damp dark cellar where they found a large number of manuscript volumes lying about on the floor in complete disorder. Most of the covers had been torn off and all were eaten by worms and rats and mouldy with damp.

To the surprise of the monks Carlyle and Hunt set themselves at once to the unpleasant task of examining every volume. Most were ecclesiastical works, gospels, liturgies and polemical theology, but, for the first time they found a substantial number of classical authors, Homer, Plato, Aristotle, Hippocrates, Galen and others. None was of any unknown work but their hopes were greatly raised. They offered to buy some of the oldest copies, but the Abbott—more scrupulous than his colleagues in monasteries they had so far visited—declared he could not sell any church property without the express approval of the Patriarch.

From Batopaidi the travellers visited every one of the twenty-four monasteries on Athos. They were very diverse. Some, like Batopaidi, were large and well-organized and contained several hundred monks. Others had less than ten inhabitants. For the most part the monks were poor, ignorant, illiterate, and superstitious, but occasionally, they met an educated man, usually one who had come from elsewhere. Carlyle and Hunt examined every library and made a detailed catalogue of each but again they were to be disappointed. In none of them did they find a single unknown classical fragment. The libraries were generally in much the same condition as at Batopaidi, sometimes even in the open air. Everywhere the monks attached more value to the printed editions. But although there was nothing new, some of the libraries did contain valuable ancient copies of the New Testament and other works in which Carlyle was interested. He soon learnt to offer his money in private to the abbot and so overcome his scruples about selling church property. In one monastery the abbot said a substantial number of their manuscripts had already been sold to the Venetians.

From Athos Carlyle and Hunt went by sea to Athens, having abandoned the plan to search for manuscripts in mainland Greece because of the danger from bandits. They arrived at about the same time as Lady Elgin's mother and father who were now on their way home after their holiday at Constantinople.

All the new visitors had expected to find Lusieri and the artists at work on the Acropolis but their arrival coincided with the Disdar's sudden refusal to give them permission to enter. They made various attempts, in the name of the ambassador, to persuade the Disdar to change his mind but without success. The Disdar was prepared to let the ambassador's friends visit the fortress but not his artists—presumably working on the same principle that nowadays sometimes forbids photography. They therefore added their efforts to those of Lusieri and Logotheti in pressing Elgin to seek a strong firman from the Porte.

At the end of May Mr. and Mrs. Nisbet left Athens for Malta and home. They had arranged to have sent on, as a decoration for their house, a number of pieces of coloured marble and porphyry which they had noticed at various ancient sites and also an ancient marble throne with which they had been presented by the Archbishop of Athens.

Carlyle went home with them and this is almost the last we shall see of him. He took with him a few dozen manuscripts collected from various monasteries and several hundred oriental manuscripts which he had bought in the bazaars. He was a disappointed man. Not only had he failed to find what he had come for, but he had spent a large sum of money and ruined his health in the process. His expectation that Elgin would help pay his expenses proved unfounded and the early friendship gave way to dislike.[14] He returned to his quiet life of scholar and churchman and died shortly afterwards. The fate of the manuscripts will be related later.

So ended this quest for the remains of the libraries of the Byzantines. It had been almost a total failure. Throughout the nineteenth century many others were to follow Carlyle and undertake journeys and visit monasteries even more remote than he had ventured to. Although much was discovered of interest to scholars, the intoxicating hope of coming upon some of the famous lost works of antiquity has yet to be fulfilled.

Chapter 8

The Conquest of Egypt and its Results

IN the fourteen months since he landed secretly in France in November 1799, Napoleon Bonaparte had not been idle. He had made himself undisputed leader of the country, had pacified a rebellion in the Vendée, established a new constitution, made far-reaching economic reforms, and laid the foundations of a new legal system. He had also overcome the resistance of all the countries opposed to France with the exception of Britain and Turkey. Naples and Austria were crushed by military force, Spain brought into a subservient alliance, and Russia had been induced to change sides.

Then in January 1801 he turned his attention at last to the army shut up in Egypt and began to gather a force at Toulon to reinforce it. It was put under the command of Admiral Ganteaume who had been on the first expedition to Egypt but whose principal distinction was his successful command of the squadron that brought Bonaparte secretly home.

The British had watched their allies crumble away one by one with only the capture of Malta to console them. But they did not repeat the mistake of withdrawing from the Mediterranean which they had made when the first alliance against Revolutionary France had collapsed. Instead they made preparations to send their own expedition to Egypt to expel the French by force. An army of 17,000 under General Sir Ralph Abercromby began to assemble at Malta at the same time as the French relief force of Admiral Ganteaume was getting ready at Toulon. In addition a smaller British force assembled at the Cape, ready if need be, to attack Egypt from the Red Sea.

General Abercromby made his preparations well. The force, having been collected at Malta, was taken by sea to Marmoris, on the coast of Asia Minor opposite Rhodes. It was then allowed to recuperate from the voyage and was put through a full programme of training in amphibious landings to prepare it for the invasion of Egypt. Abercromby brought most of his supplies with him but he was still in need of food, horses, and various other stores. For these he applied to Lord Elgin, who was not only the chief British authority in the area but a close friend and neighbour at home. Elgin exerted himself vigorously and, at his own expense, bought vast quantities of stores for the expedition. Asia Minor was scoured to provide horses; special shipyards were established to build boats; and grain ships were sent all over the Eastern Mediterranean. For all this Elgin paid and ran up bills of many thousands of pounds on behalf of the British Government. But one incidental result was that the rate of exchange of the pound fell and Elgin's salary became considerably less valuable accordingly.[1]

The French preparations on the other hand were inept and uncoordinated. General Menou, who had succeeded General Kléber as Commander-in-Chief in Egypt, was much more interested in trying to colonize Egypt than in the military side of his job. Although well warned that an invasion was imminent, he did nothing to reinforce his units stationed near the coast, and even after the invasion fleet was sighted off Aboukir, he stayed in Cairo for ten days before going to the coast. Admiral Ganteaume's relief force at Toulon behaved equally badly. It set sail for Egypt in February but returned to port after a few days without even making contact with the enemy. Bonaparte was furious and ordered it to sea again, but Admiral Ganteaume, more afraid of the British than of Bonaparte, returned to Toulon for a second time after sighting a British naval squadron. He was safely at Toulon when the decisive battle for Egypt took place.

The British Expeditionary Force landed at Aboukir Bay in Egypt on 8 March. They were vigorously opposed from the shore with artillery and musket fire but their training at Marmoris paid off and they established a beachhead. The French on the coast—

whom Menou had not reinforced—were quickly overcome and the force moved inland. Menou continued to make every possible mistake. He waited until the British were consolidated ashore and then attacked with only a fraction of the forces at his disposal. The result was that he was severely defeated and had to retire to Alexandria.

The British were now able to bring in reinforcements by sea and to concert plans with the Turkish army which had again lumbered down from Syria. The Turkish army contained the remains of General Koehler's ill-fated British Military Mission although Koehler himself and his wife had died some months before. The chief loss on the British side was the death of General Abercromby who died of wounds suffered in the assault. He was succeeded as Commander-in-Chief by General Hutchinson who proved equally vigorous and effective.

In early April the ancient dykes around Alexandria were breached so that the sea poured in round the outside of the city. The British were then able to put the city, including General Menou himself, under siege. By June the main body of the rest of the French forces were compelled to retire within the gates of Cairo and it too was put under siege. And so the French were shut up in two places and it seemed as if a long time would elapse before they could be forced to surrender.

At Cairo a mixed army was drawn up outside the city consisting of Hutchinson's British, various Turks under the Grand Vizier and the Capitan Pasha, and 1,500 Mamelukes who for the first time for five hundred years had become suddenly pro-Turkish. No one was more surprised than the besiegers when the French general in Cairo suddenly announced that he was prepared to capitulate on the same terms as the famous Convention of El Arish. His terms were accepted, an armistice was arranged, and the British took over the city in July. General Menou in Alexandria declared when he heard the news that he would fight to the last man to uphold the honour of the French Republic.

Menou's resistance at Alexandria had one small hope to justify it. Bonaparte had ordered Admiral Ganteaume at Toulon to try going to sea for the third time. The Toulon force, according to

Bonaparte's strategy, was to sail to Libya and land 5,000 troops; they were then to make their way to Egypt through the desert. That Bonaparte expected these troops to achieve this feat of endurance after three months on board ship is perhaps a measure of the boldness of his strategic imagination but, fortunately for them, Admiral Ganteaume was still not a hero. He did set sail for the third time from Toulon and some of his ships actually reached the Libyan coast, but the locals looked hostile and he scurried back yet again to the safety of Toulon without going any nearer to Egypt. How he faced Bonaparte after this is not recorded.

After the failure of Ganteaume's third excursion even General Menou was obliged to admit that he could do nothing more. His change of mind was confirmed when the forces that had been besieging Cairo began to join in the siege of Alexandria. Seven days after declaring he would fight to the end, General Menou capitulated and the last French resistance in Egypt came to an end. The terms he obtained were those he had denounced as shameful and treasonable when his countrymen at Cairo had capitulated and, of course, were those of Sir Sidney Smith's Convention of El Arish. In September the French forces in Egypt were conveyed back to France by the Royal Navy. Egypt was completely in the hands of the British and the Turks. Suddenly it appeared to the chancelleries of Europe that nothing now stood in the way of a renewal of peace.

The success of the British expedition to Egypt made Elgin one of the most highly favoured men in Turkey. The Turks were of course delighted at the prospect of recovering Egypt from the French and actually governing it themselves for the first time for some hundreds of years. They could not do enough to show their appreciation to the country that had made this possible.

Elgin was given (again) all the honours of the Ottoman Court. He was presented with an aigrette from the Sultan's turban, the Order of the Crescent (set in diamonds), more pelisses, and more caparisoned horses. He was put through all the elaborate cere-monial that he had received when he first arrived. He was now so much more practised at it than the majority of the Turkish participants that he was able to put them right when a mistake in etiquette occurred in the course of it.[2] Lady Elgin too was given the unprecedented honour of being received by the Valida, the Sultan's mother, to whom she was conveyed by a large escort of black eunuchs.[3]

When the news came through of the final triumph in Egypt the Turks arranged a splendid national celebration. For seven days Constantinople was illuminated. There were fireworks displays, music, and salutes of guns every evening. Scenes from the Egyptian war were acted out in miniature by the warships in the harbour.[4] On the first night of the celebrations it rained and the fireworks did not go off very well. The Turks therefore immediately banished the man in charge of the display and appointed someone else in his place. Fortunately for him the weather kept fine for the rest of the week. The Elgins hired a special ship over which a huge illuminated star and crescent was to be hung, but the celebrations had caused a complete sell-out of all the lamps in Constantinople. The celebrations were a success nevertheless. 'It was the most beautiful night you can imagine,' Lady Elgin wrote home, 'both sides of the Bosphorus illuminated, rockets, guns, cannon going off at all corners, all sorts of music, and a sort of masquerade, and all the Turks were as merry as Christians. . . . I think they might have conquered Egypt over and over again had they but fired half the number of cannon in earnest they are now firing in joke.'[5]

The climax of the celebrations was the Sultan showing himself to his people. He lay on a silver sofa in a Green Kiosk of the Seraglio surrounded by hundreds of attendants. An immense concourse of people on shore and in boats prayed that he should 'conquer all his enemies and reward all his friends'.[6] The women prayed that he should have a son and the priests conferred on him the title of 'Selim the Conqueror'. While Elgin was at a conference Lady Elgin rowed about and looked at all the sights. She did not realize that it was forbidden to pass near the Sultan and ordered the sailors to row past him. The Sultan—who not long before regarded it as intolerably degrading to cast his eyes on a foreigner —nodded amiably to her and, when she had gone past, picked up a telescope and watched her into the distance. Lady Elgin noticed that the discipline of the Seraglio seemed to have been relaxed for the occasion. She saw some of her friends, the ladies of the Harem, looking out of the windows and waving to her although the Black Eunuchs kept a close watch on these improprieties.

It was not only the Ambassador who benefited from the sudden love for the British. All British warships were given free provisions and refitting facilities in Turkish ports. The captain of one which happened to be in Constantinople at the time of the celebrations received a diamond snuff box and the other officers a gold one. All the officers who took part in the Egyptian Expedition—some eighteen hundred in all—were given a gold medal and, needless to say, a pelisse. General Hutchinson's brother who was in Constantinople acting as a messenger from Egypt, received a pelisse, a diamond aigrette, a watch set in diamonds worth £2,000, twenty-five purses of money, a diamond snuff box, and shawls and embroidered stuffs worth £7,000.[7]

There were other, more imaginative and practical, gifts which Elgin persuaded the Turks to bestow. For one thing Elgin persuaded the Turks to release the French subjects who had been put in prison in all parts of the Ottoman Empire.[8] It was contrary to the usage of civilized nations to imprison mere civilians and Elgin told the Turks so. They were duly impressed and Ruffin, the French Chargé d'Affaires, emerged from the Seven Towers where he had been since 1798. One wonders what the Turks thought two years later when Elgin himself was imprisoned in France as a result of a change in the usage of civilized nations.

The release of the French precipitated another act of favour to Elgin. Since 1799 he and his embassy had lived in the French Palace while the rightful owners were in the Seven Towers. Another embassy building was clearly necessary. Elgin persuaded the Turks to bestow on him a site of land suitable for building a permanent British Palace and at the same time persuaded the British Government and Levant Company to put up the money for the building. He brought over the hunchback architect Balestra, one of the artists who were working for him at Athens, and set him to work on a design. The result was a very close copy of Elgin's own house in Scotland, Broomhall.[9]

Another gift was the release of Maltese slaves. For centuries the Knights of St. John had employed Maltese as crews for their ships as they conducted their latter-day crusades against the Turks. Many had fallen into Turkish hands. They were kept in chains in a prison called the Bagnio and used as slaves in the Constantinople Dockyard. But now Malta was British and the Maltese British subjects. Elgin persuaded the Porte to release them from slavery. One hundred and sixty were discovered and given freedom. Most had been in captivity for six or eight years but a few had been there much longer and two for no less than forty-eight years. Tents were pitched for them in the grounds of the British Palace until they could be taken back to Malta, and the Capitan Pasha—who was responsible for the dockyard—even gave them 48 piastres each as they left his service.[10]

The success in Egypt brought Elgin to the pinnacle of his diplomatic career. He now enjoyed a position of influence at Constantinople such as no Christian ambassador had ever approached. The Government at home were well pleased with his success and told him so in an official letter.[11] All the aims of the embassy had been achieved and Britain was now the dominant power in the Eastern Mediterranean. However successful the French might be on the Continent of Europe this was one sizeable victory that could be claimed against them.

Elgin might well look forward to further dazzling triumphs even though his old friend Lord Grenville, who had helped him on his career so far, had now been replaced as Foreign Secretary by Lord Hawkesbury. But apart from the official letter of commendation there was no sign from home that the Government wanted to do more for him—there was no knighthood, no United Kingdom peerage that would save him the necessity of being elected to the House of Lords, as a Scottish Representative Peer. Elgin was never constrained by modesty in these matters. He drew up a 'Memorial to the King' and sent it to the Foreign Secretary with a request that it should be submitted. The Memorial gave a blow by blow account of Elgin's career to date setting out the various successes and emphasizing the huge personal expense that they had involved him in. It finished with a straight-forward request for a mark of Royal favour.[12] But again Elgin was unlucky: no public honour was forthcoming. A few months later Elgin wrote to Lord Keith, the naval Commander-in-Chief, asking him to explain in his despatches what an important part he had played in the conquest of Egypt. He deserved an honour, he wrote, adding disingenuously: 'I have never had one mark of favour nor ever asked one in my life.'[13] But it was no good. The prize which he passionately desired all his life escaped him at even this most propitious moment.

Chapter 9

The Firman

WHEN Admiral Ganteaume's French relief force began to gather at Toulon the British intelligence system got to work. Last time a force had gathered there they guessed it was intended to invade Ireland: it went, of course, to Egypt. This time the British Government guessed that the French were about to invade Greece. When Elgin passed on this titbit of intelligence to the Turks they acted upon it at once. They sent out an order to all the military governors in the European provinces telling them to put their fortresses into a state of readiness.

Among those who received the order was the Disdar of Athens and his first—and seemingly only—action was to forbid Lusieri and the other artists of Lord Elgin to enter the Acropolis to draw and mould the sculptures. The prohibition came into force in May 1801 shortly before Carlyle and Hunt, and Mr. and Mrs. Nisbet, arrived in Athens. Logotheti and Lusieri both wrote to Elgin asking him to obtain a firman to allow the artists to continue their work, but it was the evidence of the Nisbets that persuaded Elgin to persevere. He had been half-inclined to abandon the whole enterprise because of the constant difficulties but, when the Nisbets told him of the great excellence of the work that had been done before the prohibition, he decided to ask the Porte for a firman. He opened negotiations with the Capitan Pasha on 14 June, the day he received their letter.[1]

A few days earlier Hunt arrived back at Constantinople from Athens and was able to give Elgin an eye-witness account of what was happening and what was needed. He drew up a memorandum on the type of firman that he thought was required.

July 1, 1801. Mr. Hunt recommends that a Ferman should be procured from the Porte, addressed to the Voivode and Cadi* of Athens, as well as to the Disdar, or Governor of the Citadel; stating that the artists are in the service of the British Ambassador Extraordinary, and that they are to have not only permission but protection in the following objects:—

(1) to enter freely within the walls of the Citadel, and to draw and model with plaster the Ancient Temples there.

(2) to erect scaffolding and to dig where they may wish to discover the ancient foundations.

(3) liberty to take away any sculptures or inscriptions which do not interfere with the works or walls of the Citadel.[2]

This document is of great interest in view of later events. Most strikingly, it does not seek specific permission to remove sculptures *from the buildings*, although an interpretation that this was intended could be put on it. The emphasis is still very much on the original objects of the artists—to draw, to model, and to take away any choice pieces they found lying about. The exception in the last section is evidently to allay any Turkish fear that digging on the Acropolis or the removal of ancient stones from the modern walls would affect the military strength of the fortress.

On 17 June General Hutchinson received the surrender of Cairo and the success of the Egyptian expedition was finally assured. On 6 July, Elgin obtained the firman he had asked for.[3] These two events were intimately connected: indeed, allowing for the time news took to travel and the ceremoniousness of all Turkish business, one followed at once after the other. Elgin himself acknowledged that he was making little progress in the negotiations for a firman until suddenly the Turks began to shower all kinds of favours on their British allies. The granting of the firman was just another gift to be compared with the aigrettes, pelisses, horses, snuff boxes, medals, and other favours lavished on the British.

The firman was a letter addressed to the Voivode and Cadi* of Athens signed by the Caimacan Pasha who was still acting Grand

* The Cadi was the Chief Justice.

Vizier. It was to be conveyed to them by Philip Hunt. It is in two parts, the first stating the request of Lord Elgin, the second granting it point by point. It is clearly based on Hunt's memorandum of 1 July. Like most official documents it is drafted so as to be understandable by a half-wit and is so repetitious that only the most indefatigable reader is likely to read it to the end. But despite its appearance of being exact and comprehensive, it becomes ambiguous at the most crucial point. The text is as follows, translated from the Italian version given to Hunt.

It is hereby signified to you, that our sincere Friend, his Excellency Lord Elgin Ambassador Extraordinary from the Court of England to the Porte of Happiness, has represented to us, that it is well known that the greater part of the Frank Courts are anxious to read and investigate the books, pictures* and other works of science of the ancient Greek philosophers: and that in particular, the ministers, philosophers, primates and other individuals of England have a taste for the pictures remaining ever since the time of the said Greeks and which are to be seen on the shores of the Archipelago and in other climes; and have in consequence from time to time sent men to explore and examine the ancient buildings, and pictures. And that some Dilettanti of the Court of England being desirous to see the ancient buildings and the curious pictures in the City of Athens, and the old walls remaining since the time of the Greeks, which now subsist in the interior part of the said place; he [i.e. the Ambassador] has therefore engaged five English painters now dwelling at Athens, to examine and view, and also to copy the pictures remaining there, 'ab antiquo': And he has also at this time expressly asked us that it may be written and ordered that as long as the said painters shall be employed in going in and out of the citadel of the said city, which is the place of observation and in fixing scaffolding round the ancient Temple of the Idols there; and in modelling the said ornaments and visible figures, in plaster or gypsum; and in measuring the remains of other ruined buildings there; and in excavating when they find it necessary the foundations in order to discover inscriptions which may have been covered in the rubbish; that no interruption may be given them, nor any obstacle thrown in their way by the Disdar or any other person: that no one may meddle with the scaffolding or implements they may require in their works; and that when they wish to take away any pieces of stone with old

* '*Pitture*' presumably intended to mean 'sculptures'.

inscriptions or sculptures thereon, that no opposition be made thereto.

We therefore have written this letter to you and expedited it by N.N.*, in order that as soon as you shall have understood its meaning, namely, that it is the explicit desire and engagement of this Sublime Emperor endowed with all eminent qualities to favour such requests as the above mentioned, in conformity with what is due to friendship, sincerity, alliance, and good will subsisting 'ab antiquo' between the Sublime and ever durable Ottoman Court and that of England and which is on the side of both those Courts manifestly increasing; particularly as there is no harm in the said pictures, and buildings being thus viewed, contemplated, and drawn. Therefore after having fulfilled the duties of hospitality, and given a proper reception to the aforesaid Artists in compliance with the urgent request of the said Ambassador to that effect, and because it is incumbent on us to provide that they meet no opposition in walking viewing or contemplating the pictures and buildings they may wish to design or copy; and in any of their works of fixing scaffolding, or using their various instruments; it is our desire that on the arrival of this letter you use your diligence to act conformably to the instances of the said Ambassador as long as the said five artists dwelling in that place shall be employed in going in and out of the citadel of Athens which is the place of observation; or in fixing scaffolding around the ancient Temple of the Idols, or in modelling with chalk or gypsum the said ornaments and visible figures; or in measuring the fragments and vestiges of other ruined buildings; or in excavating when they find it necessary the foundations in search of inscriptions among the rubbish; that they be not molested by the said Disdar nor by any other persons; nor even by you to whom this letter is addressed; and that no one meddle with their scaffolding or implements nor hinder them from taking away any pieces of stone with inscriptions and figures.† In the aforesaid manner see that you behave and comport yourselves.

Signed with a signet

Seged Abdullah Kaimmacam[4]

The ambiguity in the firman is even more pronounced than in Hunt's memorandum. There is a great difference, as many were

---

* In the translation given by Hunt to the Select Committee in 1816, Hunt rendered this 'by Mr. Philip Hunt, an English gentleman, Secretary of the Aforesaid Ambassador'.

† This part reads: '*e non si faccia opposizione al portar via qualche pezzi di pietra con inscrizioni e figure.*'

later to say, between permission to excavate and remove and permission to remove and excavate. The first implies that one can take away anything of interest that is dug up: the second lets one take away anything of interest from whatever place one likes. The interesting thing about the firman, if one reads the last part closely, is its clear indication that the Turks, if they considered the point at all, only intended to grant permission to excavate and remove. After all the tedious detail about things which the artists are to be permitted to do the permission to remove is very much an afterthought.

Certainly at the time the Elgin family themselves put that interpretation on it. 'I am happy to tell you,' Lady Elgin wrote on 9 July to her parents:

Pisani* has succeeded *à merveille* in his *firman* from the Porte, Hunt is in raptures for the *firman* is perfection and P. says he will answer with his whiskers that it is exact. It allows all our artists to go into the citadel to copy and model everything in it, to erect scaffolds all round the Temple, to dig and discover all the ancient foundations, and to bring away any marbles that may be deemed curious by their having inscriptions on them, and that they are not to be disturbed by the soldiers etc. under any pretence whatever. Don't you think this will do? I am in the greatest glee for it would have been a great pity to have failed in the principal part after having been at such an expense.[5]

The 'principal part' was of course Elgin's scheme that he had pressed ever since before he left England of drawing, modelling, and removing selected pieces from the debris scattered around the Acropolis.

Lord Elgin himself wrote to Lusieri to tell him that the firman had been obtained and to exhort him to seize the moment to do all he could. It is evident that he too was still thinking entirely of obtaining drawings and representations to improve British artistic taste.

Besides the general work (by which I mean that which had been begun at the departure of Mr. Hunt) it would be very essential that the *Formatori* should be able to take away exact models of the little

* Pisani was the chief interpreter to the British Embassy.

ornaments *or detached pieces if any are found** which would be interesting
for the Arts. The very great variety in our manufactures, in objects
either of elegance or luxury, offers a thousand applications for such
details. A chair, a footstool, designs or shapes for porcelain, ornaments
for cornices, nothing is indifferent, and whether it be in painting or a
model, exact representations of such things would be much to be
desired. Besides you have now the permission to dig, and there a great
field is opened for medals, and for the remains both of sculpture and
architecture.[6]

There is no suggestion that Elgin thought he had obtained permission to remove from the buildings.

Governments have only themselves to blame if they draft
ambiguous instructions which are then misinterpreted. If one
believes, however, that the Turks had any interest at all in
preserving the Parthenon, they had bad luck. The removals only
took place as a result of a series of accidents all of them involving
the Reverend Philip Hunt. First of all, the firman would not have
been drafted in the form it was if Philip Hunt had not happened
to be in Athens in May when the trouble started and in Constantinople in July when the good news from Egypt came
through. Secondly, the firman would not have been given the
interpretation that was put on it if Hunt had not happened to be
the man who conveyed it to Athens. The reason he was sent back
to Athens within a few weeks of his return to Constantinople was
tied to larger events in the world outside. It was only because he
had to go in any case that he was chosen to take the firman.

Despite the imminent conquest of Egypt, Admiral Ganteaume's
squadron still lay at Toulon and, after its three ineffective sorties,
the British Government became more and more convinced that
the French were intending to invade Greece. Elgin decided,
therefore, on advice from home, to send someone to Greece to
visit the pashas in the area and impress on them the folly of
coming to any arrangement with the French, to report on their
military strength, and to make preparations for the country to
receive a garrison of British troops if this should prove necessary.
Elgin would normally have sent one of his private secretaries to

* My italics.

do this, but Hamilton was in Egypt and Morier in England on other missions: the only man available for the job was the chaplain and Hunt was appointed temporary private secretary for the purpose.[7] Since Hunt was going immediately to Athens on his diplomatic mission it seemed sensible that he should be asked to convey the firman to the Voivode, and the Porte agreed to this arrangement.

Hunt left Constantinople in the middle of July. He was armed with numerous powerful documents from the Porte commending him to the local authorities as an important friend of the Sultan and apart from the usual retinue of servants, he was accompanied by a Mou Bashir or official of the Porte, to see that he was accorded the right treatment. He also took with him a large collection of the wherewithal of Turkish diplomacy, chandeliers, firearms, telescopes, jewellery, pieces of cloth and other presents. And of course, as on all his travels, he was instructed by Lord Elgin to keep his eyes open for antiquities. He arrived in Athens on 22 July having picked up some inscriptions and statues at the Dardanelles on the way and having survived the usual encounter with pirates. He was met by Logotheti and put up in his house as the only other quarters in the town were taken by a party of English travellers including Edward Dodwell and William Gell, both college friends of Hunt's.

The situation had changed since Hunt was last in Athens. Logotheti and Lusieri had succeeded without a firman in obtaining permission for the artists to enter the Acropolis from time to time about a month beforehand. But they had again had to pay heavily —about five guineas a time—and were subjected to constant insult, interruption and extortion from the soldiers, the Disdar, and the Disdar's son. Dodwell and Gell who were trying to make drawings on the Acropolis were subjected to the same treatment.

When Hunt heard what had been going on he immediately called on the Voivode to make a protest and invoke the terms of the firman. He was accompanied by the Mou Bashir. The Voivode—to whom the firman was addressed—was the superior of the Disdar, and the Mou Bashir was the superior of the Voivode. The interview was a tempestuous one.

Hunt began by demanding that all Englishmen should be allowed to visit the Acropolis at any time they wanted without interference. The Voivode, after reading the firman, said he was mortified to hear that the Disdar had treated any Englishman with disrespect or had demanded money: he implied that he did not believe them. But Hunt was able to substantiate the complaints of the artists and of Dodwell and Gell from his own experience last time he was in Athens. The Disdar's son was then sent for, his father being ill. He came in barefooted and trembling and the Mou Bashir announced at once that he was to be sent into exile. Hunt then interceded and obtained a pardon for him, but the Mou Bashir hinted strongly that if there was another complaint, he would be sent as a slave to the galleys. At some stage of the meeting Hunt presented the Voivode with some brilliant cut-glass lustres, firearms, and other presents.[8] The effect was immediate. The conference ended with assurances that the Acropolis would be open to all Englishmen from sunrise to sunset and that Lord Elgin's artists would have all the facilities which the firman demanded.

After this triumph Hunt immediately pressed home his advantage. A huge labour force of Greeks was hired and men brought from a ship in the Piraeus to supervise them. All the inscriptions lying about the Acropolis were collected; extensive excavations were begun; and the Caryatid porch was cleared of its modern obstructions. Then, a few days later, Hunt made the decisive move. He asked the Voivode for permission to take down the most perfect of the surviving metopes from the Parthenon itself.

The Voivode hesitated before granting this permission. But Hunt, with the judicious mixture of threats and bribes that had been so successful at the first interview, carried the day again. Events had turned further in his favour during the intervening days. The old Disdar had died and his son had hopes of succeeding to the office that had been hereditary for over a century. As Hunt told Elgin, 'He is now submissive to all our views in hopes of your speaking favourably for him to the Porte'. Since the choice was between the galleys and the disdarship his change of attitude is understandable. Only Logotheti, the British Consul, had doubts. Unlike the others he was a Greek and an archon of Athens at that. He was 'timid', Hunt reported, '[He] did not enter *con amore* with the idea of taking the sculptures from the Parthenon and ventured to hint that the Voivode durst not extend the firman to such a point'.[9] But a consul is not in a strong position to oppose the wishes of an ambassador. Hunt was firm. The Voivode was soon persuaded to believe that the firman granted permission to remove from the buildings or that at any rate he had the power to grant the permission himself.

Some of Hunt's answers to questions from the Select Committee when the legality of Elgin's actions was being investigated fifteen years later, make it clear that both he and the Voivode realized the terms of the firman were being exceeded. They hint at much more.

'Do you imagine,' Hunt was asked, 'that the firmaun gave a direct permission to remove figures and pieces of sculpture from the walls of temples, or that that must have been a matter of private arrangement with the local authorities of Athens?' 'That was the interpretation,' Hunt answered, 'which the Vaivode of Athens was induced to allow it to bear.'

'In consequence of what was the Vaivode induced to give it this interpretation?'

'With respect to the first metope, it was to gratify what he conceived to be the favourable wishes of the Turkish Government towards Lord Elgin, and which induced him rather to extend than contract the precise permissions of the firmaun.'[10]

Earlier in his interview before the Select Committee Hunt was asked: 'Was there any difficulty in persuading the Vaivode to give this interpretation to the firmaun?' He replied 'Not a great deal of difficulty.'[11]

And so, with not a great deal of difficulty, the vital twist to the firman was given. On 31 July the ship's carpenter with five of the crew mounted the walls of the Parthenon and with the aid of windlasses, cordage, and twenty Greeks succeeded in detaching and lowering down without the slightest accident the best of the surviving metopes. Further presents were given to the

Voivode while it was actually in the air.[12] The next day another metope was successfully removed.

They were taken at once with the aid of a gun carriage to the yard of the British Consul where the Calmuck was given the job of drawing them. They were then conveyed, with very great difficulty and only with the help of the large cart that had once belonged to Fauvel, along the four-mile track to the Piraeus. At the beginning of August Hunt wrote in delight to Lord Elgin:

'These admirable specimens of Greek sculpture which have been repeatedly refused to the gold and influence of France in the zenith of her power, I have now embarked with other precious fragments of antiquity on board the ship that brought me here. I trust they will reach England in safety where they must prove of inestimable service in improving the National Taste.'[13] Hunt declared that the two metopes were the 'chef d'œuvre' of sculpture and persuaded himself that one contained a representation of Theseus and the other of Pirithoos.[14] Lusieri said there was nothing so perfect of their kind in the whole universe.[15]

But the enthusiasm of Lusieri and Hunt was nothing to that of Lord Elgin. 'The object that I had in view', he wrote from Constantinople when he heard the news, '. . . now seems to promise a success beyond our most ardent hopes. I venture to flatter myself that my purpose will be attained in a fashion to put the names of my artists on an elevation that no one has approached since the time of the originals whose perfection you are about to revive.'[16] This last statement is astonishing for its pomposity, even in an age which included Bonaparte, Nelson, and Philip Hunt.

Thus it was that Elgin obtained his firman and thus did his agent put it into execution. The legality of Hunt's actions and of the later removals made under the authority of the firman was debatable, to say the least, but once the first fateful breach had been made the way was open for the removal of anything he liked. There is no reason to doubt, however, that one of the motives that induced Hunt to remove the first sculptures from the Parthenon was his vivid appreciation of the great danger to which they were exposed. 'It grieved me to the heart,' he wrote to

Lord Upper Ossory when the first metopes were taken down, 'to see the destruction made daily by the Janissaries of the fortress. They break up the finest bas-reliefs and sculptures in search of the morsels of lead that unite them to the buildings after which they are broken with wanton barbarity.'[17] * Lusieri reported the same story to Lord Elgin and it is confirmed by the accounts of travellers.

Something has been said earlier about the equally great damage which the travellers themselves caused. Lord Elgin himself said in a dignified defence to the Select Committe in 1816:

Every traveller coming added to the general defacement of the statuary in his reach: there are now in London pieces broken off within our day. And the Turks have been continually defacing the heads; and in some instances they have actually acknowledged to me that they have pounded down the statues to convert them into mortar: It was upon these suggestions, and with these feelings, that I proceeded to remove as much of the sculpture as I conveniently could; it was no part of my original plan to bring away any thing but my models.[19]

If anyone suspects that these were only justifications invented after the event, the evidence of the sculptures themselves is surely decisive. In 1749 the traveller Dalton drew twelve figures in the west pediment of the Parthenon: by the time Lusieri arrived in 1800 there were only four. Five slabs of the frieze drawn by Stuart between 1750 and 1755 had completely disappeared. One slab of which a mould was taken by Fauvel as recently as 1790 was utterly destroyed. The metopes tell a similar story.[20]

Equally, however, there was another, perhaps less worthy motive. As the first metope was being lowered from the Parthenon the Disdar's son—no doubt anxious to please after his uncomfortable experience a few days before—said to Hunt that the Comte de Choiseul-Gouffier had given his father 800 piastres for the adjoining metope; but that as it was being taken down the rope broke and it was dashed to a thousand pieces.[21] This story

* Before telling the story of his success at Athens to Lord Upper Ossory Hunt prudently asked Elgin's permission. 'I know there are envious people', he wrote ominously, 'who will not fail to represent what has been done here as a violence to the fine remains of Grecian sculpture'.[18]

was untrue—Choiseul-Gouffier never succeeded in obtaining any sculptures from the building itself.[22] It was, however, just the sort of story to suit Elgin's book and he never doubted it.[23] The excuse that the French had started it carried great weight with British public opinion which was beginning to regard anything the French did with deep loathing. By 1839, when the Elgin Marbles were safe in London, the author of the British Museum catalogue could let his imagination loose. Choiseul-Gouffier was the first to remove a sculpture from the Parthenon, he said. 'The machinery he first used was defective, the ropes failed and the marble was broken to pieces; fresh tackle was then procured from Toulon and the removal proceeded satisfactorily.'[24] This was all rather unfair on Choiseul-Gouffier whose motives were as honourable, and whose methods as efficient, as those of Elgin himself.

Nevertheless the main point does emerge. If the accessible sculptures of the Parthenon had not been taken by Elgin they might equally have been taken by the French. In 1801 it must have seemed only a matter of time before someone, French or British, acquired the right combination of opportunity and resources to attempt wholesale removals. It happened to be Elgin. No one today can feel passionately because most of the marbles went to the British Museum rather than to the Louvre, but we can understand Elgin's pride in having saved them from the French. After all, his main object from first to last was to improve the national taste of Great Britain.

Chapter 10

'The Last Poor Plunder from a Bleeding Land'

THE first set of excavations on the Acropolis produced a rich harvest. The home of one of the Turkish soldiers at the west end of the Parthenon was bought and pulled down. Underneath the excavators found some colossal fragments of the west pediment that had been thrown down by the explosion of 1687—the Torso of Poseidon, the Amphitrite, the Hermes, and some other pieces. These are among the finest statues in the round that survive from classical Greece. Excavations were then begun on the south side and a number of other fragments and parts of the frieze were uncovered. Saws were sent for from Constantinople to cut off the back parts of the heavy marble blocks on which the sculptures were carved, and thus lightened the artists were able to transport them down to the Consul's yard.

At another likely site on the Acropolis a house stood in the way and the owner was unwilling to sell. Some months later permission was obtained from Constantinople to buy it compulsorily and pull it down. But the excavations—which went down to the rock—yielded nothing. The Turk whose house it was declared laughingly that he had used the marble from the statues found on that spot to make the mortar for his house.[1]

Turks and Greeks vied with one another in gratifying the wishes of Elgin's agents and, according to Hunt, no one made any objection or even expressed regret.[2] More statues and fragments were dug up and an increasing number of vases, coins and other antiquities. The British Consul Logotheti, forgetting his scruples, made Elgin a present of some antiquities that had been lying in his yard for many years and the people of Athens were delighted to sell any fragments that they found. The labour force employed by Lord Elgin grew and grew. The greatest number of acquisitions, however, came from the buildings themselves. Scaffolds were erected, masons established on the Acropolis and a large number of porters engaged. Elgin's ambition had now gone far beyond drawings and moulds. 'I should wish to have,' he wrote to Lusieri, 'examples in the actual object, of each thing, and architectural ornament—of each cornice, each frieze, each capital—of the decorated ceilings, of the fluted columns—specimens of the different architectural orders and of the variant forms of the orders,—of metopes and the like, as much as possible. Finally everything in the way of sculpture, medals, and curious marbles that can be discovered by means of assiduous and indefatigable excavation. This excavation ought to be pushed on as much as possible, be its success what it may.'[3] Despite all this activity, the original objects of the expedition were not forgotten. Elgin's moulders, architects, and artists were kept busy on all the monuments of Athens, making moulds and compiling an accurate record of their architecture and sculpture. When the moulders had difficulty in making moulds with the earth to be found near Athens, Elgin chartered a vessel to bring a more suitable type from Melos.[4] It was hardly the scientific archaeology we know today but it was far superior to the simple treasure-hunting indulged in by all previous collectors in Greece or Italy.

When the Caryatid porch of the Erechtheum was first cleared of modern accretions Hunt suggested that the whole building could be removed and rebuilt in England. 'If your Lordship,' he wrote, 'would come here in a large Man of War that beautiful little model of ancient art might be transported wholly to England.'[5] Elgin, who of course had not even been to Athens, seized on the idea and wrote to Lord Keith to ask for a ship to call there.

I have been at a monstrous expense at Athens where I at this moment possess advantages beyond belief. . . . Now if you would allow a ship of war of size to convoy the Commissary's ship and stop a couple of days at Athens to get away a most valuable piece of architecture at my disposal there you could confer upon me the greatest obligation I could receive and do a very essential service to the Arts in England. Bonaparte has not got such a thing from all his thefts in Italy. Pray kindly attend to this my Lord.'[6]

But for the time being no ship could be spared and, for the time being, the Caryatid porch survived. The artists had to content themselves with sawing off choice pieces selected to illustrate the various details.

Meanwhile Philip Hunt had gone on his diplomatic tour of Greece to strengthen the local pashas against the French. On his travels he visited many of the famous classical sites. Ali Pasha of Ioannina promised to send Elgin any antiquities he found in his province and said he had recently broken up some statues that 'only seemed to want breath'[7] to make them real. At Thebes Hunt obtained at a great price from a local peasant an exquisite cameo of a female centaur suckling her infant. At various places —notably Olympia—he recommended that Elgin should pay for excavations. At Mycenae he cast covetous eyes over the Lion Gate but decided regretfully that it was too far from the sea for there to be hope of removing it. At Eleusis, the site of the Temple of Demeter and home of the Mysteries he saw what he thought was the colossal statue of Demeter herself and suggested that it was well worth taking away.

While Hunt was on his travels Elgin engaged one of the survivors of the Koehler mission to act as supervisor at Athens. He was Thomas Lacy, a captain in the Royal Engineers. But Lacy was a great disappointment. He accepted the job—and who can blame him?—mainly as a means of escaping from Egypt and the ill-fated assignment that he had been sent on three years before. 'Congratulate me,' Lacy wrote to Hunt, 'I have at length found means to escape from the Mission and shall now be at leisure to devote myself to my friends. In two days I embark for Athens to plunder temples and commit sacrilege, a proper finish to my diplomatic career.'[8] Lacy did not stay long at Athens. He quarrelled with Lusieri and went off in a huff on a tour of the classical sites. Very soon he disappeared from the scene entirely.

Lacy's time would have been better spent in applying his engineering knowledge to the problem of removing sculptured marbles from Greek temples. Some of the removals were not very skilful. The blocks on which the metopes and frieze were carved were an integral part of the structure of the building and could not easily be separated from it. In some cases, the buildings were damaged as the artists attempted to get at the sculptures.

The traveller Edward Dodwell was a witness of these attempts. He had benefited from Hunt's firman and spent his days sketching on the Acropolis. He was now on the best of terms with the new Disdar, to whom he gave a bottle of wine (forbidden to Moslems) whenever his dinner was sent up. He wrote:

> During my first tour to Greece I had the inexpressible mortification of being present when the Parthenon was despoiled of its finest sculpture, and when some of its architectural members were thrown to the ground. I saw several metopae at the south east extremity of the temple taken down. They were fixed in between the triglyphs as in a groove; and in order to lift them up, it was necessary to throw to the ground the magnificent cornice by which they were covered. The south east angle of the pediment shared the same fate; and instead of the picturesque beauty and high preservation in which I first saw it, it is now comparatively reduced to a state of shattered desolation.[9]

Another witness of the dilapidations was Edward Daniel Clarke who arrived in Athens in the course of his long tour in October 1801. Since his violent quarrel with Carlyle and Hunt in the Troad he had been to Cyprus, the Holy Land, Egypt, and the Greek Islands. His antipathy to Hunt was so great as to make him a doubtful authority but his account has, in some particulars at least, the ring of plausibility.

> Some workmen, employed under his [Lusieri's] direction for the British Ambassador, were then engaged in making preparation, by means of ropes and pulleys, for taking down the metopes, where the sculptures remained the most perfect. The Disdar himself came to view the work but with evident marks of dissatisfaction; and Lusieri told us that it was with great difficulty he could accomplish this part of his undertaking from the attachment the Turks entertained towards a building which they had been accustomed to regard with religious veneration and had converted into a mosque. We confessed that we participated the Mahometan feeling in this instance and would gladly

see an order enforced to preserve rather than destroy such a glorious edifice. After a short time spent in examining the several parts of the temple one of the workmen came to inform Don Battista that they were then going to lower one of the metopes. We saw this fine piece of sculpture raised from its station between the triglyphs: but the workmen endeavouring to give it a position adapted to the projected line of descent, a part of the adjoining masonry was loosened by the machinery; and down came the fine masses of Pentelican marble, scattering their white fragments with thundering noise among the ruins. The Disdar, seeing this could no longer restrain his emotions; but actually took his pipe from his mouth, and letting fall a tear, said in a most emphatic tone of voice 'τελος!'* positively declaring that nothing should induce him to consent to any further dilapidations of the building. Looking up we saw with regret the gap that had been made; which all the ambassadors of the earth, with all the sovereigns they represent aided by every resource that wealth and talent can now bestow, will never again repair.†[10]

There can be no doubt that the Parthenon suffered severely as a result of Lusieri's efforts. Virtually the whole of the surviving cornice on the south side was thrown to the ground to allow the metopes to be extracted. A drawing made by William Gell in 1801 during the first removals show the cornice at both ends of the colonnade almost complete and the metopes well preserved underneath:‡ a water-colour by Hobhouse painted in 1810§ looks very sad by comparison—the cornice and metopes have entirely disappeared. All that was then left of the best cornice of the Parthenon was a series of jagged blocks sticking up like broken teeth. Only one metope was left on the south side, the one at the extreme west. Fortunately it was one of the finest and best preserved of all and there it still stands in solitary splendour, a

* 'The end!' or 'Never again!' The Disdar did in fact allow many more sculptures to be removed.
† Clarke told this story to Lord Byron who incorporated it in a note to *Childe Harold's Pilgrimage*, Canto II, stanza XII. See p. 191.
‡ Plate II. Gell, like Dodwell and Clarke, disapproved strongly of Lusieri's activities. In the picture the Disdar can be seen remonstrating with Lusieri against the destruction, wagging his finger at him. Lusieri, his arms folded, leans nonchalantly against a column, unmoved by the Disdar's pleas. A water-colour by Dodwell which also shows Lusieri's scaffolding is at Broomhall.
§ Plate III (b).

last example of the sculptor's and architect's skill. One suspects, however, that the reason it was left was the sheer physical difficulty of removing it. It is surmounted by a huge block which forms part of the pediment: to remove it would have required very great destruction indeed.

Yet, although we may sympathize with the travellers' indignation, it was partly their own activities which induced Elgin to go ahead. Dodwell was an eager antiquarian whenever he had the chance and eventually built up a large collection. He even obtained the head of one of the male figures from the western pediment which was said to have been knocked off by a British sailor.[11] Since this fragment is now lost, the last pedimental head to survive so late except for one in Paris and that on the Theseus, it would have been preferable if he had left it for Lord Elgin. Dodwell also took a few architectural fragments from the Parthenon.

Clarke too was an eager collector and part at least of his anger at Elgin's removals can be explained by simple jealousy. At Alexandria he had found an undistinguished sarcophagus which he convinced himself was the tomb of Alexander the Great.[12] His judgements about the antiquities he obtained in Greece were equally imaginative. The piece he was most proud of was an inscription bearing the words *ΕΥΚΛΙΔΑΣ ΕΥΚΛΙΔΟΥ ΕΡΜΙΟΝΕΥΣ* which, he said, he 'bought of a consul from under the very nose of the ambassador's chaplain and his host of gothic plunderers'.[13] Clarke imagined, with touching naïvety, that he had discovered the tomb of *the* Euclid and could hardly wait to present it to Cambridge University. Unfortunately the Euclid whose tomb he had found was not the famous geometer.

Clarke also obtained a small marble relief which, with his usual confidence, he pronounced to be 'nothing less than a fragment of one of the metopes belonging to the Parthenon and therefore . . . the undoubted work of Phidias'.[14] There was an embargo on removing anything from the Acropolis except into Elgin's storehouse, but Clarke persuaded the Disdar to claim it as his own and give it to him secretly. He need not have worried. The fragment is not from the Parthenon at all but is a coarsely-carved piece of an old grave stone.* Clarke's friend the Disdar also sold him some architectural fragments from the Erechtheum. As a few of these are now lost somewhere in England[15] we may wish that Clarke too had left collecting to Elgin.

Clarke's greatest triumph was to secure the colossal statue from Eleusis that Hunt had pronounced worthy to be added to the Elgin collection. This enormous and battered statue—it weighed over two tons—representing a woman with a basket on her head, had been noticed by travellers for many years before. Like so many antiquities it was regarded with peculiar veneration by the local inhabitants, and like so many antiquities it had been much sought after by collectors, including the Comte de Choiseul-Gouffier. Eleusis in ancient times was a shrine of Demeter, the goddess of corn and fertility, and the behaviour of the Eleusinians showed that the pagan tradition of worship of Demeter was still flourishing. A traveller who visited Eleusis in 1765 reported that the local inhabitants regarded the fertility of the land as depending on the statue and Clarke found that they lit a lamp before it on festival days.[16] They told him that as often as foreigners came to remove the statue some disaster occurred and that the arm of any person who touched it with violence would fall off.[17]

Clarke determined to have it and acted quickly and secretly to forestall Elgin's agents. He wrote:

I found the goddess in a dunghill buried to her ears. The Eleusinian peasants, at the very mention of moving it, regarded me as one who would bring the moon from her orbit. What would become of their corn, they said, if the old lady with her basket was removed? I went to Athens and made application to the Pacha, aiding my request by letting an English telescope glide between his fingers. The business was done.[18]

* When the first part of *Childe Harold's Pilgrimage* was published in 1812 Clarke obviously felt some embarrassment about his possession of his 'fragment of the Parthenon'. He persuaded himself that his fragment was 'the solitary example of sculpture removed from the Parthenon without injuring what time and the Goths had spared' (*Travels* II, 2, p. 475). He chose to ignore the fact that many of the Elgin Marbles were excavated and only some were removed from the buildings. His words echo *Childe Harold's Pilgrimage*, II, XII:

> But most the modern Pict's ignoble boast,
> To rive what Goth, and Turk, and Time hath spared.

The English telescope which did the trick Clarke had obtained from Lusieri who temporarily abandoned his loyalty to Elgin and connived with Clarke for the purpose.[19] Clarke was just in time. Shortly afterwards Elgin sent Lusieri a telescope made by the best maker in London as a gift for the Voivode. His instructions were, 'Make good use of it. I still hope you will find the means to procure for me the colossal bust of Ceres at Eleusis.'[20]

But permission from the Voivode of Athens was not enough. Ropes and poles were obtained from Athens and the jetty at Eleusis had to be repaired. And the locals had to be persuaded. On the night before the statue was due to be removed an accident occurred which seemed to confirm the opinions of the Eleusinians. While they were conversing with the Turkish officer who brought the firman, an ox broke loose from its yoke and butted violently at the statue with its horns, and then ran amuck over the plain of Eleusis, bellowing loudly. The Eleusinians joined in the clamour and there was nearly a riot. They had always been famous for their corn, they shouted, and the fertility of the land would cease if the statue was removed.

Calm was restored and next day the Eleusinians agreed to obey the Voivode. The local priest, arrayed in full vestments, struck the first blow to remove the rubbish. Contrary to public expectation his arm did not fall off, and after many hours work a force of one hundred men and fifty boys eventually succeeded in hauling the statue to the shore where it was loaded into a ship Clarke had chartered. Elgin generously forgave Clarke for 'plucking the jewel from his crown', and allowed it to go home in a warship from Smyrna.[21] In the first year the corn crop was good and the Eleusinians believed that their goddess would return. In the next year it was not so good and they feared she must have deserted them. Gradually they convinced themselves that only witchcraft could have carried her off. The goddess did, however, have some revenge. The ship taking her to England foundered off Beachy Head and it was only with great difficulty that she was recovered from the sea bed.[22] She now stands in a corner of the Fitzwilliam Museum at Cambridge. An object which had probably been worshipped longer than any other in the world is now regarded as a second-rate architectural fragment and hardly engages the attention of the casual visitor.

As time passed and Elgin's schemes became ever more ambitious another threat to his activities, far more dangerous than the protests of disgruntled travellers, appeared on the horizon. The French were on their way back. With the expulsion of the French from Egypt it was only a matter of time before peace between France and Turkey was restored. If a French Ambassador re-appeared at Constantinople Elgin could be sure he would do everything in his power to put an end to the removals at Athens —even if only to keep open the possibility that the marbles might later be taken by France.

At Athens Louis-François-Sébastien Fauvel, who had so dominated the antiquarian scene before the arrival of Lusieri, was expected to return and no one could doubt his attitude. Fauvel had been in prison when the artists first arrived in 1800, but even from there his influence had still been felt. He managed to suborn some of Elgin's artists. The Calmuck and the architects were suspected by Lusieri of concealing drawings and measure-ments with the intention of selling them to Fauvel: they had to be closely supervised and regularly searched. In June 1801 the French prisoners at Athens, including Fauvel, were sent to Constantinople and he was thus out of the way at the critical moment when Hunt arrived with his famous firman.[23] But even in Fauvel's absence the French found ways of sabotaging Elgin's operations. A French doctor who had managed to escape internment by claiming Danish citizenship, kept cutting off the water supply to Lusieri's store and so hindered the washing of the antiquities and the refreshment of the workers. Lusieri also protested that the Doctor 'has made and continues to make efforts to stop our acquisitions by sowing foolish ideas in the weak minds of the Turks'.[24]

While the Franco-Turkish war continued the French property at Athens was in theory at least sequestrated. As we have noticed, however, this did not prevent the Turks from giving Lusieri the large cart and tackle that had belonged to Choiseul-Gouffier and subsequently Fauvel. As they were the only effective equipment in all Athens it is extremely doubtful if Lusieri could have succeeded in removing the Parthenon marbles without them. But besides this tackle, there still remained in the cellars of the Capuchin Monastery the collection of antiquities that Fauvel had in his possession when he was arrested. They included the metope from the Parthenon that Fauvel had obtained for Choiseul-Gouffier when it fell from the building in a storm fourteen years before. Lusieri, whose antipathy to Fauvel was stronger than his enthusiasm for Lord Elgin, suggested various schemes to seize the collection by force or, at least, to buy it.[25] He did not succeed.* Soon the return of French influence put all such ideas out of the question.

A few months later it was learnt definitely that Fauvel himself was coming back, and this time as an official representative of the French Government. The news brought dismay to the British camp. Lusieri was afraid for his precious cart and suggested that another should be specially made at Naples. He also recommended that the Calmuck should be sent away from Athens as he was too unreliable when Fauvel was around. The French abbot of the Capuchin Monastery was afraid he would incur official displeasure for having allowed Elgin's agents to mould the frieze of the building. The formidable Fauvel did not, however, reach Athens until January 1803.

The French influence had also appeared at Constantinople. Peace between France and Turkey was concluded in October, and Elgin, as expected, had to hand back the Embassy building. In December Count Sébastiani arrived as the personal agent of Bonaparte and was well received by the Turks. 'There is a smart French Beau,' wrote Lady Elgin, 'just arrived from Paris to sign a treaty of Peace with the Turks, he arrived two days too late. He has called upon us and was excessively civil; there is another young man come with him, they are both equipped *parfaitement à la mode* and are both handsome: I wish you could see the fuss

---

* Choiseul-Gouffier later accused Elgin's agents of having taken some of his antiquities from a storehouse in the Piraeus,[26] but although Luisieri attempted to do this there is no evidence that he ever succeeded.

everybody makes of them.'[27] It seemed that Turkish gratitude to the English was already on the wane and Elgin had better seize his moment at Athens while it lasted.

In the spring of 1802 he decided to pay a personal visit to Greece to see the situation for himself and give directions on how the operations should be advanced. He had asked permission to go in 1800 but the Egyptian expedition and troubles with Spencer Smith had intervened.[28] He wrote again in July 1801 on the day after the firman was obtained, and permission was granted.[29] His second child was born in August 1801 and Lady Elgin was pregnant for the third time when they set off, but he could not let family difficulties stand in his way. It was necessary to act at once to get everything away from Athens before the French could persuade the Turks to put a stop to it. Lady Elgin produced another reason: 'If it were not for leaving the little girl this would be the most desirable tour possible; for travelling through this country while Elgin's ambassadorial titles and pomp remain, is certainly a very great advantage. We mean to take a number of servants to cut a dash.'[30] They arrived at Athens at the beginning of April 1802.

Elgin was absolutely delighted at what had been done by Hunt and Lusieri. 'It would be sacrilege to speak hastily of such wonders and the Justice done them'[31] he wrote, referring to the antiquities of Athens and the work of the artists. Gifts were showered on the Voivode and other Turkish dignitaries, and Lusieri was given authority to increase the vast expense. Elgin did not in fact see many of the Parthenon sculptures as most had already been packed up for shipping, but what he did see greatly increased his enthusiasm. While he was in Greece the horse's head representing the waning moon—perhaps the finest of all the Elgin Marbles— was taken from its corner in the east pediment.

Elgin urged his agents on, telling them to dig and buy and take away. No effort or money was to be spared to get what was wanted from the Acropolis and that work was to have priority over everything else. Lady Elgin instructed Lusieri to put about a story that she had a new set of powerful firmans which settled any lingering doubts about the legality of the removals.[32]

Individual Greeks who were unwilling to sell their antiquities at a reasonable price were brought before the Voivode and compulsory purchase orders were issued.[33] By 2 June Lady Elgin was able to announce, 'We yesterday got down the last thing we want from the Acropolis so now we may boldly bid defiance to our enemies.'[34] In the ten months since Hunt first arrived with the firman more than half of the Parthenon sculptures in the Elgin collection had been taken from the Acropolis. They included at least seven metopes, about twenty slabs of the frieze, and almost all the surviving figures from the pediments.

Elgin now extended his operations beyond Athens. He spent several weeks on an exhaustive tour of the classical sites of Greece and, everywhere he went, he collected more antiquities and sent back streams of instructions to Lusieri. The monasteries round Athens were to be searched; columns were to be taken from Daphne; excavations were to be started at Eleusis; the architects, if they could be spared from the Acropolis, were to be sent to supervise diggings at various parts of the Peloponnese; the feasibility of large-scale excavations at Olympia was to be looked at again. At Mycenae Elgin was so impressed by the ruins that he ordered excavations to be started at once with the result that he was able to obtain the best surviving pillars and some vases on his way back.

In the course of the tour the Ambassador and his party made a ceremonial entry into Tripolis to pay his respects to the Pasha of the Morea. Even in the remote provinces Turkish magnificence was not stinted. Lady Elgin gave her usual vivid description.

Three Parade Horses were sent for Elgin, Mr. Hunt and Dr. Scott besides a great many led Horses all with the most brilliant furniture, the Lieutenant Governor and the first Chamberlain riding by their side, the Dragoman of the Morea preceding, and a train of at least six or seven hundred on Horseback following. All the Inhabitants of the Town in their best dresses and well armed lined the Avenues to the Gate, and as we approached, the Great Cannon were fired from every Fort round the Walls of the City. One man out of a large embroidered box kept flinging money to the Children and poor People on the road. There was something extremely grand in that. In the Evening we alighted at the house of the Dragoman of the Morea which was assigned for our residence, and were waited on by the officers of the Pasha and Bey to congratulate us on our arrival, and an immense Supper of 30 or 40 dishes dressed in the Turkish style were sent from the Pasha's Seraglio.[35]

The next day the audience with the Pasha took place and there were the usual gifts of pelisses, shawls, and horses. More important for Elgin—whose collection of these commodities must by now have exceeded his wants—the Pasha gave approval for excavations and removals anywhere in his province.

In the middle of June having completed his progress through Greece, Elgin left Athens in H.M.S. *Narcissus* on his way back to Constantinople. He left behind instructions that would keep an army of excavators busy for months if not years. He sailed round to Marathon where he ordered more digging, and then set off across the Aegean calling at several islands to pick up antiquities. There was no temptation to hurry back to Constantinople. Not only had plague broken out but the Pasha of Roumelia was in revolt and reported to be only twenty-four hours' march from the capital. Lady Elgin as usual was almost continuously sea-sick.

Near Delos the *Narcissus* sighted a pirate ship attacking a British merchantman. They gave chase but the pirates landed on the island and started to fire at the *Narcissus* from the cliffs. The Captain ordered the *Narcissus* to fire at the pirate ship until she sank and then sent a party of marines ashore to attack the pirates. Twenty-five were captured.[36]

On 1 August Elgin arrived at Smyrna and stayed for a while with the Levant Company merchants who were settled there. The visit was extremely unpleasant. Not only was it so hot that plague was expected but he took ill before they arrived and there was already an epidemic of whooping cough among the children. But the worst part was that the Smyrna merchants had believed all Spencer Smith's complaints about Elgin and received him with marked coldness. Moreover, relations were not improved by Elgin's discovery that many of the merchants had been profiteering out of the Egyptian war.[37]

At last at the beginning of September, after a tour that had lasted six months, Lord and Lady Elgin arrived safely back at Constantinople, having escaped bandits, plague, and insurrection. They were just in time for the birth of their third child. But Elgin had now had enough. He was tired of the East and his health had not improved as he had expected. All the objects of the embassy had been achieved and his own schemes had succeeded far beyond his most optimistic hopes. He was anxious to return to England to promote his political career and put his collection of marbles in order. Permission to end the Embassy Extraordinary was given by the Government and it was arranged that he should leave Constantinople for home in January 1803.

At Athens throughout the summer and autumn of 1802 more removals and excavations took place. Six continuous slabs of the Parthenon frieze were taken from the building and two more metopes. Another slab of the frieze was discovered in excavations. Four slabs of the frieze of the Temple of Athena Nike were discovered built into the fortifications of the Acropolis and successfully removed. Examples of all the architectural details were taken —capitals, bases, cornices, and pieces of pillar from the Parthenon, the Propylaea, the Erechtheum, and the Temple of Nike: the piece of the Parthenon capital had to be sawn in two before it could be moved. Other antiquities began to arrive at Athens as a result of the excavations ordered on Elgin's tour. The colossal headless statue of Dionysos which stood above the Monument of Thrasyllos on the south side of the Acropolis was removed on the day the Voivode was given a horse and green cape. Lusieri even suggested that Elgin might be able to remove the Monument of Lysicrates in its entirely if he offered enough money to the Capuchin Abbot and Elgin urged him to try.

The haste with which everything had to be done caused a few more casualties. On 16 September Lusieri reported 'I have, my Lord, the pleasure of announcing to you the possession of the 8th metope that one where there is the Centaur carrying off the woman. This piece has caused much trouble in all respects and I have even been obliged to be a little barbarous.'[38] The barbarity was no doubt the destruction of part of the building as had been necessary several months before with other metopes in the presence of Dodwell and Clarke. Another slab of the frieze—the great central slab on the east side—was taken from the Acropolis wall to which it had been built many years before. On its way down to the Piraeus it broke into two pieces in a straight line down the middle: fortunately it broke at a place where there was no carving.

So the Elgin collection continued to grow. Besides the marbles a large number of coins and vases were accumulated and there were, of course, the drawings and measurements of the artists and architects and the numerous casts made by the moulders. Elgin knew how to keep the supply flowing. A seemingly inexhaustible amount of money was poured into Athens, and horses, telescopes, and shawls were heaped on the Voivode and Disdar until even they must have had enough. Perhaps most important of all, Elgin obtained from the Porte written documents saying that the Turkish Government approved of all that the Voivode and Disdar had done on his behalf. These documents were intended to reassure the Voivode and Disdar that they would be protected if policy changed in favour of France. Lusieri handed over the documents as one of the bribes. It is a pity no copy has survived: they would seem to prove Elgin's contention that the Turkish Government condoned everything he did.

Removing the marbles from the Acropolis to the storehouse was one thing: shipping them to England was quite another. It was by no means easy in time of war to ship heavy packages on the long sea voyage. There were a great number of British ships in the Eastern Mediterranean as a result of the Egyptian campaign but not many of them called at the Piraeus, and their captains, naturally enough, were not eager to weigh down their ships with heavy useless cases. When peace came in March 1802 matters were slightly easier, but even then the British were under treaty to evacuate Malta by mid-summer and Malta was an essential staging post.

Fortunately for Elgin no one seems to have questioned his assumed right to use the King's warships and transports to carry home his collection of marbles. He was able to impress on the naval authorities and his agents on the spot the importance of getting everything away before the French could intervene. Wonders were achieved. The marbles came to England by a variety of routes mostly by way of Alexandria and Smyrna. Almost all were unloaded at Malta and found their way from there as opportunity offered.

The first two metopes that Hunt obtained when he arrived at Athens with the firman were put on board the ship that brought him there. She was a Ragusan merchantman, the *Constanza*, and took them to Egypt. Hunt went with them and when the ship had to put into Halicarnassos and Cnidos in storms he carried off more antiquities from both places. The ship that brought Lacy on his unsuccessful mission, on the other hand, H.M.S. *Cynthia* refused to take any cases at all on board and sailed off after only thirty-six hours in harbour. It was probably as a result of this experience and because of the increasing threat from the French that Elgin decided to devote his own ship, the *Mentor*, to the task. He had originally bought the *Mentor*—she was a small brig— to take him on his tour of Greece but this had been postponed from 1801. The *Mentor*'s first voyage in December 1801 was to take ten cases of marbles and moulds from the Piraeus to Alexandria. This was hardly a big cargo in view of the large number of cases that began to pile up at Athens but it was all she would take. Elgin wrote to Malta to try to buy a bigger ship but for some reason nothing came of this idea. A small brigantine, the *Dorinda*, was chartered in his name and later took away a few cases.

In March 1802 the frigate H.M.S. *La Diane* took some cases and in May H.M.S. *Mutine* some more, but they continued to pile up quicker than they could be taken away. Lusieri began to be afraid for the dispersal of the collection and issued the following notice

If any of the articles require being cased it would much oblige Lord Elgin to make cases for them similar to the others; and if any of the cases etc are without Direction, it will be esteemed a great Favour to make them in strong letters with the Name of His Excellency The Earl of Elgin, Ambassador Extraordinary and Plenipotentiary at the Porte, Downing Street, London.[39]

Lady Elgin was in Athens when H.M.S. *Mutine* came in and she used her charms to persuade the captain to take more than he really wanted. The captain, Captain Hoste, said he could take nothing but Lady Elgin relates to Elgin then on tour what happened.

> I began by saying as the Capt. was going straight to Malta & there being no Enemies to encounter I ventured to propose his taking them. It would be doing me a very great favour as you were extremely anxious to get them off & *I* sh^d feel so proud to tell you how well I had succeeded during your absence—*Female* eloquence as *usal* succeeded, the Capt. sent me a very polite answer, & by peep of Day I send down the three cases.[40]

Later in the same day Lady Elgin wrote that she had persuaded Captain Hoste to take two more cases largely by giving him and his friends lavish hospitality and by giving what she called 'Backcheses' to the workers. The next day she wrote again in triumph:

> But in hopes that I shall be the *first* to tell you what I have done for your—Know that besides the *5* cases I have already told you of I have prevaled on Capt. Hoste to take *Three* more, two are already on board & the third will be taken when he returns from Corinth. How I have faged to get all this done, do you love me better for it, Elgin? . . . And *how* I have pushed Lusieri to get cases made for these three large pack-ages! I beg you will shew delight (Lay aside the Deplomatic Character) to Capt. Hoste for taking so much on board. I am now *satisfied* of what I always thought; which is how much *more* Women can do if they set about it than Men. I will lay any bet had you been here you would not have got half so much on board as I have. As for getting the other things you wished for down from the Acropolis it is *quite impossible* before you return. Lusieri says Capt. Lacy was, upon his *first* coming here, against the things being taken down but at last he was keener than anybody & absolutely wished you to have the whole Temple of the Cari-something, where the Statues of the Women are.[41]

The *Mentor*, Elgin's own ship, returned to the Piraeus to pick up her second cargo in June having safely deposited her first in Egypt. She had on board William Richard Hamilton, Elgin's private secretary, who now reappears on the stage. Hamilton had been sent to Egypt in June 1801, exactly a year before, to help superintend the evacuation of the French (Elgin did not want to risk a repetition of El Arish), but the evacuation had gone so smoothly that he had been able to go on a tour of Upper Egypt with Clarke.

When he was in Egypt Hamilton had assisted in securing for the British Government another famous archaeological treasure, the Rosetta Stone. The Rosetta Stone is a slab of black basalt which contains an inscription of a decree of 196 B.C. The inscription itself is not of great interest but it is repeated on the slab in three languages, Greek, Demotic Egyptian, and Hieroglyphs. As soon as it was discovered its importance in providing a clue to the decipherment of hieroglyphic was recognized and, in fact, it was by comparing the three scripts, starting with the proper names, that Young and Champollion were first able to read the writing of ancient Egypt.[42] The Rosetta Stone was uncovered by Bonaparte's engineers in July 1799 as they were repairing some fortifications and the French generals immediately took possession of it. After the successful British invasion of Egypt, however, General Hutchinson, on Hamilton's advice, insisted on writing into the terms of capitulation that the Rosetta Stone and certain other antiquities should be handed over to the British. When the news of the cease-fire came through, Hamilton rushed to see General Hutchinson to press on him the importance of securing the Rosetta Stone. It was concealed in General Menou's own house covered by cloths but a detachment of gunners, accompanied by Hamilton, went in and removed it.[43] It is now in the British Museum. By the time of Hamilton's death in 1859 the story of his exploit had so grown that his obituary said he rowed out in a small boat to a plague-infested French warship and, at great personal danger, succeeded in removing it.[44]

Hamilton arrived in Greece with the *Mentor* just in time to see Elgin before he left for Constantinople at the end of his Greek tour. He was immediately put in general charge of the operations at Athens and asked to stay to supervise the loading of the *Mentor* for her second voyage. He had instructions from Elgin to put on board absolutely everything that the captain could be persuaded to accept without danger to the ship and, if possible, to charter other vessels to get the marbles off as soon as possible.

The artists and workmen worked extremely hard for several weeks to take the marbles to the Piraeus and load them into the ship. On 16 September the *Mentor* sailed. She had on board seventeen cases including fourteen pieces of the Parthenon frieze, four pieces of the frieze of the Temple of Athena Nike, and various other marbles including the ancient throne given to the Nisbets by the Archbishop of Athens. The *Mentor* did not, however, take any of the larger (and best) sculptures—the figures from the pediments —as Captain Eglen, the captain of the *Mentor*, could not be persuaded to enlarge his hatches to get them in. When Elgin heard that Captain Eglen was unwilling to do this he at once wrote a rather testy letter to say he was sending the captain of H.M.S. *La Diane* to overrule Captain Eglen's opinion if, in his view, the hatches could be enlarged without danger.

Captain Eglen's . . . conduct in that respect has been unpardonable. The officers of the frigates at Smyrna assured him that this opening might be made without injury to the vessel. It is troublesome, it is true, but nothing in comparison with the object. . . . It is only his obstinacy that would have found the difficulties that he raised at Athens. My brig is come from England for my acquisitions. That is its purpose.[45]

As things turned out, however, it is extremely fortunate that Elgin was too late and the *Mentor* did not take the heavy sculptures. Two days after she left Athens she ran into a storm and struck a rock at the entrance to the harbour of the island of Cerigo. She sank at once in twelve fathoms of water. Only by great good luck did Hamilton—who was hoping to return home —and the crew, manage to scramble ashore. The story of the efforts to recover the *Mentor* and her cargo will be told later. It was a long and expensive business. The loss of the *Mentor* was, however, only an incident of the continuous struggle to ship the marbles away which was pressed on with despite the disaster.

H.M.S. *La Victorieuse* was sent from Constantinople in November to see if she could lend a hand at Cerigo. Philip Hunt took passage in her as far as Athens and, before she had left for Cerigo, he managed to get a few more cases away.

There are twelve or fifteen cases of Sculpture at the Piraeus, ready for embarking, but many of them are too large for the hatchway or Stowage of such a Ship as the Victorieuse: but Captn. Richards observed that if his decks had not been so encumbered by the spars he has on board for weighing the Mentor, he could have taken some of the Smaller ones. It is not easy to describe how much our Commander required being humoured. His Hobby horse seems to be that every action of his life shall appear to originate from himself; and he is more jealous than can be conceived of the most trifling requests or even suggestion coming from anyone but such as the strict rules of service authorize a Superior Officer to give him. On my first hinting to him the danger your acquisitions here were in on any change of Interests in Turkey, he mentioned a number of difficulties and concluded by saying he had been unable even to take Lady Elgin's chest on board at Constantinople, but after a walk with me among the ruins of Athens, he melted into good humour, and has taken two cases on board containing parts of the Frieze of the Parthenon in good preservation, and which Lusieri ranks with the most valuable in your Lordship's possession.[46]

Next day Hunt emulated Lady Elgin's efforts with the *Mutine* and persuaded the *Victorieuse* to take another case.

But although about fifty cases of sculptures had thus left the Piraeus by various means, there were still about fifty left at Athens including the heaviest and most difficult ones containing the pedimental sculptures, seventeen cases of the frieze and two metopes. And the danger from the French seemed to be growing. A French Ambassador—in addition to Sébastiani—was already on his way to Constantinople with an escort of five warships and the Chief of the Capuchin Monastery, so far from selling the Monument of Lysicrates, was told to withhold all co-operation.

Then on Christmas Eve 1802 Hunt had a stroke of luck. H.M.S. *Braakel*, a troopship under the command of Captain Clarke, brother of 'Eleusinian' Clarke, ran aground at the Piraeus. She was in imminent danger of sinking for lack of hands to unload her and pull her off. Hunt immediately took charge of the situation. In the middle of the night he hurried to see his old friend the Voivode and demanded that he should send a hundred men to the Piraeus at once. The Voivode was hesitant but Hunt insisted that the gates of his palace should be immediately shut and 'the requisite number pressed for service out of the gaping multitude of Greeks and Albanians who were in the courtyard'.[47] The manœuvre completely succeeded, and after a night of excitement during which the whole of Athens seems to have gone to the Piraeus to watch the spectacle, the *Braakel* was saved.

Captain Clarke was rather ashamed of himself for having so endangered his ship. As Hunt said: 'A Naval person can hardly believe that the *Braakel* ran smack on a boldish shore with a wind *off* the land—in a clear night, and fine weather. It is attributed to a terrible obstinacy on the part of the Master who had the Midnight watch when it happened.'[48] Captain Clarke, however, was so grateful to his brother's enemy that he agreed to take all the cases he could and even to land his crew to help in bringing them to the Piraeus. He stayed at the Piraeus for five weeks solely to take the marbles and built a special raft to float the heaviest pieces out to the ship.[49] No less than forty-four cases were embarked—by far the biggest shipment to date and by far the most important. But for Captain Clarke's bad seamanship it is doubtful if the most important part of the Elgin collection would have left Athens.

In the eighteen months between the obtaining of the firman and his departure for home Lord Elgin had done all that he had set out to do and far more. The indifference of the Turks, the jealousy of travellers, and the intrigues of the French had all been overcome. The buildings of Athens had been drawn, measured and moulded in detail never before attempted and the greatest part of the best surviving sculpture had been moved into his storehouses. Much of it was already on its way home and there was good hope of recovering the rest. It was a stupendous achievement.

But the cost had been enormous—just how enormous will appear later. In his last despatch to the Foreign Office Elgin made another despairing plea, using almost exactly the same words as he had done in a letter to Lord Grenville in May 1799. He asked yet again that his appointment might 'be placed on the footing of an extraordinary embassy in respect to salary as it has been in rank, display, business, and expense'.[50]

Lord Elgin left Constantinople with his suite for the last time in H.M.S. *La Diane* on 16 January 1803. In one of his last letters to Lusieri he urged yet again more removals and more excavations. 'If I had still three years', he wrote, 'and all the resources I have had, I would employ them all at Athens. . . . The slightest object from the Acropolis is a jewel'.[51]

Chapter 11

Prisoner of War

PEACE between France and Great Britain was signed at Amiens on 25 March 1802, but few expected that it would last. There were a number of causes for this—French interference in Ireland, British refusal to give up captured colonies—but one especially concerned Lord Elgin.

Colonel Sébastiani, the smart French beau whose arrival at Constantinople Lady Elgin had announced in December 1801, had been named as French 'commercial agent' in the Levant. In fact, however, he was on a political and military reconnaissance to see whether it was feasible for the French to invade Egypt for a second time and also march into the Balkans. Elgin realized this at once and, although he kept on close personal terms with Sébastiani, frequently inviting him to dine when he was at Constantinople, he sent Philip Hunt to Greece to keep a watch on him on his travels there. Hunt arrived at Athens in the *Victorieuse* at the end of November and darted about Greece trying to 'counteract such impression as he may have attempted to make on any class of the inhabitants contrary to the interests of Great Britain and the Ottoman Porte'. 'The loss of the *Mentor*,' he wrote to Elgin, 'and your lordship's antiquarian researches will furnish me with reasons sufficiently plausible for my journey.'[1]

Although the British Government were thus kept informed of what Sébastiani was up to, they did not expect Bonaparte to be quite so undiplomatic as he was. In January 1803 Sébastiani's report was published in the official Paris newspaper the *Moniteur*. The pretence that his mission had been commercial was dropped. The report set forth the opportunities that would be open to France in the Eastern Mediterranean if there was a war immediately. Six thousand men, it said bluntly, would be enough to reconquer Egypt and the British general was mediocre.[2] Maybe the publication of Sébastiani's report was intended to provoke Britain to war. Certainly it added greatly to the tensions between the two countries. After protracted negotiations war broke out again in May 1803.

Lord Elgin, of course, knew little of the frantic diplomatic activity between London and Paris when he left Constantinople for home in January. As far as he was concerned peace had at last returned after years of war, and he was anxious to enjoy it as anyone. His ship called at Athens, Cerigo (where he saw the remains of the *Mentor*) and Malta and then went on to Italy. He spent Easter at Rome, and decided to make the rest of the journey by land by way of Florence, Marseilles, and Paris. He arrived in France early in May. On 18 May war was declared. On 23 May came a decree of the First Consul.

All the English enrolled in the Militia from the age of 18 to 60 holding a commission from his Britannic Majesty, who are at present in France, shall be made Prisoners of War, to answer for the Citizens of the Republic who have been arrested by the vessels or subjects of his Britannic Majesty before the declaration of war. The Ministers, each as far as concerns him, are charged with the execution of the present decree.

The Ministers, on instructions from the First Consul, showed unusual zeal. They interpreted the decree to apply not only to those actually holding a commission in the militia, but also to those who might conceivably do so in the future. Since all British male subjects had a liability to serve if the country was invaded and all could, in theory at least, become officers, this meant that every male British subject was considered a prisoner of war. Lord Elgin was not excluded.

'We intended remaining a week or ten days at most at Paris when we arrived from Constantinople', wrote Lady Elgin bitterly.

I must have made some sad mistakes in writing to you if you did not always understand that. We were most positively assured by all the French Generals and Commanders and Ministers between Leghorn and this, that even should war be declared, we might go through France in the utmost security. We only knew war *was* declared at Lyons, it was then too late to go back—and with assurances, how could one imagine that an ambassador would be arrested; never since the world began was such a thing done before.* The night we arrived here, E. finding Lord W.† gone, immediately wrote to M. de Talleyrand to ask whether he had better set off for London instantaneously, or whether we might remain a few days to rest after our long journey. M. de Talleyrand's answer (which unfortunately I lost in my Imperial‡ or I would have sent it you) was that we might remain as long as we pleased and that we should have our passports whenever we pleased. The very next morning Elgin was declared prisoner of war. Who could expect that?[3]

It is difficult to imagine the horror with which this latest outrage of Bonaparte was greeted all over Europe. One of the conventions of the gentlemanly wars of the eighteenth century had been that only the armed forces of the contesting kings took part. Civilians were exempt and carried on business as usual. In fact during the eighteenth century wars the Dover to Calais packet had usually continued to run uninterrupted, and gentlemen on the Grand Tour suffered only minor inconvenience. Whether or not the British had illegally seized French ships, Bonaparte was forcing one more step towards total war.

The decree produced a good bag of prisoners, although not as many as had been hoped. After ten years of war, the English upper and middle classes could hardly wait to get back to the Continent. In the few months of peace it is estimated that no less than two-thirds of the then House of Lords visited Paris, including five dukes, three marquises, and thirty-seven earls. No wonder the French called the visitors Milords. The decree netted about five hundred, of whom about half were aristocracy and gentry and the remainder professional men and merchants. Nearly all these *détenus* were rich, and quite apart from their value as hostages, they contributed significantly to France's invisible exports.

On 27 May Elgin gave his parole and the children were sent

---

* Except of course in Turkey, but Turkey did not count as a civilized country.
† Lord Whitworth, the British Ambassador. The departure of the Ambassador was a sign that war was imminent.
‡ Lady Elgin's luggage was stolen.

on to England. But at this stage he was confident that he would soon be released. He appealed to everyone of importance within reach—the American Ambassador, the Russian Ambassador—and even wrote a personal letter to his old friend the King of Prussia.4 But his greatest hope—ironically enough—lay in Count Sébastiani, the French agent with whom he had played cat and mouse in the East, and whose report in the *Moniteur* had been one of the causes of the war. Lady Elgin wrote:

Sébastiani professed everything, came repeatedly to us, and stayed hours talking politicks. We have been anxiously expecting him these two days but alas! no Sébastiani has appeared. What is that a sign of, Ma? We heard today from good authority that this evening he was to make his great push for us, so probably tomorrow morning we shall see him. He told me that Madame B[onaparte] interested herself extremely for me and that she said she would use all her influence for us?5

But Sébastiani did not succeed and Elgin had a letter from Talleyrand confirming that he must stay. Elgin then called on the Chief Justice and reminded him of how scrupulously he had respected the capitulation in Egypt—giving passports to the returning French in his own name. But nothing could be done. The decision was Bonaparte's and he would not change it. Lord and Lady Elgin therefore settled down to wait. Life was not unpleasant. Having given their parole they were at liberty to lead their own lives, reporting to the authorities every now and then. They lived in the Hotel de Richelieu.6

In July all the English were expelled from Paris. As his health was not good, Elgin obtained permission to leave Paris and move to Barèges, a fashionable spa near the Pyrenees.7 There he settled down to take the cure and Lady Elgin amused herself in entertaining the international society. She wrote:

Barèges . . . is the most dreary place I ever saw, immense high hills without a tree. There is but one ride that one can call practicable and that one continues going down hill for an hour and a half, there are many beautiful spots at an hour or two's distance from this, but Barèges itself is most miserable. However I firmly believe it has saved Elgin's life, he gets better every day; he gets up at six or seven o'clock in the morning and goes out a shooting for four or five hours with the

Duke of Newcastle,* then about one o'clock he goes out a riding with me. He has now begun to take the baths twice a day, when he returns from shooting, and at 11 o'clock at night; he remains almost an hour each time.[8]

The evenings were spent at dinner parties, concerts, and whist. Social life at the spa was little different from life at home, or indeed from life at Constantinople.

At Barèges Lord Elgin was joined by Philip Hunt. After his shadowing of Sébastiani in Greece he had joined Elgin's ship at Athens but he had left him at Malta and he had made his way to Venice independently. There he decided to come home by land, and although, like Elgin, he received assurances that he could travel safely through France, he too was detained and put on parole.[9]

At Barèges there appeared yet another character in the story but one whom the Elgins had not met. As usual Lady Elgin is the source for this account of their first meeting.

Le Comte de Choiseul-Gouffier is here, he is very pleasant. Poor man he has been most unfortunate; after having lost almost all he possessed, he had just money enough to buy a Villa near Paris and set his heart upon the idea of placing the marbles etc he had collected at Athens: he has just received information that the Frigate on board which his Antiquities were placed, has been taken by the English. The tears were really in his eyes when he told me. He said after having lost his fortune and very nearly all the Antiquities he had with so much trouble and expense collected at Constantinople† and having hid these for so many years, and having now sent for them, he is completely overcome by the loss. It is very hard upon him, he has been entreating Elgin to write to Ld Nelson about them.[10]

Choiseul-Gouffier had indeed been very unfortunate. He had returned from exile to France in 1802, forgiven for his temporary disloyalty, but his titles and fortune were gone. His only interest in life was his collection of antiquities. He succeeded in reclaiming most of the sculptures, including the Parthenon metope, that had been seized by the Government during the Revolution, but the

* Another *détenu*.

† Lady Elgin means when he was at Constantinople: the antiquities were at Athens.

Louvre insisted on retaining his most precious piece, the slab from the Parthenon frieze.[11]

This piece had lain in the cellars of the Louvre from the time of its arrival in France until January 1802 when it was suddenly brought into prominence by Bonaparte himself. At one of his periodic inspections to see how the Louvre was filling up with the looted treasures of Europe he asked Visconti, the Director, if the Museum possessed any work by Phidias. Visconti replied that the only monument which could reasonably be attributed to that artist was a relief taken from Athens by Fauvel. The First Consul expressed his astonishment that a piece so precious was not yet on exhibition but Visconti replied that it was too mutilated and must first be restored. The work of restoration was immediately put in hand (fortunately without much damage to the original) and the slab took an honoured place in the Louvre where it still remains.[12]

With the First Consul himself displaying such a lively interest in the sculptures of the Parthenon, the French Government decided to help Choiseul-Gouffier to recover the rest of his collection that still lay at Athens, including the Parthenon metope that had come down in the storm. This collection had a curious history and one can readily imagine Choiseul-Gouffier's tears when he heard it.

Fauvel had returned to Athens in January 1803 (just in time to meet Elgin as he called there on his way home) and had taken repossession of Choiseul-Gouffier's collection. He was delighted to be back and to see his side winning again. He decided to play the same trick on Lusieri that had been played on him while he was in prison, and to seize his rival's collection, the marbles belonging to Lord Elgin. Like Lusieri's previous plot this too failed although the French Ambassador was in favour of it. Only the lack of shipping prevented his putting it into execution.[13]

In May 1803, however, the French frigate *l'Arabe*, sent by Bonaparte's express command, arrived at the Piraeus to pick up the collection belonging to Choiseul-Gouffier. To Lusieri's disappointment and Fauvel's delight the whole collection was successfully put on board and the ship sailed. But Fauvel's glee was misplaced, for war broke out before *l'Arabe* could reach France and on June 14th 1803 she was captured and taken as prize by H.M.S. *Maidstone*. By the law of prize, then as now, the value of any enemy property captured was divided among the crew of the ship which made the capture. *L'Arabe* herself was sold at Malta but Nelson directed that the cases of marbles be sent unopened to England in case the Government wanted to buy them. He wrote to Sir Joseph Banks, the President of the Royal Society, asking him to advise the Government on whether to buy them. 'One of our frigates has taken . . . some cases of I know not what but I suppose things as choice as Lord Elgin's. . . . As they are the property of the lowest seamen they cannot be presented, as I would have been truly happy to have had it in my favour to give them to the Royal Society or to the Academy of Arts.'[14]

The cases arrived in due course at the Customs House in London but the Government declined to buy them. A duty was levied on them—unfairly since Clarke brought his through at a nominal charge of one farthing[15]—and the owners were advised that they were not worth taking away. One wonders what price the same auctioneers, Messrs. Christie, would put on a Parthenon metope if they were asked to advise today. The cases were therefore left at the Customs House to await a clearance sale. They were still there in 1806 when they were rediscovered by Lord Elgin.

When Elgin met Choiseul-Gouffier at Barèges in August 1803 he knew nothing of these events. Choiseul-Gouffier for his part knew only the barest outline. Nevertheless it is astonishing that he should appeal to Elgin. After all it had been from Elgin's agents that he had been hiding the marbles for so many years. And he probably knew something at least of Elgin's schemes to seize them by force. A few months before this Fauvel had reported that Elgin's agents had stolen the piece of marble which he had years before sawn off the back of the Parthenon slab (now in the Louvre)* in order to reduce its weight.[16] In another letter,

---

* Fauvel almost certainly wanted this marble to provide materials for the restoration of the Louvre slab ordered by Bonaparte. It was quite useless to Lusieri and there seems to be no reason beyond spite why he should want to steal it from him.

reporting gleefully the loss of 'the barbarian Elgin's' ship at Cerigo, Fauvel accused Elgin's agents of breaking up sculptures for the sheer pleasure of doing so.[17]

The two noblemen met at a time when their agents at Athens were engaged in a bitter rivalry, but there was no acrimony. They were both European noblemen of the old kind and with a common interest in classical archaeology. Despite Napoleon they were true to the old standards. Elgin wrote to Nelson on Choiseul-Gouffier's behalf asking that the Parthenon metope should be sold back to Choiseul-Gouffier. Unfortunately for the Comte the collection was already in England when Nelson received the letter and he could do nothing. Choiseul-Gouffier, for his part, added his efforts to try to get Elgin released.

When the season finished at Barèges the Elgins moved to the nearby town of Pau. Life there began pleasantly enough too but, as the months went by, events took a sinister turn. Many of the *détenus* were obtaining their release by bribery or influence but it was clear that Elgin was being treated as a very special case. Elgin thought at first that he was being kept in case Bonaparte wanted an unofficial ambassador—and this was also Sébastiani's explanation—but the real reason was quite different. It lay in the personal animosity of Bonaparte.

All sorts of untrue stories had grown up about Elgin's activities at Constantinople. It was said that Elgin had attempted to double-cross the French at El Arish—on the contrary, he was one of the few who came out of the muddle with honour. It was also said that he had deliberately ill-treated the French interned in Turkey and had caused a French diplomat called Beauchamp to be put to death. This too was untrue. Elgin had intervened successfully with the Porte to relieve the sufferings of the French in the Seven Towers and, so far from causing Beauchamp's death, he had rescued him from being beheaded as a spy by Sir Sidney Smith and had later given him money and passports to return home.

Bonaparte at first seems to have believed some of these stories although his dislike of Elgin did not depend on their being true. For a time the French Government deliberately spread them and they appeared in the newspapers. Before long Lady Elgin reported that at Pau everyone was saying, '*Ah, c'est ce Milord Elgin qui a si maltraité nos compatriotes à Constantinople!*'[18] Luckily Elgin had a very powerful advocate in Sébastiani, and Lady Elgin wrote:

He swore positively that there was not the least ill will to E. personally, but on the contrary his conduct to the French in Turkey had gained him great good will. S. said for his own part he would declare whenever he was called upon, that E.'s behaviour to the French was certainly handsome, and that many Frenchmen had told him so—the first Consul was perfectly acquainted with it—and we know for certain that Sébastiani has said this in two or three Assemblies.[19]

Nevertheless it was wartime and a war that became more brutal every day. The stories persisted. Another story sprang up. It was said that a French general called Boyer who had been captured in the West Indies and was now a prisoner of war in England was being ill-treated in prison. This too was quite untrue—General Boyer was enjoying a quite comfortable life on parole. But true or false the stories had their effect. On 9 November Bonaparte issued an order that an officer of Boyer's rank should be arrested in reprisal for the ill-treatment of General Boyer.[20] Lord Elgin was the officer selected and was arrested a few days later and taken to the fortress of Lourdes.

At the time of the arrest Lady Elgin was in Paris trying to arrange for a visit home for herself and to counteract the false stories. Her energy was quite astonishing. She went straight to Talleyrand and charmed him by protesting her helplessness. She saw him often after this first meeting and corresponded through him with Bonaparte himself. She also sent out streams of letters to all her acquaintances, English and French, whom she thought might help. Talleyrand did what he could. He said it was now accepted by the Government that Elgin had not been responsible for the ill-treatment of prisoners at Constantinople; the view now was that it was Spencer Smith. After some negotiations with Bonaparte, Talleyrand offered to release Elgin altogether if the British would release General Boyer in exchange, but it was no good. Lady Elgin wrote a long plaintive letter to the Foreign Secretary and asked her father to stir up political support for the move, but the British Government took their stand on the principle that a genuine prisoner of war (Boyer) could not be exchanged for a civilian illegally detained (Elgin). There was no exchange.[21]

Meanwhile Lord Elgin himself had gone into prison at Lourdes. It is pathetic to see how he and so many of his French friends struggled vainly in their various ways to respect the gentlemanly conventions of the past even with the Government in the hands of a ruthless modern dictator and a most bitter war raging between the two countries.[22]

The commandant of Lourdes was an old friend of Elgin's. He had spent three months with him at Barèges the previous summer where both were on the social round. At Lourdes, however, to Elgin's great surprise and mortification, he received his prisoner with studied coldness and austerity, and even made him pay for the furniture of his cell. The Prefect of the Department, on the other hand, when he heard of Elgin's arrest, protested '*J'aurais volontiers donné cinquante mille écus de ma poche que ceci ne fut pas arrivé chez moi*'[23] and immediately came and passed the whole day with him accompanied by his suite.

A few days later a sergeant of the guard came mysteriously to Elgin's cell and gave him a letter. The letter purported to be from a fellow prisoner and said that if Elgin wanted to talk to him he could do so at the window. Elgin tore the letter to pieces, gave the sergeant a louis d'or, and told him that if he or anyone brought another unofficial letter he would at once deliver it to the commandant. The commandant occasionally spoke to Elgin of the mysterious fellow prisoner and seemed to be keen that Elgin should speak to him.

After only a fortnight Elgin was released from Lourdes and returned to Pau. Soon afterwards, when he was at breakfast, the woman of the house where he was lodging brought him a packet of letters which he saw was from the man who had tried to communicate with him at Lourdes. One letter said the writer had been caught in an attempt to set fire to the French fleet at Brest. It asked Elgin to forward the other letter to the Comte d'Artois who was the leader of the anti-Bonapartist *émigrés* in England.

The plan to sabotage the French fleet was to be revived. Elgin kept the woman in the room, threw all the letters in the fire, and told her that he refused to receive any letters except by the official post. He then told the whole story to the Prefect.

When Elgin had left Lourdes the commandant had immediately dropped his air of sternness and seemed disposed to renew their friendship on the old terms. He told Elgin that his speedy liberation was due to the failure of the attempts he had been ordered to make to trap him into some anti-Bonapartist intrigue. The letters had been written in Paris, and sent down by confidential agent, in the expectation of seizing them when they were in Elgin's possession.

This attempt to frame Elgin failed because of his good sense and high respect for the old-fashioned code of honour. Elgin himself only half believed that the French Government—which included so many of his friends—were implicated in the trickery, but in this he was probably wrong. He was only one of a number of British diplomats that Bonaparte attempted to discredit in the interests of propaganda. Curiously, one of the others was John Spencer Smith who had recovered from his disgrace at Constantinople and was British Minister in Württemberg. The French tried to plant on him documents addressed to *émigrés* recommending the assassination of Bonaparte.

After Elgin's release from Lourdes, he and his wife settled down to a normal life at Pau waiting patiently for permission to return to England. They lived for a time at Orleans but in the summer they returned to Barèges for the season. The Empress (Bonaparte had now become the Emperor Napoleon) was expected there and society was grander and more glittering than it had been even in the days of the *ancien régime*. In the winter the Elgins returned as before to Pau and settled down again to enjoy country life. Lady Elgin wrote:

The situation is most delightful, such a variety of beautiful rides and drives, you would be quite enchanted. As E. and Hunt were here so long before, we are allowed to remain perfectly quiet—they only go to town to present themselves occasionally to the Authorities. I have not seen a soul; almost all the families are in the country, but in winter

Pau is the greatest of places, balls, great dinners and suppers, and plenty of card playing tho' unfortunately only for sous. E. with all his ill luck, says of a long evening he could never contrive to lose more than half a crown.[24]

In the spring of 1805 they were allowed to return to Paris. To bid farewell, the prefect and the local general each gave a grand dinner in their honour. Lady Elgin was by now bored with the Bordeaux road so they went on a tour by way of Toulouse, Lyons, and Nîmes. The journey took nearly a month.

No sooner had they arrived in Paris than disaster struck. The Elgin's fourth child, who had been born at Barèges just over a year before, suddenly died. Lady Elgin was desolated and wrote home:

Pray for me, my dearest Mother, take me in your arms; Your prayers will be heard tho' mine were not listened to. I have lost my William, my angel William—my soul doated on him, I was wrapt up in my child. From the moment of his birth, to the fatal night it pleased God to call him, I have devoted myself to him. I am resigned to the Will of the Almighty but my happiness is destroyed for ever . . . *My William, my adored William is gone . . . gone . . . and left me here.* Bless your miserable child.[25]

Lady Elgin was already pregnant with a fifth child and her health was feared for. Elgin persuaded Napoleon, on humanitarian grounds, to allow Lady Elgin to return to Britain to bury the dead child in the family vault:[26] he himself was not permitted to go. Lady Elgin, accompanied by Philip Hunt, left France in October 1805.

As it turned out, Napoleon's solitary act of kindness to Elgin was an injury in disguise. About the time of Lady Elgin's return, another *détenu* was released, Robert Ferguson of Raith, a rich young man, heir to a large neighbouring estate in Fife. He was released because of his contributions to science—he was a F.R.S.[27] The Elgins had met Ferguson in Paris soon after the decree in 1803 and both recognized an old childhood friend. In the close-knit society of the British prisoners in Paris they were thrown very much together and Lady Elgin wrote that he lived 'constantly with us'.[28] Ferguson was named as the godfather of the child who

died. When Lady Elgin was on her own in Paris trying to negotiate Elgin's release from Lourdes it was natural that she should
turn to him for help. He was again there to comfort her when her
child died. By an unlucky chance Lady Elgin was now again
separated from her husband and given over to the care of this
man, just at this most dangerous moment.

But even before Lady Elgin had left for England Napoleon
struck at Lord Elgin again. He was suddenly arrested for a second
time and sent to prison at Melun. 'When I was in Paris a prisoner
in the year 1805,' he told the Select Committee eleven years later,
'living in Paris, perfectly tranquilly with my family, I received a
letter from an English traveller, complaining of Lusieri's taking
down part of the frieze of the Parthenon. The next morning a
common gens d'arme came and took me out of bed, and sent me
into close confinement away from my family. Such was the
influence exercised by the French to prevent this operation.'[29]

One may be sceptical about whether Elgin's second arrest was
due to French opposition to his activities in Athens—particularly
in view of his friendship with Choiseul-Gouffier. More probably
he was merely included in a general move to clear Paris of the
British—a policy which Napoleon tried unsuccessfully from time
to time to enforce.[30]

If the various acts of victimization against Elgin in France were
connected at all with his activities in Greece, they probably arose
out of sheer frustration. Elgin later claimed (and there is no reason
to doubt him) that he could have obtained his liberty at any time
he chose and named any price he wanted, if he would only agree
to cede his collection to the French Government.[31] Napoleon,
who bought, seized, and extorted works of art from all over
Europe to make the Louvre (temporarily) the greatest collection
ever likely to be assembled in one place, was quite capable of
making such an offer. He was the first man to set a proper value
on the sculptures of the Parthenon (although his motives were
perhaps imperial rather than artistic). The thought of the hated
Elgin possessing such treasures must have been hard to bear.

Lady Elgin's return was the start of another series of attempts
to get Elgin released. The King of Prussia, who had interceded

unsuccessfully two years before, tried again, and so did the Emperor Alexander of Russia but without success. *The Times*, on recounting this news, remarked:

One of Bonaparte's confidential ministers is said to have declared at the time that such high intercession was only calculated to prolong his Lordship's captivity as Bonaparte could not deny his pride and gratification of rejecting it; and it was observed that if the application had come from any learned Society in this country on the ground that his Lordship was an enlightened and liberal patron of the arts and had recovered many remains of antiquity at a great expense it is not improbable that the application might have succeeded as he affects to be a friend of the Arts.[32]

The confidential minister, one suspects, was Choiseul-Gouffier, or Talleyrand reported by Choiseul-Gouffier, and the source of the story Lady Elgin.

The idea was certainly worth a try—several *détenus* including Ferguson had been released on grounds of their scientific or artistic accomplishments—but one suspects it was a complete misjudgement of Bonaparte's character. A letter was drawn up by the Royal Society of Antiquaries and the Royal Academy addressed to the Institute of France.

The rage of war ought not to interrupt the intercourse of men of science and we rejoice in the progress and success of your labours. Being always ready on our part to lend assistance to your scientific men who may visit this country we beg leave to represent the following case to your consideration.

A British Nobleman, an Ambassador, embued with the love of the arts and sciences, has, at a great expense, remitted to England a very large collection of ancient monuments of Grecian art. But these precious remains have neither been published nor exhibited, to the great disappointment of artists and the learned world, because in his absence it is impossible to form any arrangements for that purpose. These noble fragments of antiquity remain packed in large cases and moulder in obscurity, exposed to the dangers of negligence and various accidents. Withdrawn from the destructive ignorance of the Turks who have already converted into lime too many similar monuments of Grecian genius, they have passed into learned and civilized Europe without conferring any of the numerous advantages that might otherwise have been expected to arise from their study and inspection, to sculpture, architecture, painting, and the sciences in general.[33]

This approach too failed like the others. It is uncertain why the French at last changed their mind. There had been an increase in the number of prisoners unofficially exchanged although neither the French nor the British Government abandoned the principle on which each had taken its stand. Perhaps it was easier for the French to let Elgin go in an unofficial secret exchange because he was an ambassador, or perhaps they simply gave in at last to pressure of world opinion. The approach which finally did the trick was one direct to Napoleon from Lord Grenville during his few months as Prime Minister. But even in releasing Elgin the French managed to do him a disservice. When Talleyrand brought the passports he also brought a document for Elgin's signature which made him promise that he would return to France whenever the French Government required. This parole was never rescinded and Elgin, ever true to the principles of *noblesse oblige*, regarded himself as bound by it right up to Napoleon's downfall.[34]

Elgin finally reached England in June 1806. It was a most unhappy homecoming.

Chapter 12

Lusieri on His Own, 1803–1806

MEANWHILE in Greece Elgin's work went on. When he left the East in January 1803 all the artists except Lusieri left with him. They had become lazy and were intriguing with the French, and, in any case, most of the work Elgin wanted in the way of moulds and figure drawings had already been done. Ittar, one of the architects was, however, employed for a year in Italy to make fair copies of his drawings. They were finished and sent to England without incident. They are now in the British Museum.* Theodor the Calmuck too was engaged to go to England to complete his drawings and engrave them. It was these engravings that Elgin hoped would improve the artistic taste of his country. Unfortunately, without supervision, the Calmuck's propensity for drink severely limited his output and his drawings were never engraved. He did, however, enjoy two years at Elgin's expense.[1]

In Greece the main job to be done was to try to salvage the *Mentor* and her cargo of marbles which lay at the bottom of Cerigo harbour. Hamilton, who was on board the ship when she sank, established himself ashore at Cerigo for several months. By offering very large sums of money to passing ships, and by importing expert sponge divers from Calymnos and Cyme at the other side of the Aegean, he succeeded in recovering four out of the seventeen cases of marbles on board. Quite independently, Elgin had shown his usual energy in one of his last acts before he left Constantinople. He despatched an Italian messenger called Pietro Gavallo with elaborate instructions, the gist of which was

---

* Every time Ittar came to copy 'Egina', as in Italian he called the island of Aegina, he wrote 'Elgina'.[2] The inhabitants of Aegina show no disposition to commemorate Lord Elgin in this way. An example of his work is shown as Plate V.

that any King's ship he came across was to be ordered at once to Cerigo and no effort or expense was to be spared to salvage the *Mentor*. Elgin also made a contract with a Greek shipowner from Spezzia called Basilio Menachini by the terms of which Basilio became British Vice-Consul at Spezzia in exchange for lending ships and aid to recover the *Mentor*. Besides all this activity, Philip Hunt, who was on his mission following Sébastiani, started to do what he could from Athens. It is hardly surprising, with so many masters trying to direct the salvage operations, that a muddle occurred.

H.M.S. *La Victorieuse* was the first ship to arrive at the scene at Cerigo. It had been arranged that she should rendezvous there with one of Basilio's ships and that between them they should try to raise the *Mentor* entire. The *Victorieuse* lay at Cerigo for thirteen days waiting for Basilio's promised ship to arrive from Spezzia but she did not come. At last, as she could wait no longer, the *Victorieuse* attempted to raise the *Mentor* by herself. But when she had lifted her two fathoms from the bottom the cables gave way and the *Mentor* fell back to the bottom. The *Victorieuse* then sailed away.[3]

Only two hours after she had gone Basilio's ship at last arrived. Hunt wrote to Hamilton from Athens to explain what had happened.

It is not easy to describe my vexation on receiving a letter from Mr. Basilio, our Vice-Consul at Spezzia, saying that he was ready to sail for Cerigo with two large ships and 120 men to co-operate with the Brig of War agreeable to Lord Elgin's written instructions, when Mr. Pierre, Corriere Straordinario di S.M.B. etc dissuaded him most strongly by saying the *Mentor* had gone to pieces ('e tutto perso, e tutto dispatto').[4]

How Pietro Gavallo got hold of this quite false information is unknown. It was probably a rumour returning full circle from some story he himself had told about the sinking of the *Mentor*. His incompetence cost Elgin very dear. By the time the muddle was sorted out, it was well on in December and too cold for the divers. All hopes of raising the *Mentor* before the winter storms dashed her to pieces had now to be abandoned.

The divers returned to Cerigo the following spring and worked there all through the summer. As expected the *Mentor* was now quite beyond salvage and great holes had to be cut in her decks to get at the cases of marbles inside. We may be grateful that the heavy figures from the pediments were not on board as Elgin had instructed: they would probably still be at the bottom of the sea. And the great slab of the frieze which had broken in two as it was taken to the Piraeus would probably not have been recovered if it had been in one piece. In 1803 five out of the thirteen remaining cases were all that could be rescued. As the marbles were recovered they were half buried on the beach and covered with seaweed, brushwood and heavy stones in an effort to protect them.

In the spring of 1804 the divers returned yet again to Cerigo and worked there for the whole of the second summer. At last in October, over two years after the *Mentor* first sank, the remaining eight cases of marbles were brought ashore. The last was the ancient throne which the Archbishop of Athens had given to Mr. and Mrs. Nisbet when they were in Athens in 1801.

Nelson, to whom Elgin had written from France, ordered a ship specially to Cerigo to pick up the collection on the beach and all the marbles found their way safely to England. The whole operation had cost Elgin about £5,000. If any proof is needed that he had a genuine concern for preserving the Parthenon marbles and was not simply—to use Clarke's favourite phrase—looking for material 'to decorate a Scotch villa',⁵ the episode of the *Mentor* alone would provide it.

Meanwhile Lusieri was still busy at Athens. Elgin had obtained permission from the King of Naples to prolong his employment at Athens and he was overjoyed. By now he was so immersed in Elgin's schemes and so fond of Greece that he could imagine no other life. He wrote to Elgin:

Here, My Lord, is my plan! It is to execute here the best works of my life, and to devote myself to them with all my strength in order to succeed. I must do more still and I much want to try it, so that some barbarisms that I have been obliged to commit in your service may be forgotten. I must work quietly. When the work of collecting is going on so furiously, how can I find the time to draw, or have the head for it?[6]

In the first few months after Elgin left, Lusieri secured another long run of the frieze and three more metopes. Among the witnesses of his operations was Robert Smirke, the architect, one of the candidates whom Elgin had rejected in 1799 when he was trying to engage an English artist to accompany him to the East. Smirke had again met Elgin at Rome on his way to Greece, but when he arrived in Athens he deliberately said nothing to Hamilton and Lusieri about the opportunity he had let slip four years before. He showed no enmity or jealousy towards Lusieri and, for the most part, approved of his efforts to send the Parthenon marbles to England. Yet, like Dodwell and Clarke earlier, he too was distressed at the destruction to the Parthenon which this rescue operation involved, and wrote:

It particularly affected me when I saw the destruction made to get down the basso-relievos on the walls of the cell [the frieze]. The men were labouring long ineffectually with iron crows to move the stones of these firm-built walls. Each stone as it fell shook the ground with its ponderous weight with a deep hollow noise; it seemed like a convulsive groan of the injured spirit of the Temple.

Nevertheless when Smirke left the Acropolis he was careful to take a few choice pieces of the Erechtheum with him: these, of course, are now lost.[7] Lusieri also about this time took one of the Caryatids of the Erechtheum. This last has probably caused more anger than any other of Elgin's acquisitions but, in spite of later stories, it seems to have been carried off without incident. The gap where the Caryatid had stood was filled with a bare brick pillar to prevent the building falling down.

But Lusieri's difficulties became greater and greater. It was virtually impossible to communicate with Elgin in France and Hamilton returned to England as soon as he had put the operations at Cerigo on a sound footing. Morier, alone of Elgin's Embassy, remained in the East—he went to Ioannina as British Consul-General—but Elgin's relations with him were distinctly cool after he had published an unauthorized account of the Convention of El

Arish.[8] Lusieri was left to fend for himself as best he could. His status with the Turks, now that he was deprived of powerful protection, fell lower and lower and, more important, his status with Elgin's bankers fell too. He found it increasingly difficult to obtain money or credit.

The French, the main opponents, were not slow to take advantage of the change of fortune. At the very moment when Elgin and Choiseul-Gouffier were the best of friends in France, Lusieri and Fauvel were engaged in a bitter struggle in Athens. Fauvel, with the agreement of the French Ambassador at Constantinople, planned to seize Elgin's cases which were still at Athens and only the lack of shipping to take them away prevented this happening.[9] He also constantly urged the Turkish Government to issue a firman ordering the removals to cease. In February 1804 Lusieri wrote:

I must stop. Fauvel has frightened all the Turks. After a number of extravagant fanfarronades he told the Disdar that he had received an order from his Ambassador to take a note of all the marbles that your Excellency has taken and to send it to him. Let him do whatever he likes, though he may get firmans empowering him to take, I very much doubt his succeeding without his paying. Then we shall see.[10]

The new British Ambassador, Drummond, was very lukewarm towards Lusieri's activities. Although he took off some of the marbles in his ship he made no effort to obtain a renewal of the firman which Lusieri told him was necessary. In the middle of 1805 the long-expected blow fell. The British Consul Logotheti received a letter from the British Embassy saying that no more statues or columns were to be taken away. So after nearly four years of almost constant removals the operations on the Acropolis came to an end.

Shortly before the final ban came Lusieri had a narrow escape, and wrote:

Two very rich English gentlemen were on the point of offering as much as 50,000 piastres,* to obtain the frieze. Happily I was told of it,

---

* Nearly £4,000 by current rates of exchange. Lusieri must surely be exaggerating. It is extremely difficult to imagine the Turks refusing this.

and I made them see that it was impossible, that it was necessary to have firmans, but that in any case I would not have let Your Excellency be second to anybody. In consequence they did nothing and will do nothing. I will work at this new acquisition with all the necessary vigour, and, I hope, My Lord, that the frieze will be yours.[11]

This part of the frieze was in fact secured. It was no doubt one of the rich travellers that Lusieri had frustrated who wrote the complaining letter to Elgin which he believed sent him to prison at Melun. If the letter really was the cause of Elgin's imprisonment he had hard luck. The act of destruction which condemned him was the last he ever committed against the Parthenon.

Among the visitors to Athens during the last days of Lusieri's removals from the Parthenon was a future prime minister, the Earl of Aberdeen, then aged twenty. He conducted large-scale excavations near the Acropolis and spent money freely in building up a collection of antiquities. He was shown round Athens both by Lusieri and by Fauvel and at the Parthenon noted 'the devastation which is indeed continual'.[12] It is possible that he had a hand in making the princely offer to the Voivode for part of the frieze. Among the antiquities that he sent to England were pieces of the Parthenon—including a fine fragment of a metope—of the Propylaea and of the temples at Sunium and Eleusis. These, one need hardly add, are now lost.[13] Later Lord Aberdeen was to join the school of connoisseurs who attempted to deny the merit of the Parthenon sculptures.

Although removal of statues was now forbidden, excavation was not and Lusieri started a great campaign of diggings at many sites in Athens, the Piraeus, and Attica. An extremely fine collection of vases and coins was accumulated including some huge marble vases and one of bronze. But the English travellers, of whom there were an increasing number, were a constant worry. Dodwell had now reappeared, combining as before condemnation of Elgin with aggrandizement of his own collection, and so had William Gell who had drawn the picture of Elgin's first removals reproduced in Plate II. Lusieri wrote of them:

They conduct themselves in such a way as to disgust everybody, and I think that those who come after will not find the same civility either here or at Argos. These gentlemen have wanted to undertake diggings without firmans, without asking permission of the Voivode, or of the landowner, and without making any return. The Voivode has been so much disgusted that he has stopped them from going on, letting all know that he would not allow anyone whatever to dig except me.[14]

Lusieri's relief was short lived. In October 1805, after over a year of successful excavations, the Voivode ordered a complete ban on all diggings by Lusieri and everybody else. Gell seems to have had a hand in this decision. He told Fauvel and the French community that Lusieri's activities were disapproved of by the British Ambassador. They of course immediately told the Voivode. The poor Voivode was a newcomer to this situation. He had arrived to take up office after the last of the Parthenon sculptures was taken down but found himself accused nevertheless of having accepted a bribe of 150 purses for allowing the removals. He was being asked to repay that sum—equivalent to 75,000 piastres or about £6,000. A total ban certainly seemed the best policy.

And so Lusieri's operations came to a complete halt. Removals and excavations were both forbidden: all he could do was draw, the purpose for which he had originally been engaged, but he was short of materials for even this innocuous activity. In the same month, October 1805, the supply of money finally failed. Elgin's bankers at Constantinople refused to give him a piastre more, understandably since they were refused more money by Elgin's bankers in London. Lusieri's position was desperate. He repeated his pleas to Drummond the British Ambassador but without success, and Morier, Elgin's former private secretary who was now Consul-General at Ioannina, refused to help him. It must have been particularly galling to receive about this time one of the few letters from Elgin in France that reached him. This simply urged him to further excavations in Attica, Eleusis, Megara, Corinth, Argos, Epidaurus, Salamis, and Aegina. Lusieri only kept himself alive by borrowing money at extortionate rates of interest.

Meanwhile the cases of marbles still lay at the Piraeus. Apart from the few taken from Cerigo which were salvaged from the *Mentor* and a very few taken to Constantinople by Drummond, no marbles left Greece during all the time that Elgin was in France. In 1806 forty cases containing many of the best of the Parthenon sculptures as well as the results of all Lusieri's labours in 1804 and 1805 lay at the Piraeus—a perpetual invitation to Fauvel. Lusieri dutifully mounted guard over this second Elgin collection. In the autumn of 1806, to his great relief, he heard of Elgin's release.

Chapter 13

Homecoming

WHEN Elgin returned to England in 1806 he was full of high hopes. He was still only forty and, although he had been abroad for nearly seven years, there seemed no reason to suppose that his career, which had begun so brilliantly, should have suffered more than a temporary set-back from the wasted years in France. But Elgin's hopes were quickly shattered. As soon as he returned he sustained a series of cruel misfortunes which laid his whole life in ruins.

The first was the destruction of his family life.[1] Lady Elgin had returned to England nearly nine months before her husband and had lived first with her parents in Portman Square and later by herself in Baker Street. In January 1806, while Elgin was still in France, her fifth child was born and it was then that he had his first indication that something was wrong. Lady Elgin wrote to say 'that she had suffered so much from this event that she would never subject herself again to that intercourse with him which might be productive of such effects'.[2]

When Elgin returned from France a few months later he was surprised to find that his wife persisted in her resolution, but he accepted the situation—perhaps remembering that Lady Elgin had been pregnant in every year of their marriage. His disappointment was increased by anxiety that he might not now leave an heir to his ancient title: the only surviving son was an epileptic. Shortly afterwards, however, some letters came into his possession which left no doubt that his wife was involved in an affair with Robert Ferguson of Raith. 'You must exasperate him,' ran one of Ferguson's letters, 'you must consider his approach as a violation of your person, and force him to a separation.'[3] Lady Elgin's letters were even more conclusive that he had long since lost her affection. In one she wrote:

He [Elgin] was very much agitated indeed, but he said nothing—after tea he got up suddenly and went into his room for a couple of hours. He coughed dreadfully which he always does when he is annoyed. I told him of my wish to go and see where my beloved William is laid—and that I wished to go alone. Friend, it was you that placed that adored angel there. There is something... I cannot account for but I feel as if he was our own. E. went out early this morning. I have not met him. I must do him the justice to say he has taken upon himself to keep his promise, but I hardly think it possible he can go on with it ... What a desperate horrible idea that nothing but death can make us free. I shudder when I dare think of it and too thoroughly I feel I cannot live without you.[4]

There was much more in the same vein and long precise instructions about how the illicit correspondence should be continued. It was clear that several of Elgin's friends were helping to pass letters, including even Alexander Straton whom Elgin had promoted to the post of secretary at Constantinople when Spencer Smith was dismissed.

Elgin decided he must divorce his wife. Under English law of the time this could only be done by a civil action for damages against Ferguson, followed by a (very expensive) private Act of Parliament. Divorce on grounds of adultery was, however, permitted by Scots law. Elgin decided on two trials—first a civil action under English law, then a divorce action in Edinburgh. The first trial took place in London in December 1807. Elgin's counsel brought in Hamilton, Morier, and several others to testify how happy the Elgin family had been right up until the last months in France. Of Ferguson it was said, 'He was indeed a very dangerous inmate [of Elgin's family] after he had planned a scheme of seduction; his manners were soft and alluring; he had been accustomed to study all the weaknesses of the female heart and the methods of taking advantage of them; and was well practised in the arts which render gallantry successful.'[5] Ferguson, in his defence, could only claim that no adultery had taken place in France 'even in the voluptuous and fascinating capital of the

French Empire where temptation is ever busily at work' but that, when Lady Elgin was alone in England 'without the protection of her husband and possessing sweetness that might rivet an anchorite —charms that could command and fascinate the coldest heart —he, all alive to such unequalled excellence and beauty, fell a devoted victim to such a shrine.'[6] Elgin was awarded damages of £10,000. The broadsheet mongers[7] found a lively market for their pamphlets as the people enjoyed the disgrace of a noble family.

The second trial took place in Edinburgh, in March 1808. For some reason Lady Elgin's lawyers decided to contest the case and indulged in a number of stratagems to try to win it. They first tried to claim that one of Lady Elgin's servants who was desperately ill in a hospital in London could not give evidence even by proxy. Another servant, who could have been an important witness, was quickly sent out of the country to prevent her having to give evidence. Then they claimed that Elgin had condoned his wife's adultery, and had even obtained a large sum of money from her as the price of condonation. Lord Elgin was only able to obtain his divorce after a long succession of servants and hotel chamber maids had proved the adultery in humiliating detail. Even for a divorce case it was a sordid affair.

The second blow which fell on Elgin on his return from France was the virtual termination of his public career. When he was first in France it was suggested that he might go as Ambassador to Russia, and he had welcomed the idea more as a means of regaining his freedom than because he was attracted by the prospect.[8] Later, while still in France, he was urging his friends to press for his appointment as Ambassador to Austria but this too did not come off.[9] No diplomatic post was offered to him. The parole which Talleyrand had exacted as the price of Elgin's release had been a cruel blow. No government could dare to take the risk of employing a man who was under such a severe restraint.

There still remained the other two careers on which he had embarked as a young man—the army and politics—but here too the story was the same. He had been promoted colonel in 1802, but there was no real prospect of success in the army for a

I. Lord Elgin as a young man, from an engraving in the British Museum.

II. The Parthenon in 1801, from a water-colour by William Gell in the British Museum.

III. (a) The South East corner of the Parthenon after the removal of some of the metopes, from a water-colour by Lusieri in the National Gallery of Scotland.

(b) The same corner after all the metopes had been taken, as shown in Hobhouse's *Journey*, 1813.

Western front of the Temples of Erectheus Minerva Polias & Pandrosus.   Acropolis.

L. B. 61

IV. Lusieri on the Erechtheum, from a water-colour by William Gell in the British Museum.

V. A Tight-Rope Display in Athens, 1800, showing the Theseum and the fortifications of the Acropolis, from a drawing by Sebastiano Ittar.

VI. (*a*) The Elgin Museum at Burlington House, 1816, from a drawing by an unknown artist, Greater London Council collection.

(*b*) Some of the Elgin Marbles in the courtyard of Burlington House, from the same collection.

VII. The Elgin Marbles at the British Museum in 1819, from a painting by A. Archer in the British Museum.

VIII. (a) An English view of the Elgin Marbles in 1816, from
a cartoon by Cruikshank.

THE ELGIN MARBLES

"*The Times* considers absurd the proposal that the marbles should be returned to Greece."

THE GOOD MERCHANT: "Quite right, too. Why should the Greeks get mixed up in this? At the most, we could
return them to the Turks from whom we bought them!"
—*Tachydromos*, Athens.

(b) A Greek View in 1961 from the Athenian newspaper *Tachydromos*.

man who had seen no active service and was in chronic bad health. As for politics, in 1807 Elgin lost his seat in the House of Lords which he had held since 1790 as one of the sixteen representative peers for Scotland. The only life that was open to him, therefore, was that of a country nobleman.

There was, however, just one indication that he had not been entirely forgotten. Lord Grenville offered him the green ribbon of the Knights of the Thistle—the honour that Elgin so eagerly wished for and which had so often been refused—but he was denied even this comfort. Grenville left office before the honour could be bestowed and his successor did not renew the offer. The only honour that Elgin ever received after his return from Turkey was the Lord Lieutenancy of Fife and even this crumb he was allowed to enjoy for only two months.[10]

To complete his misery Elgin was now deep in debt, and his divorce now deprived him of the prospect, on which he seems to have relied, of eventually adding the Nisbet fortune to his own. By the standards of some noblemen he had never been rich, nor was it really true, as Dundas had said many years before on launching him on his career, that he was 'easy in his circumstances'.[11] The income from his Scottish estates was only £2,000 a year[12]—a paltry sum for a man of his class and one which would not have appealed to even the plainest of Jane Austen's heroines.

Elgin had never during his diplomatic career expected to live within his salary nor could he ever have hoped to do so. Nevertheless he paid higher than most for the privilege of public service. His salary at Constantinople was £6,600 but, to take one item only, the domestic expenditure in the British Palace during the first year of the embassy had been £8,500.[13] Elgin had still to pay the salaries and expenses of his numerous staff, the upkeep of a large house he rented outside Constantinople, the cost of couriers and postage, and all the other multifarious expenses of a large and important Embassy. What is more, the vast expenditure made necessary by the British invasion of Egypt had caused a decline in the exchange-rate of the pound, reducing the value of his salary to about £4,400; and Elgin had spent many thousands of pounds buying supplies for the army in Egypt, not all of which he had recouped from the Government before he left Constantinople.[14] Although on his return from France in 1806 the Government gave him a further £10,000[15] this was only a part of what he had spent, quite voluntarily, out of his own purse on tents, horses, gunboats, medical supplies, and other equipment. Elgin never ceased to complain that the sum was inadequate and ten years later he was still pestering the Government for recompense, claiming, with justice, that if he had been permitted to return to England in 1803 when his success was in everybody's mind, he would never have been treated so shabbily.[16] This disaster to his finances was yet another result of his detention in France. To add to his embarrassment public opinion did not really believe that he was short of money.[17] For years afterwards the story was current that Elgin had made a fortune in Turkey in the style of a Nabob in India—a result, no doubt, of exaggerated accounts of the diamonds, pelisses, and caparisoned horses that changed hands at his audiences at the Porte.*

Elgin could have surmounted these disappointments if it had not been for his expenditure on the antiquities at Athens. This had been enormous. The original plan of drawing and taking casts was to have cost only £620 per year in salaries with something similar for expenses and materials. The expenditure had grown in proportion as the schemes became more ambitious. For the period when he himself was in the East—that is excluding any expenditure Lusieri had incurred in his name since 1803— Elgin estimated his expenditure on his collection as follows:

Pay and Expenses of the Artists over three and a half years	£9,200
Conveyance of the Artists to and from the East and their journeys there	£1,500

* Nelson, warning his brother off a diplomatic career in 1804, wrote:
 Corps Diplomatique is road to ruin. I never knew or heard of anyone who made a fortune at it and it is very easy to spend one: indeed without much more prudence than is considered right a minister cannot exist upon his salary. We must not judge because perhaps Lord Elgin at a particular moment got money at Constantinople, and even a Scotchman I dare say would have been richer with his interest if he had set up as a master tailor.[18]

Pay of Workmen employed at Athens and else-where	£15,000
Storage of Marbles at Malta	£2,500
Cost of the *Mentor* and Salvage Operations	£5,000
Cost of landing, moving and arranging the collection in England	£6,000
TOTAL	£39,200[19]

Gradually, in the months after his return from France, Elgin's affairs were sorted out. When all the bills were totted up the full extent of his difficulties was brought home to him. It came as quite a shock. 'All the money I had drawn upon public account', he wrote later, 'the whole proceeds of my patrimonial estate, my wife's fortune, and every private fund at my disposal had been absorbed; and a debt was awaiting me of about £27,000 accumulated during my foreign life.'[20] This financial difficulty lost him another of his friends. Philip Hunt, who had played such an important part in collecting the marbles and who had shared Elgin's misfortunes in France, finally recognized that the hopes of an independent fortune with which he had entered Elgin's service were never going to be realized; it is doubtful whether he received anything at all. In bitter disappointment Hunt broke off all relations with his former patron and transferred his services to the Duke of Bedford.[21] Of the party which had set out in the *Phaeton* with such high hopes seven years before only the loyal and amiable Hamilton now remained to help Elgin in his difficulties.

Last, and probably least, of the important questions which demanded Elgin's immediate attention when he returned from France was what was to be done with the collection of marbles. The main cargo of fifty cases—mostly the marbles that Hunt had put on board the *Braakel*—had arrived in England in January 1804. Since Elgin was in France, his mother the Dowager Countess had accepted responsibility for them, and they were assembled first at the house of the Duchess of Portland in Westminster and then moved nearby to the Duke of Richmond's.

From France Elgin at one stage had told his mother to hand the collection over unconditionally to the British Government but she had not complied. Another idea, to form the marbles into a public exhibition in London, had also fallen through. When Elgin returned the cases still lay unopened.²²

Besides the main cargo, some smaller lots had also arrived at different times and still lay at the various sea ports where they had been landed. Agents were sent to look for them and they were soon collected in. At the London Customs House one of Elgin's agents bought twenty-six unidentified cases of antiquities at a clearance sale at a cost of a pound each, thinking they must be Elgin's. Most of the cases contained casts or original marbles of little interest, but when one of them was opened it was found to contain a metope from the Parthenon. Although Elgin did not realize so at the time, these were the very cases that the Comte de Choiseul-Gouffier had been so concerned about when he met Elgin at Barèges. They had lain at the Customs House awaiting a buyer ever since Nelson had sent them as prize after the capture of the French frigate which was taking them to France. And so the metope which had had such an eventful history since it fell from the Parthenon in 1787 now joined the Elgin collection.²³

The Duke of Richmond, understandably, was unwilling to have fifty huge cases containing 120 tons of marbles lying in his house and garden for any longer than was necessary. Elgin, for his part, was equally anxious to remove the collection which had already cost him so much into a place where it could be both sheltered and seen. After all he had not yet seen the collection himself and was naturally eager to open his parcels. No doubt arguing to himself that it was too late to skimp now, he plunged into further expenditure. He rented a large house at the corner of Piccadilly and Park Lane which had a large garden behind. Here he built a spacious shed or penthouse where the marbles could be laid out. It took three months to build the shed and a further four to unpack and arrange the marbles. This temporary museum was finally ready in June 1807. The shed was about fifty foot square and the marbles were arranged to form a symmetrical picturesque composition to face the visitor as he entered. There was no attempt to lay out the collection systematically: sculptures, inscriptions, and architectural fragments were piled indiscriminately on one another. In the centre stood the Caryatid and all the other marbles were arranged around her according to size. The torso of Hermes, perched precariously on an inscribed column, was balanced at the other side of the room by the horse's head on top of a piece of pillar from the Erechtheum. The total effect was rather like a vignette of classical ruins so common in the travel books of the time.

Another important decision had still to be taken. Were the marbles to be restored? In the eighteenth century, the golden age of classical antiquarianism, it was the universal practice when an ancient statue was discovered, to repair the battered nose, add the missing limbs, and generally to give the imagination free play to restore the statue in entirety to what it once may have looked like. In Italy a flourishing industry produced numerous detailed and artistic compositions from the most unlikely collections of oddments. A restored statue looked better as an ornament to a room and invariably fetched a higher price than a mutilated one. The best sculptors were employed in making restorations and many a famous antique statue contained more modern than ancient parts.[24] Unfortunately in order to tack a new piece of marble on to a weathered or battered surface the rough surface must first be filed smooth. There is thus no going back. If a restored piece is wrong it cannot subsequently be taken off: the smooth modern joints thus exposed are extremely unsightly; they so resemble the finished surface that the spectator is confused, the essential form of the statue is lost, and it is very difficult to imagine what the original was like.

When Elgin's sculptures were being collected in Greece it never occurred to Hunt or Lusieri that they would not be sent to Italy for restoration. Hamilton had been more imaginative. He argued to Elgin that it would be dangerous to send the sculptures to Italy where they might easily fall into the hands of the French, that restoration would be expensive, and also, and here he was ahead of his time, 'that few would be found who would set a higher value on a work of Phidias or of one of his Scholars, with a modern head and modern arms than they would in their *present state'.*²⁵

Nevertheless when Elgin left Greece it was his firm intention to have his sculptures restored in Italy and, in fact, this seems to have been one of his chief reasons for going to Rome on his way back. Characteristically he decided that nothing but the best would do and he offered the job to the most famous sculptor in Europe, the apostle of neo-classicism, Antonio Canova. We may be thankful that he did, for Canova was a great enough artist to recognize his own limitations and is reported to have said

That however greatly it was to be lamented that these statues should have suffered so much from time and barbarism, yet it was undeniable that they had never been retouched; that they were the work of the ablest artists the world had ever seen; executed under the most enlightened patron of the arts, and at a period when genius enjoyed the most liberal encouragement, and had attained the highest degree of perfection; and that they had been found worthy of forming the decoration of the most admired edifice ever erected in Greece: That he should have had the greatest delight and derived the greatest benefit from the opportunity Lord Elgin offered him of having in his possession and contemplating these inestimable marbles. But (his expression was) it would be sacrilege in him or any man to presume to touch them with a chisel.²⁶

Canova had gone on to say, however, that if Elgin was insistent on having the marbles restored there was a man in England who could do the job as well as he, and that man was his own pupil, John Flaxman.²⁷

So the question remained during the three years of Elgin's detention in France, but he was too much a man of his generation to depart so easily from the prevailing fashion. As Canova had suggested, he now offered the work to 'the English Phidias', John Flaxman. Flaxman was willing to do it but was hesitant. The restored parts would be inferior to the original, he said modestly, and would be a constant source of dispute; the job would be long and, even when finished, might not increase the financial value of the collection. Most important of all Flaxman estimated the cost of the work at over £20,000.[28] We may be glad, for once, that Elgin was deep in debt. Lavish though he was in pouring out money on his precious marbles he could not possibly afford sums of that magnitude. The scheme was shelved and though it was later revived (Elgin wanted to offer a prize to the best suggestions for restoration)[29] by that time the fashion for restoration had gone out and he was persuaded to drop it. The sculptures of the Parthenon, rescued from Turkish ignorance, had a narrow escape from a fate almost as bad.

Chapter 14

The Second Collection

ARRANGING the marbles that had reached England was only half of Elgin's antiquarian worries on his return from France. At Athens there still lay a second collection of marbles, vases, coins, and other antiquities almost as fine as the first, over which Lusieri was still loyally standing guard. Abused by the Turks, conspired against by the French, largely abandoned by the official British authorities, and cut off from all supplies of money, Lusieri by 1806 was in a pathetic state. Elgin's release in the middle of the year was just in time to save him. There was an immediate improvement. Money and materials began to flow again, and although there could now be no question of further removals of sculpture from the buildings, excavations were re-started, despite the absence of authority, by the usual stratagem of bribing the Voivode. The famous cart which had been taken from Fauvel in 1800 was again repaired and brought into service. Lusieri proposed that he should go for a time to Naples to have the best of the vases cleaned and restored by the skilled men that had worked for Sir William Hamilton. Before anything could be decided, however, Lusieri's fortunes suddenly took a further plunge. He was suddenly obliged to fly for his life. As so often in the story larger political events had intervened.

In 1806 the period of Anglo-Turkish friendship and alliance that Elgin's Embassy had inaugurated came to an abrupt end. While Napoleon was engaged in fighting the Russians in Germany the French Ambassador in Turkey (Elgin's old friend Sébastiani) persuaded the Turks to break their treaty with Russia in favour of France. War between Russia and Turkey broke out and Britain tried to prop up her failing ally Russia by declaring war as well. A British fleet (including Sir Sidney Smith) passed the Dardanelles to make a demonstration of force outside Constantinople, but Sébastiani used the confused period of negotiations that followed to put the Dardanelles forts into a state of readiness, and the Turks inflicted heavy damage on the British ships as they returned through the straits. A small British force made an attempt to invade Egypt but little was achieved. It was an ignominious and futile war but its results were far-reaching. Within a few weeks all Lord Elgin's diplomatic successes of five years before were swept away. The Turks were more hostile to the British than ever before.

When the news of the outbreak of war reached Athens, Lusieri decided to leave. It was out of the question that he could take any of the marbles with him but he did make arrangements with his old friend the Voivode to take some of the best vases. At the very moment when the vases were about to be embarked the Voivode changed his mind. The vases were seized and Lusieri had to flee secretly at night to avoid arrest. He eventually reached Malta without any money or even spare clothes. From Malta he returned to Sicily where, characteristically, he still had drawings to finish that he had begun before 1799.

As usual the French prospects rose as the British sank. The departure of Lusieri was the signal that his enemy Fauvel had been waiting for. The two rivals had been casting covetous eyes on one another's collections ever since Fauvel's return in 1803 and each had planned, on at least one occasion, to seize the other's by force. Fauvel now had the biggest chance of his life. He took repossession at last of the cart he had lost in 1800 and made plans for the second time to seize Elgin's collections at Athens. The cases containing the vases were broken into and the vases sent overland to Ioannina for forwarding to the Louvre. But the real prize, the sculptures, were a far more difficult problem. The muleteers from Ioannina declared decisively that such heavy loads could not be taken across country by land. Fauvel could only wait therefore until a French ship could call. There could be no doubt that sooner or later Napoleon would arrange this, if only in revenge for the loss of Choiseul-Gouffier's collection in *l'Arabe*.[1]

But Elgin, after all his efforts, was not going to allow his precious collection to fall into the hands of the French without a fight. He wrote to the Governor of Malta and to Lord Mulgrave,[2] the First Lord of the Admiralty, asking them to send a warship to the Piraeus to provide a demonstration of force and a transport ship big enough to embark the marbles. To Sir John Stuart, the military Commander-in-Chief, he suggested another idea, in a letter from Broomhall:

> The only combination which occurs to my mind from hence is supposing it possible that a secret communication could be made to the authorities at Athens, I mean the Voivode, making it worth his while to permit, or connive at, the removal of such of the effects as were easily transported to the Port—Perhaps then a demonstration of disembarking a few marines, especially if there were more than one ship of war in the offing, might justify his compliance, and could easily be done, while there was not a possibility of any resistance being made.[3]

To strengthen his plea Elgin promised that he would hand over any marbles thus rescued free to the British Museum. Needless to say, these gallant officers who were engaged in a desperate war against French cruisers, were not enthusiastic about sending their warships to pick up cargoes of marbles. Their replies were only moderately encouraging.

In April 1808, despairing of success by these means, Elgin decided to send an agent of his own to the East to supervise matters on the spot. He engaged Stephen Maltass, an employee of the Levant Company who knew Greece and Turkey well, to go to Sicily and concert with Lusieri on how best to get the collection away from Athens. The main hope was to persuade the naval authorities to send a ship but another more daring scheme was to be suggested. This was nothing less than the seizing of Fauvel and the Athenian magistrates by force and holding them as ransom while the marbles were embarked. Maltass was equipped with a large sum of money, silver pistols, and English watches in case an opportunity occurred of bribing the Turks, and he was instructed to ensure that any warship that went to Athens had in company a strong transport ship, horses, tackle, and, of course, a large cart.

Maltass arrived in Sicily in July. The military authorities

continued to be evasive about sending a ship to Athens but Lusieri was keen. He even began to build a cart. If a seizure by force was to be attempted, however, Lusieri declined to take part. Maybe, as Elgin suggested, it was because he had 'formed a tender connexion'4 in Athens and did not want to jeopardise his chances of returning. But there is no reason to doubt Lusieri's own explanation. -

> Perhaps in their vexation they [the Turks] might break or burn everything in the stores and at my house; and that is the best there is. Three metopes, the best preserved, and the best pieces of the frieze, of the most picturesque part of the procession, making a sequence of several slabs, are in the town . . . One of these reliefs, which they cannot find, though they have made holes in all the corners of my house, is the despair of the Vice-Commissary [Fauvel]. They have opened all the other boxes on purpose to find it. It is finer and better preserved than all the rest.5

Fortunately for all concerned all such schemes were quickly ruled out of court. When Russia suddenly decided to ally herself with France, Britain found herself in the uncomfortable position of being at war with both the belligerents in a Russo-Turkish war. Semi-official peace negotiations with Turkey began at the Dardanelles in September 1808 and peace was signed in January 1809. The unnecessary war came to an end. Maltass went at once to Constantinople and in April obtained for Lusieri a firman allowing him to return to Athens. His mission thus successfully accomplished, Maltass disappears from the scene. But Lusieri did not go direct to Athens in spite of a ship's being specially provided to take him: he decided to take the long land route by way of Ioannina. When Elgin heard of this decision his impatience at last got the better of him and he let fly at Lusieri:

> Heavens! why the delay? How at a time like the present can you believe in the possibility of a lasting peace? What is the use of the cruel experience we have had already? For the love of God dont lose another instant at whatever cost. Take any ship that you can possibly get, either from Smyrna or Malta, to get the things into a place of safety. When you have once made them secure, then we will go forward with more confidence and calmness. But remember all I have suffered

for the last six years. Think of all the opposition you have met with and that you still have to fear. Think of all the delays inseparable from one's object in those countries. Recall the entire trust that I place in you: that I send you all the means that you can desire or that I can procure for you. Think of all that we have done; of the marvellous work at which we labour. Give yourself up entirely to the *impetuosity* of your character, as the object itself, our past success, and in short everything unite in requiring.[6]

Elgin added that he himself had decided to come to Athens in the autumn—an intention he never carried out.

Lusieri reached Athens at the end of August 1809. He presented his firman to the Voivode and took repossession of his house. The doors were all broken in; a ladder was placed permanently against the garden wall to enable anyone to go in and out at will. Everything of any value had been stolen. All the vases were gone as were a collection of presents for the Turks, all his stores, scaffolding, ropes and tackle. But to the satisfaction of everyone but Fauvel the marbles still remained.

There then began a period of frantic activity to try to get the marbles away. At Elgin's request Hamilton urged the naval authorities in the Mediterranean to send a ship to Athens, reiterating the earlier promise that any marbles thus recovered would belong to the nation and not to Elgin privately.[7] But at Athens Lusieri, taking his master's exhortations to heart, had already chartered a large vessel from the island of Hydra and obtained the permission of the Voivode to embark the collection. The marbles were actually on board and the ship was about to sail when a firman arrived from the Porte forbidding them to go. There was no alternative: the marbles had to be unloaded again, as Lusieri reported, 'in such a fashion as to cause the greatest possible pleasure to our enemies'.[8] Shortly afterwards, in response to Elgin's repeated pleas, a British warship at last arrived at the Piraeus—specially sent to take off the marbles, but it was no good. The Voivode refused absolutely to let them go. Only a firman from the Porte countermanding the first would persuade him to change his mind. The warship waited patiently for a while and then retired in disgust.

The scene of the contest to get the marbles away turned to Constantinople. The British Ambassador, Robert Adair, as a result of constant pressure from Lusieri, Elgin and the Foreign Office in London, began to apply constant pressure to the Turkish government to obtain a firman. But the Ottoman Porte could always be relied upon to produce surprises. The Turks now declared that Elgin had never had permission to remove any marbles in the first place; Elgin's activities at Athens that had been going on, with interruptions, for over eight years had been illegal from the start!⁹ One may sympathise with the Turkish point of view—the firman which Philip Hunt so skilfully engineered in August 1801 is certainly very flimsy authority for all that was done. On the other hand can one really take seriously a repudiation that was delayed for eight years until the principal part of the undertaking was already accomplished? And how was it that, before he left the East, Elgin had been able to present the Disdar with a document from the Porte which approved and commended all he had done for Lord Elgin? It is useless to look for a logical explanation or to try to reconcile the various Turkish pronouncements by legal quibbles. The Turkish Government was so inefficient that consistency over such a long period was out of the question, and, especially where money might be involved, they had no means of enforcing firmans to outlying provinces. The Turks were thoroughly bored by the whole business of ancient remains about which they had been constantly pestered since the time of Choiseul-Gouffier's ambassadorship. Their only interest in the antiquities of the despised Greeks was what use could be made of them to win friends or distress enemies—in other words as a minor instrument of foreign policy. The firmans and counter-firmans about the Parthenon marbles emanating from Constantinople between 1784 and the establishment of Greek independence are an accurate barometer of whether the French or British were uppermost in Turkish favours.

Adair was too experienced a diplomatist to take the Turkish repudiation seriously. It was only a matter of time, he knew, before the political tide would begin to turn. It took longer than he thought—nearly six months from the time he began negotiating on this subject—but he was not disappointed. On 18 February 1810 he reported to the Foreign Secretary 'with great satisfaction' that the Turks were now thoroughly dissatisfied with their new-found friendship with France and were again veering strongly towards an alliance with Great Britain.[10] Four days later—the interval having been taken up with bestowing over a hundred guineas' worth of presents—he wrote again. 'I have the honour of informing your Lordship that I have at length succeeded in obtaining the order from the Caimacan to the Voivode of Athens for the embarkation without further obstruction of the antiquities collected by Lord Elgin and now lying at Athens.'[11]

It had been a letter from the Caimacan to the Voivode that was the original authority for taking down the marbles. Now a precisely similar authority was granted to take the remaining portion of them away. If it is important to establish whether Elgin had legal authority for his activities in Greece—and the question has been debated as hotly as the question of his moral right—then the firman that Adair obtained is surely decisive. The granting of the second firman must imply condonation, if not approval, of the abuses committed with the first.

The firman reached Athens on 20 March and Lusieri lost no time in putting it into effect. By spending over £200 he succeeded in loading up his Hydriote ship by the evening of the 21st. Another British warship, H.M.S. *Pylades*, was sent specially from Smyrna to act as escort. At long last it looked as if the collection was saved. But even now Fauvel would not admit that he was beaten, and made his last bid to prevent the marbles from slipping for ever from his grasp. John Galt, the Scottish novelist, who was then in Athens in the course of a business speculation, described the final hours. He was obviously torn between a desire to join in the general condemnation of Elgin and pride in his own part in their rescue.

Two circumstances occasioned this interference on my part; an Italian artist, the agent of Lord Elgin, had quarrelled about the marbles with Monsieur Fauvelle the French consul . . . Fauvelle was no doubt ambitious to obtain these precious fragments for the Napoleon

Museum at Paris; and certainly exerted all his influence to get the removal of them interdicted. On the eve of the departure of the vessel, he sent in a strong representation on the subject to the governor of the city, stating, what I believe was very true, that Lord Elgin had never any sufficient firman or authority for the dilapidations that he had committed on the temples. Lusieri, the Italian artist alluded to, was alarmed, and called on me at the monastery of the Roman Propaganda where I then resided; and it was agreed that if any detention was attempted I should remonstrate with the governor and represent to him that such an arrest of British property would be considered an act of hostility.[12]

The presence of the *Pylades* would no doubt have given credence to the threat. But fortunately there was no need. Fauvel's protests were rejected and the Hydriote ship set sail with all her cargo on 26 March. Lusieri wrote at once in triumph to Lord Elgin:

Covering up all my past woes with eternal oblivion I wholly give myself up to joy, when I see the antiquities on board the polacca ready to set her sails for Malta. I regret that I cannot follow them as I am obliged to stay here as a surety for paying what I owe and carrying out my promises to the Voivode.[13]

The last point had not been lost on Galt who had taken passage on the ship as far as Hydra. Knowing that Elgin's bankers at Malta were proving difficult and might refuse to pay Lusieri's bills when the ship arrived, he wrote to his own banker there to instruct him to buy up the marbles if an opportunity occurred. 'Here was a chance,' he confessed later, 'of the most exquisite relics of art in the world becoming mine, and a speculation by the sale of them in London that would realise a fortune.'[14] Luckily, when the ship reached Malta, Elgin's bankers paid up and the marbles remained in his possession. What fate a collection of 'Galt Marbles' might have suffered is anyone's guess. If he had found it profitable, Galt would have dispersed them without hesitation.

Lusieri's joy at the despatch of the Hydriote ship was heartfelt, but even now, poor man, he could not taste final satisfaction.

His ship had taken forty-eight cases of marbles, including the best of the Parthenon sculptures, but she had not been large enough to take them all. Five of the heaviest cases had to be left behind and they were to prove almost the most difficult of all. It was over a year before they could be got away.

During these months of hope and despair Greece had been filled with English visitors driven by the war from the more usual haunts of the Grand Tour. John Galt came and went, as did Lord Guilford, Lord Sligo, Lady Hester Stanhope, and many others less well known. In particular, Athens was visited on two occasions by the greatest enemy Elgin ever had, Lord Byron. In the controversy between Lusieri and Fauvel these visitors took sides—mostly against Lusieri—and the whole of Athens joined in. 'It was during our stay in the place', wrote Byron's friend Hobhouse, the mildest of the visitors, 'to be lamented that a war more than civil was raging on the subject of my Lord Elgin's pursuits in Greece, and had enlisted all the Frank settlers and the principal Greeks on one or the other side of the controversy. The factions of Athens were renewed.'[15] The Fauvel party now tried to stop the last poor morsel of the Parthenon sculptures, the five cases left behind by the Hydriote ship, from being shipped away. They declared again and again to the Voivode that his actions were illegal and that he would be disowned, and they exaggerated what Elgin had done—especially the damage to the buildings—out of all proportion. Lusieri countered by saying that Fauvel wanted to take away the whole Theseum[16]—but perhaps, when one remembers that he himself had bid for the whole Caryatid porch and the Monument of Lysicrates, that is not so preposterous as it seems now. Most effective of all, they attempted to sap Lusieri's self-confidence by insinuating that Elgin was ruined and would never pay him or his bills. Lusieri, reassured on the last point, calmly continued his excavations.

Above the controversy, looking down with supreme contempt on both the contestants and all their works, was Lord Byron. He took the grand view of the situation and his prose description of it in the notes to *Childe Harold's Pilgrimage* is as eloquent and as romantic as any of his verse.

We can all feel, or imagine, the regret with which the ruins of cities, once the capitals of empires, are beheld; the reflections suggested by such objects are too trite to require recapitulation. But never did the littleness of man, and the vanity of his very best virtues, of patriotism to exalt, and of valour to defend his country, appear more conspicuous than in the record of what Athens was, and the certainty of what she now is. This theatre of contention between mighty factions, of the struggles of orators, the exaltation and deposition of tyrants, the triumph and punishment of generals, is now become a scene of petty intrigue and perpetual disturbance, between the bickering agents of certain British nobility and gentry. 'The wild foxes, the owls and serpents in the ruins of Babylon' were surely less degrading than such inhabitants. The Turks have the plea of conquest for their tyranny, and the Greeks have only suffered the fortune of war, incidental to the bravest; but how are the mighty fallen, when two painters contest the privilege of plundering the Parthenon, and triumph in turn, according to the tenor of each succeeding firman! Sylla could but punish, Philip subdue, and Xerxes burn Athens; but it remained for the paltry Antiquarian, and his despicable agents, to render her contemptible as himself and his pursuits.[17]

In another passage, written on 3 January 1810, before Lusieri's ship had sailed he declared

At this moment besides what has been already deposited in London, an Hydriot vessel is in the Piraeus to receive every portable relic. Thus, as I heard a young Greek observe in common with many of his countrymen—for, lost as they are, they yet feel on this occasion—thus may Lord Elgin boast of having ruined Athens. An Italian painter of the first eminence, named Lusieri, is the agent of devastation; and, like the Greek *finder* of Verres in Sicily, who followed the same profession, he has proved an able instrument of plunder. Between this artist and the French Consul Fauvel, who wishes to rescue* the remains for his own government, there is now a violent dispute concerning a car employed in their conveyance, the wheel of which—I wish they were both broken upon it—has been locked up by the Consul, and Lusieri has laid his complaint before the Waywode. Lord Elgin has been extremely happy in his choice of Signor Lusieri. During a residence of ten years in Athens, he never had the curiosity

* Is Byron using this word ironically, or could only the French 'rescue' the marbles?

to proceed as far as Sunium, till he accompanied us in our second excursion. However, his works, as far as they go, are most beautiful; but they are almost all unfinished . . . etc. etc.[18]

But these powerful words and the even more stirring verses to which they were to form a commentary were still hidden in Byron's notebook to burst on an astonished world a year later. While he was in Athens Byron was on the best of terms with both Fauvel and Lusieri—inspecting and comparing their collections of antiquities and drawings and using them in turn as a guide round Athens. As he himself says he even went with Lusieri on an expedition to Sunium.

But Byron had an even closer tie with Lusieri. Lusieri had married the daughter of Madame Giraud, the widow of a French merchant with whom he lodged. Byron took a fancy to Nicolo Giraud, then aged about fifteen, the young brother of Lusieri's wife,[19] and, as with all his fancies, he denied him nothing while this favour lasted. Nicolo went with Byron on his travels in Greece (helping him incidentally with his Greek and Italian) and was still writing him passionate letters five years later. Byron showered presents on the boy and even included him in his will for £7,000.[20] Lusieri seems to have done nothing to discourage this unusual friendship.

A year after the despatch of the Hydriote ship, Elgin's agents in Malta at last persuaded the Navy to send another transport, called confusingly the *Hydra*, to pick up the last of the marbles. She arrived at the Piraeus in April 1811. Byron was then in Athens waiting for an opportunity to go home and it was agreed that he should take passage in the *Hydra* as far as Malta. He sailed from the Piraeus with the last of the Elgin Marbles on 22 April 1811. Also on board were Lusieri and Nicolo Giraud, his two best friends. Byron's most bitter indictment of Lord Elgin, *The Curse of Minerva*, is dated 17 March 1811—just over a month earlier.

When the *Hydra* reached Malta the party broke up and Byron proceeded to England. At Lusieri's request he acted as messenger for a letter which Lusieri wanted to send to Elgin. Byron on his return to London forwarded the letter to Elgin as he was asked to do, but was embarrassed when Elgin offered to call on him personally to thank him. In another letter Elgin asked again to call, and said he attached much value to Byron's opinion of the researches at Athens. The two men never met, but Byron did feel obliged to give Elgin an indication of his real opinions and to warn him that he was intending to publish an attack on him.[21] How Elgin received this information is not known, but one presumes that he agreed with Hamilton to whom he sent Byron's letter for advice. Hamilton wrote:

I do not consider him [Byron] a very formidable enemy in his meditated attack and I shall be much surprised if his attack on what you have done do not turn out one of the most friendly acts he could have done. It will create an interest in the public, excite curiosity, and the real advantage to this country and the merit of your exertions will become more known and felt as they are more known.[22]

If this is what Elgin thought, it was a disastrous misjudgement.

Chapter 15

Artists and Dilettanti

BY June 1807 the arrangement of the Elgin Marbles in the shed behind Piccadilly was complete: the first collection was ready for exhibition. It was now, surely, time to begin the improvement of the arts in Great Britain which had been the original aim. Elgin still intended that eventually the marbles should be engraved and published but this was put off until the second collection should arrive and until his finances improved. Meanwhile a number of prominent artists, sculptors, and connoisseurs were permitted to view the collection and make drawings from it. The effect was startling: the whole artistic world was bowled over with admiration.

The sculptor John Flaxman, who had been asked to advise on possible restoration, was one of the first to go to Piccadilly. The pupil of the famous Canova, he had been brought up in the purest traditions of neo-classicism. His models of perfection were the Apollo Belvedere, the Laocoon, the Medici Venus and all the other Greco-Roman and Roman statues of Italy which the world then regarded as 'Greek'. These statues were almost universally held to represent the summit of artistic achievement, the greatest masterpieces of all time, and a theory of what constituted 'Ideal Beauty' had been constructed from a study of them. The statesmen and admirals in contemporary memorials, which clutter up St. Paul's and Westminster Abbey, were, in an attempt to imitate them, either embarrassingly naked or dressed as Roman Senators. Their surfaces were smooth and soapy in the manner which was then thought classical, anatomical details were slurred over, and most had more than a hint of sentimentality. Flaxman seemed destined to continue this tradition and his reaction to the Elgin Marbles is a tribute both to his honesty and to his taste. For the first time he was looking at statues which were undoubtedly Greek and the difference from his previous models was apparent to him as it had been to his master Canova.[1] He immediately declared that the Elgin Marbles were 'very far superior'[2] to all the treasures of Italy (which Napoleon had removed to the Louvre), virtually admitting that the standards on which he had based his art and whose study had brought him to the top of his profession were second-rate works. From the first day he never wavered from his opinion and no praise of the Marbles was too high. Compared with the Theseus, the Apollo Belvedere was a dancing master, he told Hamilton.[3] 'The hand of Phidias was on that'[4] he would say as he showed visitors round the museum.

Benjamin West, the President of the Royal Academy, who had tried to find Elgin an English artist before he set out for Constantinople, was equally enthusiastic. The marbles were, he said 'sublime specimens of the purest sculpture'. He declared that when the summer arrived he would devote much time to studying from them, and that he wished he were again twenty years of age instead of seventy, so that he could profit from them the more.[5] He did in fact in the ensuing months spend many hours in Elgin's cold shed sketching the marbles and incorporating the results in his huge historical paintings. When he had finished, West composed a long letter of thanks to Lord Elgin which he hoped the Academy would publish.

I have found in this collection of sculpture so much excellence in art (which is as applicable to painting and architecture as to sculpture) and a variety so magnificent and boundless, that every branch of science connected with the fine arts, cannot fail to acquire something from this collection. Your Lordship, by bringing these treasures of the first and best age of sculpture and architecture into London, has founded a new Athens for the emulation and example of the British student.

He went on to describe what he had drawn and to thank Elgin for affording him an advantage not enjoyed by Raphael, closing with a resounding peroration:

In whatever estimation the arts of the present day shall be held by those of future ages, your Lordship must be remembered by the present, and be recorded by those to come, as a benefactor who has conferred obligations not only on a profession but upon a nation; and as having rescued from the devastation of ignorance and the unholy rapine of barbarism, those unrivalled works of genius, to be preserved in the bosom of your country, which a few centuries more might have consigned to oblivion. . . . And may the materials from which those sublime sculptures have been produced be preserved from accident, that men of taste and genius yet unborn may be gratified with a sight of them; and that the admiring world may revere the Author of all things, for having bestowed on man those peculiar powers of his mind and hand.[6]

The Academy were unwilling to publish this letter, considering it too full of 'self-panegyrick.'[7] Elgin himself published it shortly afterwards.

Other artists joined in the praise. The landscape painter Farington thought the marbles were 'the highest quality of Art, a union of greatness and nature'.[8] The portrait painter Sir Thomas Lawrence became a regular visitor. The eccentric old sculptor Nollekens after finding nothing fine[9] in the sculptures, soon changed his mind and joined the artists applying for permission to sketch in Elgin's shed. Even Richard and Robert Smirke, and William Daniell, who had all been rejected by Elgin in 1799, had to admit that they had missed a great opportunity.[10] Turner, another rejected candidate, wrote enthusiastically to 'pay my homage to your lordship's exertions for this rescue from barbarism'.[11] Artists, sculptors, statesmen, ambassadors, and the whole of London society begged permission to visit Lord Elgin's museum and permits to draw were in great demand. The Elgin Marbles were the talk of the town and the museum became busier and busier.[12] William Hamilton, Elgin's former private secretary, acted as curator when Elgin was in Scotland but in 1809 he was appointed Under Secretary of State at the Foreign Office. A full-time curator was appointed and a catalogue of the exhibits printed for the use of visitors.

In June 1808 the famous prize-fighter Gregson was induced to stand naked in the museum and pose for two hours in various attitudes so that his anatomy could be compared with that of the statues. A number of artists and gentlemen each contributed five shillings (some a guinea) to witness this performance.[13] A month later another such show was held in the presence of eighteen gentlemen. This time three actual boxing matches were arranged between the best 'pugilists' of the day. The physique of Dutch Sam was much admired and so, no doubt, were the marbles.[14] On another occasion Elgin invited West and Lawrence to meet the celebrated actress Mrs. Siddons among the Parthenon sculptures. Lawrence was unable to come but wrote: 'Mrs. Siddons can nowhere be seen with so just accompaniments as the works of Phidias, nor can they receive nobler homage than from her praise. She is of his age, a kindred genius, though living in our times.'[15] Mrs. Siddons did her best to live up to this assessment. The first sight of the statues of the Fates, according to Elgin, 'so rivetted and agitated the feelings of Mrs. Siddons, the pride of theatrical representation, as actually to draw tears from her eyes'.[16]

Among the earliest of the artists who came to pay homage to the Elgin Marbles was an unsuccessful young historical painter called Benjamin Robert Haydon. Their effect on him was even more dramatic than on Mrs. Siddons. In the spring of 1807 Haydon was struggling with a picture of a Roman army being ambushed in a rocky pass and, as with most of his pictures, he was making little progress. He was perpetually rubbing out and repainting but never to his satisfaction. He was in an agony of frustration. Haydon was a man of colossal energy, passionate feelings, considerable vanity, and little common sense. He believed sincerely that he was destined by God to found a new and brilliant school of English historical painting, and he was to struggle in vain for sixty years to fulfil it. Disaster after disaster assailed him. He had the fatal disability in a painter of bad eyesight; he was constantly in debt; he was regularly arrested, and eventually he committed suicide. Although his pictures were undistinguished, his sensitivity was prodigious. He lived his intolerable life at an intensity that has seldom been matched. Everything about him was dramatic. He exulted in his occasional successes with a joy that few human beings ever touch and grovelled in his more frequent misfortunes with corresponding misery. He was introduced to the Elgin Marbles by his fellow student, David Wilkie, who had obtained a pass. The two men set off with little idea of what they were to see. Haydon's autobiography shows how he was affected both as an artist and as a professional student of artistic technique. Like Flaxman he recognized at once that here was sculpture which did not depend for its effect on a slurring over of anatomical detail or 'idealization' of nature—the style which was characteristic of the fashionable ancient statues of Italy.

To Park Lane then we went, and after passing through the hall and thence into an open yard, entered a damp, dirty pent-house where lay the marbles ranged within sight and reach. The first thing I fixed my eyes on was the wrist of a figure in one of the female groups, in which were visible, though in a feminine form, the radius and the ulna. I was astonished, for I had never seen them hinted at in any female wrist in the antique. I darted my eye to the elbow, and saw the outer condyle visibly affecting the shape as in nature. I saw that the arm was in repose and the soft parts in relaxation. That combination of nature and idea, which I had felt was so much wanting for high art, was here displayed to midday conviction. My heart beat! If I had seen nothing else I had beheld sufficient to keep me to nature for the rest of my life. But when I turned to the Theseus and saw that every form was altered by action or repose—when I saw that the two sides of his back varied, one side stretched from the shoulder blade being pulled forward and the other side compressed from the shoulder blade being pushed close to the spine as he rested on his elbow with the belly flat because the bowels fell into the pelvis as he sat—and when, turning to the Ilissus, I saw the belly protruded, from the figure lying on its side—and again, when in the figure of the fighting metope I saw the muscle shown under the one arm-pit in that instantaneous action of darting out, and left out in the other arm-pits because not wanted—when I saw, in fact, the most heroic style of art combined with all the essential detail of actual life, the thing was done at once and for ever. Here were principles which the common sense of the English people would understand; here were principles which I had struggled for in my first picture with timidity and apprehension; here were the principles which the great Greeks in their finest time established, and here was I, the most prominent historical student, perfectly qualified to appreciate all this by my own determined mode of study under the influence of my old friend the watchmaker*—perfectly comprehending the hint at the skin by knowing well what was underneath it!

Oh, how I inwardly thanked God that I was prepared to understand all this! Now I was rewarded for all the petty harassings I had suffered. Now was I mad for buying Albinus without a penny to pay for it?† . . . I felt as if a divine truth had blazed inwardly upon my mind and I knew that they would at last rouse the art of Europe from its slumber in the darkness.[17]

That evening Haydon rushed home and 'dashed out the abominable mass', from the picture of the battle he was trying to paint. All night he dozed and dreamed about the marbles and woke at five in the morning in a fever of excitement. For the next few days he tried to sketch the marbles from memory, rejecting attempt after attempt to recapture the forms he had seen. Shortly afterwards he obtained a pass to view the marbles on his own account and rushed off—Haydon always rushed— to find another of his friends, the Swiss painter Henry Fuseli. They drove headlong along the Strand, upsetting a coal cart and a flock of sheep on the way, and at last reached Park Lane. Fuseli's opinion of the marbles came up to expectation: 'Never shall I forget his uncompromising enthusiasm', wrote Haydon. 'He strode about saying "De Greeks were godes! de Greeks were godes!". . . . To look back on those hours has been my solace in the bitterest afflictions.'[18]

With some difficulty Haydon obtained permission to draw at the Park Lane Museum. His patron was extremely sceptical whether this would do his painting any good but Elgin took the larger view, remembering, no doubt, his original object of improving the progress of art. Haydon made good use of his pass. For months afterwards he spent every spare moment of his life drawing in Elgin's chilly museum. He drew for ten or fifteen hours at a time, continuing by candlelight until the porter came to close up at midnight. In his autobiography he says:

Then often have I gone home, cold, benumbed, and damp, my clothes steaming up as I dried them; and so spreading my drawings on

---

* A friend who encouraged Haydon on his artistic career when he was a boy.

† When he was a boy Haydon bought an anatomy book by Albinus for £2. 10s. 0d. to improve his knowledge of the human form.

the floor and putting a candle on the ground, I have drank my tea at one in the morning with ecstacy as its warmth trickled through my frame, and looked at my picture, and dwelt on my drawings, and pondered on the change of empires, and thought that I had been contemplating what Socrates looked at and Plato saw—and then, lifted up with my own high urgings of soul, I have prayed to God to enlighten my mind to discover the principles of those divine things— and then I have had inward assurances of future glory, and almost fancying divine influence in my room, have lingered to my mattress bed, and soon dozed into a rich balmy slumber.[19]

Some typical entries in Haydon's diary give an idea of how he worked in these tempestuous months:

8 September 1808. 'Drew at Lord Elgin's from ten till ¼ past two and from three till ¾ past five—walked about and looked at those matchless productions. I consider it truly the greatest blessing that ever happened to this country their being brought here.'[20]

31 October 1808. 'Drew at Lord Elgin's from ½ past nine to five, without intermission, perhaps I got up twice, say I lost ten minutes or 15—dined, at the Academy as usual from six to eight—9 hours and a quarter absolute drawing, not at all fatigued, not at all sore, but rather damp & cold.[21]

1 November 1808. 'I have begun this new month by rising early, praying sincerely and studying industriously: let this be the character of this month for Jesus X sake and the character of the remainder of my existence. Drew at Lord Elgin's from ¼ past nine to ¾ past 4—at the Academy ½ past 6 to 8.'[22]

The entry for 5 November would surely have pleased Lord Elgin:

'November 5—Drew at Lord Elgin's—6 hours. My taste thank God is improved wonderfully.'[23]

Such was the verdict of the artists. They at least were in no doubt about the merit of Lord Elgin's marbles. But in Regency England the artists were only part of the artistic world, perhaps not the most important one. The other part was the patrons, the rich noblemen and gentlemen who paid the artists, devoting their ample leisure to collecting and connoisseurship, or, as it was called in those days, 'virtu'. Their reaction was somewhat different.

The spokesman for the connoisseurs was Richard Payne

Knight, a man whose influence on the taste and opinions of his generation was almost equal to that later enjoyed by Ruskin. He was called the 'arbiter of fashionable virtu'.[24] He is now remembered only for his disparagement of the Elgin Marbles. Payne Knight's progress to his enviable position had been irregular but he had been unusually blessed with good luck. As a young man a diary he wrote of a journey to Sicily so impressed the great Goethe that he translated it into German and published it. This gave his career a flying start. Shortly afterwards he became an M.P. but he did not debate: he devoted himself to literary pursuits of a somewhat esoteric nature. His first work was a treatise on phallus worship which did more to shock than inform and had to be withdrawn. He then attempted a long didactic poem attacking the activities of Capability Brown and other landscape gardeners but here he felt obliged to explain its ponderous humour in meticulous footnotes. An essay on politics followed which contained a sneer at Christianity. None of these works, naturally enough, was a success.

In 1805 however Payne Knight produced a study of a subject extremely fashionable at the time, aesthetics. This was an immediate success. *An Analytic Inquiry into the Principles of Taste* became for a time the canon. After considering in turn Sense, Ideas, and Passions, and various concepts such as the sublime, the pathetic, the novel, and the ridiculous, Knight concluded, against the prevailing view, that Ideal Beauty did not exist. He allowed however that 'there are certain standards of excellence which every generation of civilized man subsequent to their first production has uniformly recognised in theory how variously soever they have departed from them in practice. Such are the precious remains of Greek sculpture which affords standards of real beauty, grace and elegance, in the human form and the modes of adorning it, the truth and perfection of which have never been questioned.'[25] As classical taste was almost the only kind then admitted, and as many of his rich contemporaries were filling their houses with 'classical' statues from Italy, this view was eminently acceptable. Whether Ideal Beauty existed or not, they were reassured that their statues were the best in the world.

Payne Knight's reputation did not rest solely on the *Analytical Inquiry*. He was also a classical scholar of considerable merit who contributed liberally to the classical journals. But most important, he had amassed a private collection of classical antiquities second to none in Europe. His cabinet included some marbles—mostly inferior works from Italy—a large number of coins, gems, and pieces of ancient jewellery, but it chiefly consisted of bronzes. During a long stay with Sir William Hamilton in Naples, Payne Knight had sifted Italy of the finest bronze statues, statuettes and pieces of armour, and his agents, backed up by his huge wealth, subsequently roamed all over Europe in search of choice specimens. Knight heard of a find of bronzes in Greece that had been taken to Russia—he immediately sent an agent there who bought them all. A Hermes with a golden necklace found near Lyons passed through the hands of three Frenchmen before Knight eventually secured it. As soon as a fine piece of bronze work appeared on the market anywhere in Europe—and many did at the time of the French Revolution— every dealer knew that Payne Knight would buy.

Ancient writers on sculpture were never in any doubt that sculpture in bronze was a higher form of art than sculpture in marble. The great Greek sculptors whose names have come down to us, Myron, Polyclitus, Phidias, Praxiteles had all, according to the sources, made their masterpieces of bronze and more precious materials, although it was well known that they also worked in marble. Payne Knight, of course, was well aware of this. Although his bronzes were for the most part small, he considered, with some justice, that his collection was far superior to the huge marbles that his friends were importing in great numbers, in a rather undiscriminating fashion, from sundry excavations in Italy. It was his intention to bequeath his incomparable collection to the Royal Academy or the British Museum where, no doubt, the Payne Knight Bronzes would perpetuate his memory.*

Ten days after Lord Elgin's arrival back in England from captivity in France in 1806 he met Payne Knight at a dinner.

---

* Payne Knight's bronzes, like almost all the antiquities referred to in this book, did in fact find their way to the British Museum.

Payne Knight had not seen the marbles which were still in the large packages that had brought them from Greece, but this did not prevent him from stating his opinion on them: 'You have lost your labour, my Lord Elgin. Your marbles are over-rated: they are not Greek: they are Roman of the time of Hadrian.'[26] Within hours Payne Knight's pronouncement was the talk of London. The Elgin Marbles which many connoisseurs had read about in reports from Athens and elsewhere were already condemned by the master—and condemned unseen at that. The master was to maintain that the Elgin Marbles were inferior works until his death eighteen years later and he was to spend ten years trying to convince other people that this was so.

In fact Payne Knight's remark was one of the silliest he ever made. The story that the Parthenon sculptures were of Roman date had no authority whatsoever in the ancient authors. It arose from an observation of a superficial traveller, Dr. Spon, who had visited Athens before the explosion of 1687 destroyed the Parthenon. Spon thought that the two of the smaller statues of the west pediment were of rather whiter marble than the rest, and suggested that perhaps the Greeks of the time of Hadrian might have replaced the original group with statues of Hadrian and Sabina, the current emperor and his wife—a fairly common form of flattery in Roman times.[27] This absurd story quickly became accepted since most subsequent travellers to Greece found it easier to get their information from the works of their predecessors than to plough through the original sources. It was believed without question by Philip Hunt,[28] and it was no doubt because they were generally believed to be inferior works, that these two sad fragments were the only original pedimental sculptures to be left on the building by Elgin's agents. Payne Knight, a classical scholar, ought to have known better. If he could not take the trouble to look up the ancient authors he could at least have read Dr. Spon, who had never suggested that the frieze, the metopes, or the other parts of the pediments were other than original.*

* Even Benjamin West originally fell a victim to this myth. He told Farington, probably as a result of talking to Payne Knight, that some parts of the Elgin Marbles had been 'very badly restored probably about the time of Adrian but it was at once seen that these parts were not the original work'.[29]

Unfortunately for Lord Elgin, Payne Knight had a ready audience for his opinion that the Elgin Marbles were inferior works. He held unchallenged sway over the Society of Dilettanti.* This society was founded about 1732 and its influence over taste in England during the next hundred years was enormous. It began as a purely social club for rich young men, and its original antiquarian activities consisted largely of meeting once a month in the Star and Garter and drinking toasts to 'Grecian taste and Roman spirit'. Most clubs of this type are a result of degeneration from more intellectual bodies but the Dilettanti grew more serious and important as the years went by. It became increasingly fashionable and soon its membership was confined to men in the highest positions in church and state: its wealth and range of activity increased correspondingly. From its earliest days members of the Society returning from the Grand Tour in Italy brought home with them vast quantities of 'classical' statues. The country houses of England became one of the greatest repositories of Greco-Roman art and a booming industry developed in Italy to excavate, reconstruct, and restore statues for the English market. In 1750, however, the Society extended its activities to Greece. It decided to support two very competent draftsmen called Stuart and Revett in making an accurate and detailed record of the surviving ancient buildings of Athens—an enterprise very similar (except for the lack of moulders) to that undertaken by Elgin fifty years later. The result was the publication in 1762 of volume I of *The Antiquities of Athens*, a magnificent folio work whose beauty and craftsmanship were enhanced by scholarship and accuracy never before attempted in classical archaeology. Two more volumes appeared in 1787 and 1794 and a fourth was in preparation: the high standard was maintained. *The Antiquities of Athens* was mainly responsible for the Grecian fashion in English architecture which began suddenly in the last years of the eighteenth century. All at once—as far as architecture was concerned—the models of Rome gave way to the models of Greece.

Besides Stuart and Revett the Dilettanti sent other expeditions

---

* The word has come down in the world since then: in the eighteenth century it did not imply superficiality.

to Greece and the Levant and published their results. All the Society's publications had the excellence and splendour of the original volumes. In an age when the classical dominated European taste, the Dilettanti were the greatest promoters of classical archaeology and the greatest connoisseurs of ancient art. At the time the Elgin Marbles arrived in England their influence was at its height and Payne Knight was their undoubted leader.

Some years before, when Elgin found himself running short of money, towards the end of his time at Constantinople, he had turned to the Dilettanti for help. It was only natural to expect that the Society which had commissioned *The Antiquities of Athens* should wish to help in bringing home the Parthenon marbles and perhaps welcome Lord Elgin himself among their ranks. Thomas Harrison, the architect who had first suggested attaching artists to Elgin's embassy, succeeded in interesting some members of the Society on Elgin's behalf and obtained an offer of a 'handsome remittance' for Lusieri. In the event the Dilettanti did nothing. At the meeting in February 1803 when the proposal was discussed someone vetoed it. There can be little doubt that it was Payne Knight.[30] His much publicized remark at the dinner in 1806 confirmed the breach between Lord Elgin and the men who were most able to help him. The Dilettanti had pronounced that the Elgin Marbles were inferior works not to be compared with the statues the Society's members had obtained in Italy.

In 1809 Payne Knight spoke again. The next of the Dilettanti Society's magnificent folios *Specimens of Antient Sculpture* which had been in preparation since 1799 was finally published. It contained engravings of sixty-three works of art in the possession of members of the Society of which no less than twenty-three belonged to Payne Knight. Payne Knight wrote the text and he allowed himself this comment on the Elgin Marbles. Characteristically he did not even mention Elgin by name.

Of Phidias's general style of composition, the friezes and metopes of the Temple of Minerva at Athens, published by Mr. Stuart and since brought to England, may afford us competent information; but as these are merely architectural sculptures executed from his designs and under his directions probably by workmen scarcely ranked among artists, and meant to be seen at the height of more than forty feet from the eye, they can throw but little light upon the more important details of his art. From the degree and mode of relief in the friezes they appear to have been intended to produce an effect like that of the simplest kind of monochromatic painting when seen from their proper point of sight; which effect must have been extremely light and elegant. The relief in the metopes is much higher, so as to exhibit the figures nearly complete, and the details are more accurately and elaborately made out, but they are so different in their degrees of merit, as to be evidently the works of many different persons, some of whom would not have been entitled to the rank of artists in a much less cultivated and fastidious age. [31]

No mention was made of the pediment sculptures.

Payne Knight had changed his ground considerably from his earlier statement that the marbles were of the time of Hadrian. In spite of himself his artistic perceptiveness shines through in some of his judgements. The Elgin Marbles are indeed architectural sculptures—an art not highly regarded in ancient times—and it is true that the quality of the metopes is irregular. Nevertheless the total effect is to damn with faint praise.

Many of the Dilettanti followed Payne Knight's lead. William Wilkins,* later architect of the National Gallery in London, was the most contemptuous, but others such as Lord Aberdeen found it prudent to be unenthusiastic. [33] No doubt they were rightly suspicious of the unmoderated praise of the artists, particularly of the assertion (which Elgin himself took care never to make) that the marbles were the work of Phidias himself. On the other hand there is at least a suspicion of a less worthy motive. The Elgin Marbles offended against all the standards of Ideal Beauty on which the great collectors had been brought up—the Elgin Marbles were large and masculine, evidently based on a sound knowledge of nature: they had little of the softness that character-ized the Apollo Belvedere and the other 'classical' sculptures of Italy. Perhaps the Dilettanti realized that by praising the Elgin

---

* In a book on the antiquities of Athens Wilkins hardly bothers to argue his case against the Elgin Marbles. He merely quotes the passage from *Specimens of Antient Sculpture* and says: 'Supported by such authority we may venture to check that mistaken enthu-siasm which venerates the sculptures as the works of Phidias.' [32]

Marbles they would be condemning, by implication, the numerous sculptures which they themselves had brought from Italy at such expense. The more thoughtful of the Dilettanti such as Sir William Hamilton had begun to suspect that there might be a distinction to be drawn between Greek, Greco-Roman, and Roman sculpture but Hamilton had died in 1803 and his successors in the Society tried to banish that uncomfortable thought from their minds.

Shortly after the publication of *Specimens of Antient Sculpture* Payne Knight's view of the Elgin Marbles received support from an unexpected quarter. The young Lord Byron, scion of the class from which Dilettanti were drawn, launched his Parthian shot at society before setting out on his travels to the East. *English Bards and Scotch Reviewers* is a satire which swipes wildly, bitterly and indiscriminately at everyone in sight: towards the end it includes these lines:

> Let Aberdeen and Elgin still pursue
> The shade of fame through regions of virtu;
> Waste useless thousands on their Phidian freaks,
> Misshapen monuments and maim'd antiques;
> And make their grand saloons a general mart
> For all the mutilated blocks of art.

In a footnote Byron adds 'Lord Elgin would fain persuade us that all the figures, with and without noses, in his stoneshop are the work of Phidias! "Credat Judaeus!" ' The inclusion of Lord Aberdeen, a celebrated member of the Dilettanti, in his tirade against the authenticity of the Elgin Marbles cannot conceal that Byron was merely underwriting the opinion of his class in general and of the Dilettanti themselves in particular. He continued to sneer at the Parthenon sculptures even when he was in Athens.[34]

Chapter 16

Elgin Offers His First Collection to the Government

FTER his return from France in 1806 Lord Elgin's way of
life changed completely. Cut off from all public life by the
loss of his seat in the House of Lords and by his parole to
Napoleon he rarely visited London. The disfigurement of his
nose made him shy of company, but even country life was not
what it might have been in happier circumstances. He could no
longer afford to run Broomhall on the scale on which Harrison
had built it in the 1790s and much of it remained unfurnished.
Most of the servants were discharged and Elgin lived as quietly
and economically as he could in one wing of the building.

In 1810 Elgin married again. His second wife, Elizabeth
Oswald of Dunnikeir, daughter of a neighbouring landowner in
Fife, was perhaps a more stable, if less interesting woman than the
first countess. She was a great comfort in his misfortunes. Eight
children were born of this second marriage and, since Elgin still
had the four surviving children of the first marriage to look after,
his financial burden continued to grow. The former Lady Elgin
had duly married Robert Ferguson of Raith and settled in his
estate not far from Broomhall. Occasionally the four children
were sent to their grandmother's home across the Firth so that
their mother could visit them.[1]

It became increasingly clear that Elgin could not afford to
keep the house in London where the marbles were stored. On the
other hand there seemed no prospect of being able to sell the
house until the marbles were removed. The collection which had
already cost him so much—and it was still only the first collection
—was rapidly becoming a millstone round his neck. All idea of

bringing it to Broomhall had long since been abandoned and even the scheme to have the marbles engraved, an essential part of any improvement of the arts that was to take place, was put off indefinitely for lack of funds. There seemed no alternative but to try to sell the collection to the Government.

Hamilton put forward the idea tentatively for the first time in May 1809. He suggested in a letter to Elgin that a number of 'respectable men, Artists, Amateurs, and members of the House of Commons'[2] should be appointed to fix a fair price based on Elgin's actual expenses, and he named among possible members of this body, West, Flaxman and Nollekens, Lord Aberdeen and Payne Knight. Hamilton, the last of Elgin's associates to stay loyal to him, was very well placed to give him advice. As Under Secretary at the Foreign Office he knew what the Government were thinking and soon afterwards (after two rejections) he was elected to the Society of Dilettanti.

But Elgin was still unwilling to open negotiations. In 1803, at the time when he had asked the Dilettanti for help, he had also approached the Government—through Flaxman—to consider building an extension of the British Museum to house his collection.[3] They had refused and Elgin was unwilling to risk further humiliation. Another scheme was investigated whereby the shed at Park Lane would be replaced by a more substantial structure and a permanent private museum established to which admittance charges could be levied. The scheme was found to be impracticable. A new museum could be built at a cost of between £1,500 and £2,000 but it would probably have to be pulled down at the end of the lease: the admittance charges were very unlikely to cover the expense. A year went by after Hamilton's suggestion and still the Park Lane house remained unsold.

In the summer of 1810 Elgin at last decided to try to sell his collection to the Government. Overtures had been received from the British Museum asking what his intentions were and public opinion seemed to be moving more towards Benjamin West's estimation of the value of the collection than to Payne Knight's. Elgin's friends urged him to seize the opportunity and he agreed. He came to London and saw the Librarian of the Museum, and also the Speaker of the House of Commons, one of the principal trustees. It was agreed to suggest to the trustees that the collection should be purchased by the nation.

The next meeting of the Trustees of the British Museum was fixed for November 1810, more than three months from the time that Elgin saw the Librarian. Elgin decided to use the intervening months to present his case to the public in the most favourable light possible. Some people had begun to question whether the marbles were indeed Elgin's property at all, seeing that he had held an official post when he collected them. It was necessary to clear the public's mind of such doubts and also to offer some reply to the assertions of Payne Knight. Elgin decided to publish his own account of his activities in Greece.

The *Memorandum on the Subject of the Earl of Elgin's Pursuits in Greece* was published anonymously late in 1810. It is a very skilful document. It gives a short, plain, and modest history of how, from the first, Lord Elgin had wished his Embassy to be of service to the arts; how he had been discouraged by the Government but had gone ahead at his own expense; and how, having seen the destruction perpetrated by the Turks and the greedy designs of the French, he had used his influence to remove to safety, with great difficulty, all the sculptures he could obtain. There then follows a brief description of the chief antiquities he had collected and of the praises lavished on them by the artists. It admits frankly that Elgin had wished to have his marbles restored until dissuaded by Canova and it reasserts that it was still his object to make his collection beneficial to the arts of his country by having engravings made that artists could buy at a reasonable price. It then offers two practical suggestions on how the marbles might be used to improve the arts—first, that a competition should be held among artists for the best restorations executed on casts, and second, that artists should be invited to witness athletic exercises performed in the presence of the marbles so that 'the variety of attitude, the articulation of the muscles, the descriptions of the passions; in short everything a sculptor has to represent' could be understood and copied. The pamphlet finishes with this thought:

Under similar advantages, and with an enlightened and encouraging protection bestowed on genius and the arts, it may not be too sanguine to indulge a hope, that, prodigal as Nature is in the perfections of the human figure in this country, animating as are the instances of patriotism, heroic actions, and private virtues, deserving commemoration, sculpture may soon be raised in England to rival the ablest productions of the best times of Greece.

The *Memorandum* is completely free of contentiousness and it does not even mention that Elgin wanted to sell his collection to the nation. It does, however, by implication, deal several blows to the fashionable opinion of the Dilettanti. Benjamin West's effusive letter of thanks for being allowed to sketch is quoted in full as an appendix, and the *Memorandum* itself emphasizes that much of the excellence of the sculptures derives from an intimate knowledge of anatomy, thereby discounting one of the standards of 'Ideal Beauty' which placed Art above Nature.

The *Memorandum* was a considerable success. Elgin himself distributed large numbers of copies to his friends and to members of the Government and other prominent men who might be able to help him. Very soon the first edition ran out. Elgin immediately put in hand a second edition which came out a few months after the first. From a stylistic point of view it was an improvement over the first. For the passages on the individual antiquities, Elgin (who of course had not been at Athens when they were collected) had relied on a long letter which Philip Hunt had composed in captivity in Pau in 1805.[4] Elgin had plagiarized this wholesale even to the extent of Hunt's idiosyncrasies of style. The Caryatid porch was a '*concetto* in architecture'; the Monument of Lysicrates 'a most precious little *bijou* in architecture'. Hamilton, sensible as always, recognized these as examples of his former friend's 'fanciful flights of eloquence'[5] and, on his advice they were cut out and the whole text sharpened up in the second edition. More appendices were added. These included an article recently published in France which showed in what high esteem the French regarded the slab of the Parthenon frieze which Choiseul-Gouffier had obtained and which Napoleon had brought into prominence.[6] Besides fortifying the judgement of the English artists who secretly still felt inferior to the artists across the Channel, this article also helped to lend weight to Elgin's contention that, but for patriotic motives, he could easily have disposed of his collection in exchange for his freedom while he was a prisoner in France. The second edition of the *Memorandum*, like the first, was given a wide distribution among influential people.

Greatly encouraged by the success of his pamphlet Elgin threw himself wholeheartedly into the negotiations. After some hopeful discussions it was decided that he should write a formal letter to Charles Long, the Paymaster General, giving the Government a detailed account of his expenses in collecting the marbles. It was agreed that this should provide a basis for the price. Elgin wrote this letter on 6 May 1811. It was very lengthy. It referred Long to the *Memorandum*, to the opportunities Elgin had turned down of disposing of the collection in France, to the universal admiration of the artists. It repeated yet again the benefits the arts of the country could expect to derive from the public possession of his collection. If an independent commission of artists and 'men of taste', had been asked to advise it would, Elgin felt sure, have endorsed this view.

And while they would have awarded a fair reimbursement of my expenses, which the state of my family and my affairs would not justify me in foregoing; they would at the same time have stamped the transaction as wholly differing from a pecuniary bargain, and would have pronounced on the service I had been the means of conferring on the Country, in a way to have presented a powerful recommendation and claim in my favour, for some mark of Royal approbation.[7]

The last part of Elgin's letter contained his estimate of his expenses. They were huge. The cost of the artists and workmen, the storage of the collection at Malta and the salvaging of the *Mentor*, he put at £33,200.* Since much of this money had been borrowed he thought it fair to include interest on this amount at five per cent. for fourteen years,† thus adding another £23,240. Expenses of moving the marbles to Westminster and then to Park

* See p. 148 for a breakdown of this figure.
† That is from 1797, two years before he set out for Constantinople.

Lane he put at £6,000. The grand total of identifiable expenses was thus £62,440. Three of the items on his list he did not put a figure to, agency fees in Turkey, money borrowed in Turkey at twelve or fourteen per cent. and 'a variety of minor expenses': these he left to the Government to fill in. No doubt he hoped the Government would round the sum up to £70,000.

The same day as he wrote this letter to the Paymaster General Elgin wrote another to the Prime Minister, Spencer Perceval. Apart from omitting the estimate of his expenses this letter was for the most part the same, word for word, as the other. But when he reached the place where he had mentioned the 'mark of Royal approbation' Elgin became more explicit. 'To a Scotch peer,' he declared roundly, 'nothing could be so desirable as a British peerage . . . I need hardly add that such an arrangement would be in the highest degree gratifying to my own feelings.'[8] He finished by suggesting, if a peerage was conferred, that he would be prepared to accept payment by instalments, or partly by annuity, if this would be more convenient.

But Elgin's hopes of thus restoring his finances and, at the same time, re-entering political life were sadly misplaced. The next few weeks were to be among the most uncomfortable in his life. The Prime Minister's reply came first. Far from using the proposed peerage to negotiate terms of payment, Spencer Perceval administered a sharp snub. 'In reply to the observations conveyed in your Lordship's letter respecting the peerage,' he wrote, 'I must candidly say that I should feel it quite impossible to recommend any arrangement of that nature as connected in the remotest degree with the purchase of your Lordship's collection.'[9]

The Paymaster General's letter was equally mortifying. The Government, Long said, were prepared to recommend to Parliament that the collection should be bought for £30,000—less than half of Elgin's expenses. Elgin was horrified and instantly declined the offer as 'wholly inadequate either to the expenses incurred, or to the acknowledged value of the collection'.[10] More letters passed in the next few days between Elgin and the Government but the Government refused firmly to depart from their offer. The Speaker too, from his knowledge of the views of 'Leading

Persons unconnected with Government' could hold out no hope.

Elgin's situation was now desperate. At long last a buyer had appeared for the Park Lane house, the Duke of Gloucester. It was urgent that the marbles should be moved out as soon as possible to ensure the sale. Elgin immediately offered his collection for exhibition to the British Institution—the rival of the Royal Academy—but they declined for lack of room.

Elgin was saved, for the present, by a timely offer of the Duke of Devonshire to store the marbles in the enclosed space at the back of Burlington House. This could only be a temporary arrangement, the Duke warned, but Elgin accepted thankfully. In July 1811 he began to cart the 120 tons of marbles up Piccadilly to Burlington House, their fourth London home. But there was no end to Elgin's bad luck. While the marbles were still in transit, the Duke of Devonshire died and there was an anxious waiting period while it was ascertained if the new Duke would agree. Fortunately he did and the removal continued. The operation cost £1,500. The new site was quite unsuitable and some of the larger marbles had to be left out in the open air, but it was something. At the end of July Elgin wrote plaintively to Spencer Perceval that his debt (which was £27,000 in 1806) had now risen to £90,000.[11] And the second collection still lay at Malta attracting heavy expenses every day.

After the failure of the negotiations Elgin retired unhappily to Broomhall. The summer passed but Hamilton reported that there was no likelihood of the Government increasing its offer. Elgin's bankers were pressing him to settle for the smaller sum and Hamilton reluctantly began to agree. Schemes were suggested to try to sell the collection to the Prince Regent or to induce the Duke of Devonshire to build a more permanent museum at Burlington House, but nothing was done.

On 11 May 1812 Spencer Perceval, the Prime Minister, was shot dead in the lobby of the House of Commons. For the time being further negotiations were out of the question.

Chapter 17

Poets and Travellers

THE first two cantos of *Childe Harold's Pilgrimage, a Romaunt by Lord Byron* were published on about 1 March 1812. Its success was instantaneous. Within three days the edition was sold out: another four editions were to go through the press before the end of the year. Suddenly, almost overnight, the young disreputable Lord Byron became one of the most famous and most sought-after men in England. The hostesses of London crowded him with invitations, fashionable young ladies vied for his attentions, the Prince Regent joined in the congratulations, and the artistic world at once forgave the youthful excesses of *English Bards*. The scurrilous versifier had become a great romantic poet, and *Childe Harold* was eagerly read in every drawing-room in England.

Lord Elgin had been well warned what to expect. Byron, conscious of his debts to Lusieri and Elgin himself, had felt obliged to tell him what was afoot. 'Lord Elgin has been teazing to see me these last four days,' he wrote to Hobhouse in July 1811. 'I wrote to him at his own request all I knew about his robberies, and at last have written to say that, as it is my intention to publish (in Childe Harold) on that topic, I thought proper since he insisted on seeing me, to give him notice, that he might not have an opportunity of accusing me of double-dealing afterwards.'[1] Despite the warning, there was nothing that Elgin could do. He seems never to have succeeded even in meeting Byron, far less mitigating his attack. His only success was that William Miller, who published the *Memorandum*, turned down an offer to publish *Childe Harold*.[2] On the other hand there is no reason to suppose that Elgin tried very hard. Most probably he felt, like Hamilton, that publicity for his activities, even unfavourable publicity, would do him more good than harm.

Lord Elgin was not to know that he was to be immortalized in one of the great poems of the century. The young lord who had used Elgin's painter as his guide to Athens and had sailed in Elgin's ship from Greece to Malta was destined to do him more damage than Payne Knight or even Napoleon Bonaparte. Contrary to public expectation, *Childe Harold's Pilgrimage* was not a satire. Only once in the body of the poem did it attack an individual with bitterness and that individual was Lord Elgin. At the beginning of Canto II Childe Harold has arrived in Greece. Sitting upon a 'massy stone, the marble column's yet unshaken base' and contemplating the ruins of the Parthenon, the Childe's melancholy gives way to anger.

> But who, of all the plunderers of yon fane
> On high—where Pallas linger'd, loth to flee
> The latest relic of her ancient reign—
> The last, the worst, dull spoiler, who was he?
> Blush, Caledonia! such thy son could be!
> England! I joy no child he was of thine:
> Thy free-born men should spare what once was free;
> Yet they could violate each saddening shrine,
> And bear these altars o'er the long-reluctant brine.

> But most the modern Pict's ignoble boast,
> To rive what Goth, and Turk, and Time hath spared:
> Cold as the crags upon his native coast,
> His mind as barren and his heart as hard,
> Is he whose head conceiv'd, whose hand prepar'd,
> Aught to displace Athena's poor remains:
> Her sons too weak the sacred shrine to guard,
> Yet felt some portion of their mother's pains,
> And never knew, till then, the weight of Despot's chains.

> What! Shall it e'er be said by British tongue,
> Albion was happy in Athena's tears?
> Though in thy name the slaves her bosom wrung,
> Tell not the deed to blushing Europe's ears;
> The ocean queen, the free Britannia, bears

The last poor plunder from a bleeding land:
Yes, she, whose gen'rous aid her name endears,
Tore down those remnants with a Harpy's hand,
Which envious Eld forbore, and tyrants left to stand.

Where was thine Aegis, Pallas! that appall'd
Stern Alaric and Havoc on their way?
Where Peleus' son? whom Hell in vain enthrall'd,
His shade from Hades upon that dread day
Bursting to light in terrible array!
What! could not Pluto spare the chief once more,
To scare a second robber from his prey?
Idly he wander'd on the Stygian shore,
Nor now preserv'd the walls he lov'd to shield before.

Cold is the heart, fair Greece! that looks on thee,
Nor feels as lovers o'er the dust they lov'd;
Dull is the eye that will not weep to see
Thy walls defac'd, thy mouldering shrines remov'd
By British hands, which it had best behov'd
To guard those relics ne'er to be restor'd.
Curst be the hour when from their isle they rov'd,
And once again thy hapless bosom gor'd,
And snatch'd thy shrinking Gods to northern climes abhorr'd![3]

With the publication of these verses, and the long rhetorical notes that accompanied them the controversy over the Elgin Marbles moved to a new battlefield. No longer did the conversation turn on the dry academic question of whether the marbles were truly 'Phidian' or not. Now the question was what right had Elgin to remove the precious remains of a weak and proud nation, what right had he to raise his hand against a building that had stood for over two thousand years. The Elgin Marbles had now become a symbol—of Greece's ignominious slavery, of Europe's failure to help her, and of Britain's overweening pride. Whatever view one might take of Lord Elgin's activities the whole basis of public opinion was altered. *Childe Harold* has dominated all discussion of the Elgin Marbles ever since.

Some weeks before *Childe Harold* was published Byron received a letter from Edward Daniel Clarke, the Cambridge professor who had quarrelled so bitterly with Carlyle and Hunt in the Troad in 1801 and had subsequently witnessed the taking down of the sculptures from the Parthenon. Clarke reported that Lord Aberdeen wished to propose Byron for membership of the Athenian Club—a club of rich young men who had visited Athens, almost an offshoot of the Dilettanti.

The letter put Byron in a dilemma. On the one hand he was genuinely flattered to be invited: on the other he was afraid of how the Athenian Club would receive the remarks on antiquarianism in his forthcoming poem. In his reply to Clarke, Byron remarked

In the notes to a thing of mine now passing through the press there is some notice taken of an agent of Ld. A's in the Levant, *Gropius* by name, and a few remarks on Ld. Elgin, Lusieri etc and their pursuits which may render the writer not very acceptable to a zealous Antiquarian. Ld. A is not mentioned or alluded to in any manner personally disrespectful but Ld. Elgin is spoken of according to the writer's decided opinion of *him* and *his* . . . Truth is I am sadly deficient in gusto and have little of the antique spirit except a wish to immolate Ld. Elgin to Minerva and Nemesis.*[4]

* In the notes to *Childe Harold* Lord Aberdeen is not mentioned by name. He is 'Lord—' exempt from even the usual partial identification of asterisks. He is, compared with Elgin, 'another noble Lord [who] has done better because he has done less'. Gropius, Lord Aberdeen's agent, quarrelled with Lusieri over the ownership of some vases, each claiming them for his master. In the early editions of *Childe Harold*, Byron tells a story that Lusieri challenged Gropius to a duel and asked Byron to arbitrate. In later editions Byron withdrew even these heavily veiled criticisms of Lord Aberdeen in an unnecessarily profuse apology.[5]

Nevertheless Byron was being a little disingenuous in telling Clarke that it was only Elgin that he wished to attack. At a late stage before publication the manuscript of *Childe Harold* contained this stanza (after xiii):

> Come then ye classic Thieves of each degree,
> Dark Hamilton and sullen Aberdeen,
> Come pilfer all that pilgrims love to see,
> All that yet consecrates the fading scene:
> Ah! better were it ye had never been
> Nor ye nor Elgin nor that lesser wight
> The victim sad of vase-collecting spleen
> House furnisher withal one Thomas hight
> Than ye should bear one stone from wronged Athena's site.[6]

Dark Hamilton is, of course, William Richard Hamilton, Elgin's private secretary. Lord Aberdeen too had removed pieces of sculpture from the Parthenon and fully deserved the charge of pilfering. 'One Thomas hight' is Thomas Hope, another

Lord Aberdeen was prepared to overlook the remarks on antiquarians but, for some reason, Byron never did become a member of the Athenian Club. The exchange of correspondence did, however, reveal that Clarke too was an old enemy of Lord Elgin and an alliance directed against Elgin's reputation grew up between the two men. In writing to congratulate Byron on the publication of *Childe Harold*, Clarke told him the story of the damage to the Parthenon cornice caused by Lusieri's operations and the tears of the Disdar when he witnessed it. Byron gratefully incorporated the story with due acknowledgement in the notes to subsequent editions of his poem.[9] Clarke, in his turn, asked permission to quote from *Childe Harold* in the enormous book of *Travels* on which he was then engaged and obtained Byron's thanks for 'preserving my relics embalmed in your own spices and ensuring me readers to whom I could not otherwise have aspired'.[10]

Clarke's *Travels in Various Countries of Europe, Asia, and Africa* can have few readers today. In its time when almost any book of travels in the Levant could command a ready market, it was very popular and, despite its forbidding length and the irrelevancy of much of its information, it quickly passed through several editions. In the section on Athens, Clarke attacked Elgin mercilessly for 'want of taste and utter barbarism'.[11] The marbles removed from their original setting, he said, lost all their excellence. Elgin was compared to 'another nobleman who being delighted at a Puppet Show, bought Punch and was chagrined to find when he carried him home, that the figure had lost all its

---

prominent member of the Dilettanti who had obtained a sculptured fragment from Athens several years before which he exhibited in his London house as a fragment of the Parthenon.[7] In another rejected stanza Byron suggests:

> Or will the gentle Dilettanti crew
> New delegate the task to digging Gell

and comments 'According to Lusieri's account he [Gell] began digging most furiously without a firman but before the resurrection of a single sauce-pan the Painter [Lusieri] countermined and the Waywode countermanded and sent him back to bookmaking.'[8]

The obvious demerits of these stanzas adequately account for their rejection. It is nevertheless possible that, in excluding them, Byron was influenced by Clarke's letter and by fear of offending the Dilettanti. Clarke himself, of course, deserved to be numbered among the 'classic Thieves'.

humour'.[12] Clarke while lavishing praise on the marbles in Athens was, by this sophistry, able to support the Dilettanti view that the marbles in London were of little value. His attack is almost as unfair as Byron's. His narrative (which described proudly the numerous removals of antiquities which he himself had accomplished) provides ample confirmation of Elgin's view that the Parthenon was being quickly destroyed and that the Turks—especially when money was offered—were quite incapable of preventing it even if they had wished. As a final piece of effrontery Clarke included in his book several views drawn by Lusieri and the Calmuck which had quite improperly come into his possession. But the British public knew nothing of what lay behind the scenes. To them it seemed simply that the opinions of the passionate poet were being confirmed by the painstaking researches of the scholar.

In addition to Clarke, more and more travellers returning from the East took up their pens and, since the war had put a stop to the Grand Tour of Italy, more travellers found their way to Greece in the early part of the nineteenth century than ever before. Almost without exception they had something disparaging to say of Elgin although equally they were all full of praise for Lusieri. The Hon. F. S. N. Douglas, while admitting frankly most of Elgin's arguments in the *Memorandum*, concluded: 'It appears to me a very flagrant piece of injustice to deprive a helpless and friendly nation of any possession of value to them . . . I wonder at the boldness of the hand that could venture to remove what Phidias had placed under the inspection of Pericles.'[13] Dodwell, himself a despoiler of the Parthenon, wrote of Elgin's 'insensate barbarism'[14] and of 'his devastating outrage which will never cease to be deplored'.[15] Hughes wrote of Elgin's 'wanton devastation' and 'avidity for plunder'.[16] Eustace in a very popular *Classical Tour through Italy* condemned Elgin fiercely without even having been to Athens.[17] French travellers combined indignation at Elgin with regret that the marbles had not gone to the Louvre.[18] Even the gentle Chateaubriand joined in the condemnation although, when he left Athens, he too had a piece of the Parthenon in his pocket.[19]

Like most of the travellers and archaeologists of his day Elgin saw nothing improper in writing his name on the monument he was so anxious to preserve.* The names Elgin and Mary Elgin with the date 1802 were carved deeply and clearly about half-way up one of the columns of the Parthenon in a place which Hunt had specially reserved in May 1801.[20] Elgin's name was soon erased but that of Mary Elgin could still be read in 1826.[21] Some travellers, understandably one now feels, regarded this as perhaps Elgin's greatest act of impertinence and gave their indignation free play. Others were a little more subtle. On one of the surviving Caryatids someone wrote '*Opus Phidiae*' (the work of Phidias): on the pillar of masonry which had been substituted for the Caryatid which Elgin removed, he wrote '*Opus Elgin*' (the work of Elgin).[22] A better joke could be seen carved on a wall inside the Erechtheum. There some donnish wit wrote '*Quod non fecerunt Goti, hoc fecerunt Scoti*.'[23]

These jibes, clearly intended to impress other travellers and not the Greeks or Turks, were gleefully recounted by travellers and taken up by the reviews. Other rhymes about Lord Elgin passed into circulation. Some managed to combine the Payne Knight view that the marbles were valueless with condemnation of Elgin. Even the ugly disfigurement of his nose was not spared and it was viciously attributed to venereal disease.

> Noseless himself he brings here noseless blocks
> To show what time has done and what the pox.†[24]

Within a few years the stories current among the foreign colony in Athens were so confused that Elgin was blamed even for actions he never committed.[25] Indignation at the Turks waned in proportion.

The most bitter attack of all was *The Curse of Minerva* by Lord Byron. Like the first part of *Childe Harold's Pilgrimage* it was

---

* Byron's name can still be read at Sunium; Choiseul-Gouffier's on the Monument of Philopappos. Lord Aberdeen and Thomas Hope carved theirs at Delphi; John Galt in the quarry on Mount Pentelicus, etc.

† Byron at one time considered making an attack on Elgin's appearance in *Childe Harold*. In a rejected version of Canto II stanza xiii he referred to Elgin as a 'man distinguished by some monstrous sign' comparing him to Attila the Hun as being 'surely horned'.[26] The horns were, of course, in Elgin's case, those of a cuckold.

The reference in *English Bards and Scotch Reviewers* to the figures in Elgin's stoneshop 'with and without noses' (see p. 179) was also surely not accidental.

written when Byron was in Athens, and originally it was intended
that the two poems should be published together in 1812 along
with some other of Byron's satires. At the last moment, however,
owing to the intervention of one of Elgin's friends, Byron decided
not to publish the *Curse* and the full version did not appear under
his name until some years later.* Yet Byron had not the heart to
suppress it entirely. In 1812 a few copies were printed and sent to
Byron's friends. To Clarke, for instance, in thanks for the story
about the Disdar, Byron wrote 'I have printed [number in-
decipherable] copies of a certain thing, one of which shall be
yours'.[28] Samuel Rogers had another,[29] and no doubt many
people had an opportunity of reading it. In 1815 a pirated copy,
much mutilated, appeared in the *New Monthly Magazine*† [30]
and others began circulating some months later. An undistinguished but bitter poem called *The Parthenon* published by
James and Horace Smith in 1813[31] bears evidence of having been
paraphrased from the *Curse*. Although Byron attempted to dis-
own the pirated versions, his authorship was clear[32] and he
openly quarried a large part of the opening section for inclusion
in *The Corsair*.

The *Curse of Minerva* begins with a very beautiful passage on
the evening falling in Greece—well worth salvaging for *The
Corsair*. The poet (as in *Childe Harold*) sits alone and friendless
within the walls of the ruined Parthenon when suddenly Minerva
herself appears. She is hardly recognizable. Her aegis holds no
terrors, her armour is dented, and her lance is broken.

> 'Mortal!'—'twas thus she spake—'that blush of shame
> Proclaims thee Briton, once a noble name;
> First of the mighty, foremost of the free,

---

* Moore in his *Life of Byron*[27] suggests that this decision was aided by a 'friendly remon-
strance from Lord Elgin or some of his connection'. This has been doubted as being
out of character but is confirmed by a reference in the Ms Journal of Edward Everett
preserved in the Library of the Massachusetts Historical Society. Everett met Byron
on 18 June 1815 shortly after Elgin's Petition to Parliament was debated. 'I asked him,'
he wrote, 'whether his poem which he speaks of as "printed but not published" in the
notes to the Corsair, would ever be given to the World. Oh No! he replied it was a
satire upon Lord Elgin, which a particular friend of each had begged him to suppress.'

† This version is very corrupt and bears the signs of having passed through several manuscript versions before reaching the printer: it was certainly not copied from the printed
version.

Now honour'd *less* by all, and *least* by me:
Chief of thy foes shall Pallas still be found.
Seek'st thou the cause of loathing?—look around.
Lo! here, despite of war and wasting fire,
I saw successive tyrannies expire.
'Scaped from the ravage of the Turk and Goth,
Thy country sends a spoiler worse than both.
Survey this vacant violated fane;
Recount the relics torn that yet remain:
These Cecrops placed, *this* Pericles adorn'd.
That Adrian rear'd* when drooping Science mourn'd.
What more I owe let gratitude attest—
Know, Alaric and Elgin did the rest.
That all may learn from whence the plunderer came,
The insulted wall sustains his hated name:
For Elgin's fame thus grateful Pallas pleads,
Below, his name—above behold his deeds!
Be ever hailed with equal honour here
The Gothic monarch and the Pictish peer:
Arms gave the first his right, the last had none,
But basely stole what less barbarians won.
So when the lion quits his fell repast,
Next prowls the wolf, the filthy jackal last:
Flesh, limbs, and blood the former make their own,
The last poor brute securely gnaws the bone.'

Minerva then observes that Venus has helped to avenge her:
Elgin's cuckolding and divorce are a punishment for his sacrilege.

'Yet still the gods are just, and crimes are cross'd:
See here what Elgin won, and what he lost!
Another name with *his* pollutes my shrine:
Behold where Dian's beams disdain to shine!
Some retribution still might Pallas claim,
When Venus half avenged Minerva's shame.'

To this outburst from Minerva the poet dares to make some
reply. Do not blame England for this terrible deed, he says.

* Byron claimed in a footnote that he was referring to the Temple of Olympian Zeus
built by Hadrian, not here subscribing to the Payne Knight view that the Parthenon
sculptures were Hadrianic.

England disowns him, the plunderer was a Scot. Just as Boeotia
was the uncivilized part of Greece, so Scotland is the uncivilized
part of Britain:

> 'And well I know within that bastard land
> Hath Wisdom's goddess never held command;
> A barren soil, where Nature's germs, confined
> To stern sterility, can stint the mind;
> Whose thistle well betrays the niggard earth,
> Emblem of all to whom the land gives birth;
> Each genial influence nurtured to resist;
> A land of meanness, sophistry, and mist.
> Each breeze from foggy mount and marshy plain
> Dilutes with drivel every drizzly brain,
> Till, burst at length, each wat'ry head o'erflows,
> Foul as their soil, and frigid as their snows.
> Then thousand schemes of petulance and pride
> Despatch her scheming children far and wide:
> Some east, some west, some everywhere but north,
> In quest of lawless gain, they issue forth.
> And thus—accursed be the day and year!—
> She sent a Pict to play the felon here.'

It was necessary for the argument that Elgin's Scottishness should
be stressed. But Byron was conscious of his own Scottish origins
and obviously did not want to be included in his own condemnation. His solution was very neat and contains one of the few hints
of humour in the poem. Just as Boeotia managed to produce a
Pindar, he said, so there was hope for a few Scotsmen, 'the letter'd
and the brave' provided they were prepared to shake off the sordid
dust of their native land.

Having heard the poet's reply Minerva bids him carry her
curse home to his native shore. Time will show that her curse is
effective.

> 'First on the head of him who did this deed
> My curse shall light—on him and all his seed:
> Without one spark of intellectual fire,
> Be all the sons as senseless as the sire:*

* Perhaps a cruel allusion to the fact that Elgin's son was an epileptic.

If one with wit the parent brood disgrace,
Believe him bastard of a brighter race:
Still with his hireling artists let him prate,
And Folly's praise repay for Wisdom's hate;
Long of their patron's gusto let them tell,
Whose noblest, *native* gusto is—to sell:
To sell, and make—may shame record the day!—
The state receiver of his pilfer'd prey.
Meanwhile, the flattering, feeble dotard, West,
Europe's worst dauber, and poor Britain's best,
With palsied hand shall turn each model o'er,
And own himself an infant of fourscore.
Be all the bruisers cull'd from all St. Giles'*
That art and nature may compare their styles;
While brawny brutes in stupid wonder stare,
And marvel at his lordship's "stone shop" there.'

After some amusing remarks about the embarrassment of the young ladies of London at seeing such huge manly statues Minerva pronounces her curse. Lord Elgin, like Eratostratus who set fire to the Temple of Diana at Ephesus, will be for ever hated. 'Loathed in life nor pardoned in the dust.' Vengeance will pursue him far beyond the grave 'In many a branding page and burning line'.

But Minerva's curse goes further. Elgin's deed is so terrible that it is not enough that he alone should be punished. Britain herself must suffer the penalty. The horrible wars on which she has embarked will soon destroy her. In the Baltic and the Peninsula she will be defeated; in the East the Indians will 'shake her tyrant empire to its base' finally at home Minerva will strike. Trade will languish, famine break out, the Government become powerless. The country itself will be invaded and ravaged. And, says Minerva, no one will be sorry. It is too late. England has brought all this upon herself.

Childe Harold's Pilgrimage and *The Curse of Minerva* have coloured the world's view of Lord Elgin's activities ever since they first appeared. This is not surprising. As satires they are very

* A reference no doubt to the displays of boxing held at Elgin's Museum in Park Lane in 1808.

good indeed. And it is no criticism of a satirist to say that he gives only one side of an argument. On the other hand the indignation of satirists is often more literary than heart-felt and Byron was no exception.

When Byron was in Athens John Galt was writing voluminously both in prose and verse. As his letters show, Galt clearly recognized that the antiquities of Greece were being quickly destroyed by the Turks and that if Elgin had not removed the Parthenon marbles the French certainly would.[33] Nor was he averse from acquiring them himself if he had had the chance.[34] While he was staying at the Capuchin Convent, however, Galt knocked out a satire on Lord Elgin which he called the *Atheniad*.[35] He showed this to Byron, who kept the manuscript for several weeks before returning it by way of Hobhouse. On his return to England Galt intended to publish his poem but, like Byron, he was dissuaded by one of Elgin's friends, in this case Hamilton.* It was not published until 1820.

The *Atheniad* is an amateurish piece of mock heroics, good-humoured enough on the whole. Where the *Curse* becomes bitter against Lord Elgin, the *Atheniad* merely shows bad taste. It was clearly never intended to be more than a literary exercise.

The gods of Olympus, dejected by the oppression of Greece, are consoled somewhat by the memory of the former glories of Athens and by the contemplation of her ruins. Then Fate takes a hand. Mercury himself is sent back to earth disguised as a man called 'Dontitos' (Don Tita Lusieri). 'Cadaverous, crafty, skilled in tints and lines, A lean Italian master of designs' Dontitos seeks out a nobleman called 'Brucides' (Lord Elgin) and tells him he will be famous if only he will rescue the Parthenon sculptures from the Turks. Brucides falls for this trap and sets to work.

> With ready gold he calls men, carts, and cords,
> Cords, carts and men, rise at the baited words.

---

* In a letter to Elgin on 17 September 1811 Hamilton wrote: 'I saw Mr. Hume a few days ago who called to give me the satisfactory intelligence that Mr. Gant had given up all idea of bringing to light the productions of his Muse, and that the absence of Lord Biron had given him time to reflect on the improper tendency of his former intentions.'[36] Hamilton's misspelling of the names of Galt and Byron shows how little known both men were at the time.

> The ropes asunder rive the wedded stone,
> The mortals labour and the axles groan,
> Hymettus echoes to the tumbling fane,
> And shook th' Acropolis—shakes all the plain.

Suddenly the gods of Olympus realize what is happening and one by one they take their revenge. First Neptune conjures up a storm and sinks Brucides' vessel at Cerigo. Minerva inspires Brucides with delirious fancies so that his diplomatic despatches are filled with talk of 'basso-relievos' and 'marble blocks' instead of military and political affairs—Brucides at once loses his ambassadorship. On the way home, however, Brucides makes a partial recovery. He lingers in Italy and France and, 'still has sprightly pleasures left'. But Minerva soon has the better of him. She drives to Paris in her golden chariot and disguising herself as Talleyrand, she persuades Napoleon to arrest all the British in France and so to possess Brucides 'a prize more precious than the Greeks of old, From Ilion stole'. Meanwhile Mars too is taking his revenge. In order to effect the transfer of a very useful cart from 'Fouvelle' (Fauvel) to Dontitos, he stirs up dreadful wars in Egypt, Russia, and Spain, and finally, in a delightful piece of bathos, causes a conflict in Athens over the wheel of this cart, which by 1810 had changed hands between Fauvel and Lusieri at least four times.

Next Venus in her turn takes her revenge on Brucides but the poet is reluctant to speak of it—he is forbidden by Juno. No doubt in the unexpurgated version Venus arranged the break-up of Elgin's marriage. Less squeamishly he reports that Cupid's revenge is to thrust a flaming torch into Elgin's face disfiguring him to look like a noseless antique bust. And finally Apollo vents his wrath by inspiring John Galt to record these great events 'in epic strains'.

> Thus wrought the gods in old Athenia's cause,
> Avenged their fanes, and will'd the world's applause.

The Curse of Minerva clearly owes some of its ideas to the *Atheniad* although its whole tone is quite different and Galt was never able to persuade Byron to acknowledge any debt.[37] Most probably it was the idea itself that Galt inspired. Perhaps Byron on reading Galt's literary effort, decided that he could do much better than his tedious companion and dashed off the *Curse*. It may be a literary extravaganza. *Childe Harold's Pilgrimage*, too, undoubtedly owes much to its literary predecessors. Its main theme—that of a reborn Greece rising against the Turks—was far from new when Byron wrote: it was already a well-known literary genre.[38] A long anonymous poem on this theme—*A Letter from Athens addressed to a Friend in England*[39]—appeared almost simultaneously with the first two cantos of *Childe Harold*. Another—William Haygarth's *Greece*[40]—was actually being written when Byron was in Athens and he knew and liked its author. All three poems show similarities of idea if not of style. Haygarth's *Greece* also has a few resemblances in construction to *The Curse of Minerva*.

Is then Byron's indignation against Elgin purely literary? Was he being no more serious in attacking Elgin than he was in his satire against the *English Bards and Scotch Reviewers*, much of whose unfairness he later regretted? Or was his attack merely a facet of the philhellenism which his later life was to show was more sincere and practical than that of his literary contemporaries and imitators? Was his main objection Elgin's 'robbery of Athens to instruct the English in sculpture',[41] or was there something about Elgin personally which roused his anger: his Scottishness, his Toryism, or his apparently typical British contempt for foreigners? The cruelty of *The Curse of Minerva* is unusually personal.

Any or all of these explanations may be true. It is impossible to say what moved Byron's embittered mind. Possibly the answer lies in Byron's sheer perverseness, his wish to be different from the careful moderation of Hobhouse and Galt. Writing of *Childe Harold* in September 1811, some months before it was published, he declared boldly

I have attacked De Pauw, Thornton,* Lord Elgin, Spain, Portugal, *the Edinburgh Review*, travellers, Painters, Antiquarians, and others,

---

* A Levant Company banker at Constantinople, author of *The Present State of Turkey*. Byron refers to this work several times in the notes to *Childe Harold's Pilgrimage*, canto II. De Pauw's contemptuous remarks on the Greeks in his book are also criticized.

so you see what a dish of Sour Crout Controversy I shall prepare for myself. It would not answer for me to give way now; as I was forced into bitterness* at the beginning, I will go through to the last. *Vae Victis!* If I fall I shall fall gloriously, fighting against a host.[42]

Byron's bravado was badly misplaced as far as Elgin was concerned. His unthinking and unfair attack fell on a man who was already almost broken by his misfortunes. *Childe Harold* and the travellers who took their cue from it dealt a blow at Elgin's reputation from which it has never recovered. Byron has much to answer for.

Lord Elgin, trying desperately to restore his finances in his Scottish retreat, was strangely silent. The world's reception of *Childe Harold* coming so soon after his rebuff from Spencer Perceval seemed merely another in the long series of misfortunes to which he was now almost accustomed. After *Childe Harold* it seemed to Elgin that every time he opened the *Edinburgh* or the *Quarterly Review*, yet another book of travels had been published with its inevitable sneers and accusations. What could be the meaning of it all? What had he done to deserve such treatment? He had only done what men of his class had been doing for over a hundred years—with the exception that his interest in antiquities had been so genuine that it had ruined him. There must be some explanation, Elgin felt. The world could not be so unjust without some cause.

Who could the arch conspirator be? Could it be his hated neighbour Robert Ferguson of Raith, the man who had seduced his wife and whom he had successfully sued for £10,000? Possibly. Ferguson who sat in Parliament as a Whig, might have persuaded his friends in those days of increasing political bitterness to attack a prominent Tory.[43] Could it be Clarke? His hatred of Elgin seemed to be unlimited, despite the many kindnesses he had accepted at Constantinople. This too was a possibility, although it was unlikely that a mere Cambridge don could exert so much influence.

But there was a man who held his grudge against Elgin more deeply than either of these. John Spencer Smith could not forget

* By the vicious review of his first poems in the *Edinburgh Review*.

the disgrace of being superseded by Elgin as minister in Turkey and then of being dismissed for incompetence and disobedience. He could not forget too that the accusations which Napoleon had levelled against Elgin in 1804 of mistreating the French in Constantinople had subsequently been transferred by the French Government to himself; and that, partly as a consequence, he was bundled out of his last diplomatic appointment in Württemberg. Here, Elgin suspected, was his conspirator. Spencer Smith's tongue was active against him in England and the merchants of the Levant Company were maligning him to travellers, English and French, in Greece and Constantinople. The Levant Company had an interest in preventing any more ambassadors extraordinary being appointed to Constantinople to break their precarious monopoly. And had not Byron dallied with Spencer Smith's wife in Malta on his way to Greece and commemorated the event in *Childe Harold*?* It all seemed to hang together.

Elgin was wrong in thinking his misfortunes were the result of a conspiracy[44] although subsequent events seemed to prove his theory. His detractors were too numerous and, for the most part, too independently minded to be so carefully disciplined. Elgin was simply unlucky. He fell, undefended, from Byron's onslaught. Had it not been for Byron, his ambition of improving British taste might have been quietly fulfilled and the honours he so ardently desired might have been bestowed; the present-day Greeks might feel as little passion that the Parthenon Marbles are in London as they do at the Venus of Melos being in Paris. Such considerations could, of course, provide very little comfort at the time.

---

* Mrs. Spencer Smith, the daughter of Baron Herbert, Austrian Ambassador to the Porte, made a dramatic and romantic escape when the French entered Venice in 1806. This was related by the Marquis of Salvo in a book published in 1807. She is described in enthusiastic terms in Byron's letters. In *Childe Harold* she is

> Sweet Florence! could another ever share
> This wayward loveless heart, it would be thine:
> But check'd by every tie, I may not dare
> To cast a worthless offering at thy shrine.
> Nor ask so dear a breast to feel one pang for thine.

Byron's relationship with her seems in fact to have been innocent enough although he perhaps pretended the contrary.

Chapter 18

Later Years in Greece

LUSIERI meanwhile, undisturbed by the controversies in England, still continued in Lord Elgin's employment. After reaching Malta in the *Hydra* in April 1811 with Byron, Nicolo Giraud, and the second Elgin collection, he stayed there for a few months reconditioning the cases in which the marbles were stored and trying to negotiate a satisfactory arrangement with Elgin's bankers. Early in July he returned to Athens.

During his short absence his own archaeological activities had been put in the shade by a new discovery and this time he was a helpless outsider among the artists of Athens. A young architectural student, Charles Robert Cockerell had arrived in Greece some months before on a tour of the Levant that was to last several years.[1] He had obtained a government commission to carry despatches as a result of his friendship with Hamilton at the Foreign Office, but once they were safely delivered he applied himself to an exhaustive and meticulous study of every ancient building he could find. He was among the luckiest of all Greek antiquarians and one of the best architects of the classical revival in England.

The very day that the *Hydra* left the Piraeus Cockerell was crossing to Aegina with two Germans and another Englishman as his companions. Recognizing the *Hydra* he went alongside and sang a favourite song of Byron's to attract his attention. Byron and Lusieri invited them on board and the two parties enjoyed a few glasses of wine together before going their separate ways. A few days later Cockerell and his party began to dig in Aegina at the temple then known as the Temple of Jupiter Panhellenius.

He wrote,

On the second day one of the excavators working in the interior portico, struck on a piece of Parian marble which, as the building itself is of stone, arrested his attention. It turned out to be the head of a helmeted warrior, perfect in every feature. It lay with the face turned upwards, and as the features came out by degrees you can imagine nothing like the state of rapture and excitement to which we were wrought ... Soon another head was turned up, then a leg and a foot, and finally, to make a long story short, we found ... no less than sixteen statues and thirteen heads, legs, arms etc, all in the highest preservation not three feet below the surface of the ground.[2]

Cockerell's party had discovered a magnificent example of a period of Greek art hitherto virtually unknown. The Aegina marbles—all pedimental sculptures—are of the late archaic period some years before the Parthenon. While they lack the extreme sophistication of the Parthenon sculptures they preserve some of the rugged monumental quality of archaic art.

Since Lord Elgin's time the Greeks had begun to learn that ancient remains had a market value. The leading men of the island presented a petition to Cockerell protesting that terrible misfortunes would fall on their land if the marbles were removed, and imploring him to cease his operations. Cockerell took this merely as an invitation to treat, and after some negotiation, bought the marbles outright for about £40 sterling. Remembering the difficulties Lusieri had suffered with the Parthenon marbles, Cockerell then conveyed the collection in great secrecy, at night, to Athens.

The foreign population of Athens, now grown greater than ever by the virtual cessation of travel in Western Europe, was given a peep at them. Cockerell wrote on 13 May,

Our council of artists here considers them as not inferior to the remains of the Parthenon and certainly in the second rank after the Torso, Laocoon and other famous statues. We conduct all our affairs in respect to them with the utmost secrecy for we sadly fear the Turks may either reclaim them or put some sad difficulties in our way. The few friends we have here and consult, such as they are, are dying with jealousy, literally one who intended to have farmed Aegina of the

Capitan Pasha is almost ill on the occasion.* Fauvel, the French consul hardly recovers the shock, although an excellent man, he does not suffer his envy to prevail against us. On the contrary he is on all occasions most obliging and has given most excellent advice to us. You may imagine the finding of such a treasure has tried everyone's character most powerfully.[3]

The Aegina Marbles were still at Athens when Lusieri returned from Malta. There is a hint of sour grapes as well as sound appreciation in his report on them to Lord Elgin. 'They are respectable for their antiquity, there are some fragments that are very fine and some that are very curious. They want the perfection and elegance of the age of Phidias.'[4]

It was obviously necessary to remove such a prize from the area of Turkish control as soon as possible. But what was to be done? There were four owners, two English and two German, each eager to possess them but equally determined that the collection should not be split. The English members of the party offered to buy out the Germans' share but without success. Fauvel, on behalf of the French Government made an extremely attractive offer of 160,000 francs but, remembering no doubt the fate of Choiseul-Gouffier's collection in 1803, he stipulated that the bulk of the money should not be paid until the marbles were safely in France. His offer too was declined. At last, on Fauvel's advice, it was decided to ship the collection to Zante (one of the Ionian Islands then under British occupation) and hold a public auction there on 1 November 1812. The marbles left Athens for Zante soon afterwards.

There then followed one of those muddles so common in the days of bad communications. Cockerell's father, hearing of his son's discovery but not of the agreement to auction, prevailed upon the Prince Regent to make an offer of £6,000 for the Aegina Marbles there and then. He also persuaded the Government to send a warship to Athens to pick them up. H.M.S. *Pauline*, a brig of war, with a heavy transport in convoy, duly

* This has usually been taken to refer to Lusieri. For years he had proposed that permission should be sought from the Capitan Pasha to allow excavations in the islands. Lusieri was not, however, in Athens at this time. Cockerell was probably referring to someone who had hoped to acquire the right to farm the taxes of Aegina.

arrived at the Piraeus in November 1811 only to discover that
the marbles had gone to Zante. Her captain was understandably
indignant at his wasted journey, but when the circumstances had
been explained to him he calmed down. He agreed to take on
board some cases of marbles for Lord Elgin that Lusieri had
collected since the *Hydra* sailed and also to go to Zante and remove
the Aegina Marbles to the greater safety of Malta. This he
accomplished without incident.

Meanwhile the forthcoming sale of the Aegina Marbles was
advertised in the newspapers of Europe and the artists of the
various countries, knowing of the excellence of the Elgin Marbles,
pressed their Governments to acquire them. In London the
Dilettanti Society, with an enthusiasm never shown for the
Parthenon marbles, persuaded the Government through Hamilton
that Great Britian must possess them at virtually any cost. Taylor
Combe of the British Museum was sent on the long dangerous
voyage with full powers. When he reached Malta he found the
Aegina Marbles had been brought there by the *Pauline* and
assumed, wrongly, that the venue of the sale had been changed to
Malta.

Taylor Combe was still at Malta on 1 November 1812 when the
sale at Zante took place. Two bidders presented themselves, one
on behalf of the French Government, the other representing
Prince Ludwig of Bavaria. The French repeated the generous
conditional offer made by Fauvel but this was not accepted: the
marbles were knocked down to the Bavarians for 130,000 piastres.[5]

Some months before, Lord Elgin's second collection of marbles,
the ones brought by the *Hydra*, left Malta on board the transport
Navigator. In May 1812 she reached Deptford. The port authorities
who were fully expecting the ship to contain the Aegina sculptures for the Prince Regent were horrified to find that her cargo
consisted solely of more Elgin Marbles. There was some acri-
monious argument about the ownership of the collection but
Lord Elgin's claim was indisputable. But, as usual, some of the
blame for an event for which he was in no way responsible seemed
to rub off on Lord Elgin.[6] His second collection at long last was
united with the first in the courtyard of Burlington House.

Gradually the story of the muddle over the Aegina Marbles came out. The Regent was affronted at being deprived of his sculptures—especially by minions of Bonaparte. Attempts were made to prove that Taylor Combe had been deliberately misled and to sequestrate the marbles at Malta, but the legality of the sale at Zante was finally upheld. The Aegina Marbles were sent to Munich where they still remain.[7] Unfortunately, they suffered the fate from which the Parthenon sculptures were saved by Elgin's poverty. They were restored. It is now difficult to distinguish the work of the Greek sculptors from that of Thorwaldsen.

Cockerell's second discovery occurred in much the same way as the first. While he was waiting for the sale of the Aegina Marbles to take place Cockerell made a tour of classical sites in Greece. In Arcadia while visiting the remote temple near Phigaleia he saw a fox darting out of the heap of stones that lay inside the ruins. Curious to discover the fox's lair Cockerell crept into the hole and at the bottom discovered a beautiful and well-preserved marble relief. He realized at once that this temple too, although built of stone, had once been decorated with a sculptured frieze and that there was every prospect of recovering it. He let the other members of the party into the secret (they were the same as the Aegina party with some others) and it was agreed to try to remove them.

With the usual presents the Porte was prevailed upon to grant a firman but as usual, in remote Greece, a firman was only permission to negotiate with the local authorities. It was accordingly agreed with the Pasha of the Morea that he should have half profits of the sale of anything that was discovered and excavations began in the summer of 1812. The temple at Phigaleia belongs to the purest classical period: it may even be by the same architect as the Parthenon. The excavators uncovered an almost complete and well-preserved frieze in high relief depicting battles of Amazons and of Lapiths and Centaurs, an example of classical architectural sculpture second only to the sculptures of the Parthenon. The excavators also discovered that the temple contained the first known example of the Corinthian order of architecture—one solitary Corinthian pillar had stood in the interior. For three months an army of between fifty and eighty men was employed digging out these treasures. In August 1812 they were on their way to the sea.

At the last minute the whole expedition almost ended in disaster. The Pasha of the Morea was bitterly disappointed that no gold had been found but, when he heard that he had been superseded in his command, he accepted £400 as his share of the spoils. The local Greeks were not so easily assuaged. A strike occurred among the porters and it was only after great delays that the marbles reached the coast. All the marbles were embarked with the exception of the unique Corinthian capital when the new pasha arrived with a party of armed troops to stop them going. The excavators had to put out to sea leaving the capital lying on the beach half in and half out of the water. They had the mortification of seeing the Turkish troops hack it to pieces in their rage and frustration.[8] The Phigaleian Marbles reached Zante safely where they were bought by the local British general on behalf of the British Government for £15,000. They arrived in London at the very time that Elgin was trying for the second time to sell his collection. As will be seen they played an important part in those negotiations.

While these great antiquarian victories were being won in other parts of Greece, Lusieri remained at Athens. But ever since the last of the Parthenon marbles had been successfully sent off Lusieri's life had changed. He was no longer the undisputed leader of the foreign artists in Athens but one of many. He no longer had the resources to carry on his researches. The price of antiquities was constantly rising as a result of the numbers of visitors and, in any case, Attica had been virtually exhausted. In 1812 Lusieri made a bargain with the Pasha of the Morea (the one that had attacked Cockerell's party) to dig at Olympia but the initial cost (500 sequins and a gold watch) was more than Elgin's bankers would allow, to say nothing of the cost of labour and transportation that would follow. Lord Elgin's antiquarian days were over.

Gradually virtually all excavation work was abandoned. Occasionally a new item was added to Lusieri's collection for

Lord Elgin, and occasionally he took up his pencil to work on his numberless uncompleted drawings, but the old enthusiasm was gone. It was so much easier to fill in his time acting as guide to the travellers and to sit late telling them about the past.[9] With advancing age and growing ill health, Lusieri's natural laziness became more and more pronounced.

The old rivalry with Fauvel continued. The great war between Great Britain and France was fought out in miniature by the two parties in Athens, each side giving a feast to celebrate the news of military victories. Their two houses, each within sight of the other on the slopes of the Acropolis and each proudly flying the flag of the warring nations were the first places in Athens that travellers invariably made for. The names of Fauvel or Lusieri, the two doyens of Athens, were passport enough for any Turkish official.

In 1813 for the last time Lusieri set the politics of Athens alight. Years before, in an attempt to sweeten the Turks towards his activities on the Acropolis, Elgin had promised to present a town clock to Athens. This suggestion was seized upon and never forgotten. Probably the only other town in the whole Turkish empire that had a clock was Thebes and the Thebans were far more proud of this than of their ancient buildings. Like all lazy people, the travellers said,[10] the Turks were very concerned about the passing of time and were continually asking the time from any foreigner who might have a watch.

The clock, ordered in 1806, arrived in Athens in 1813 to everyone's great excitement. But immediately argument broke out about where it should be sited. Lord Guilford, a visiting member of the Dilettanti, offered 1,500 piastres to have the tower built in the lower town, but Lusieri, with more loyalty than tact, insisted otherwise. The clock would be erected at Lord Elgin's expense, he said, and nowhere else but on top of the Acropolis. It seemed that, as one traveller said,[11] Lusieri wished to remind the Greeks of the despoiler of the Parthenon at every hour of the day. In the end the tower was built—with considerable murmuring from the Greeks—[12] at the expense of the town in the bazaar near the Tower of the Winds. The Turks were delighted with it. It bore the inscription

TOMAS COMES
DE ELGIN
ATHENIEN. HOROL. D.D.
SPQA EREX COLLOC
AD MDCCCXIV*

It stood until 1884 when it was destroyed by a fire.[13] Those who have some respect for Lord Elgin's memory must be grateful that its inscription was in a language that neither Greeks nor Turks were likely to understand. It is surprising that such a prominent monument to a man the Greeks soon began to hate survived so long. Scurrilous verses about it were composed in Greece as early as 1817 but it was allowed to stand.[14] During the War of Independence the clock was destroyed and afterwards the Greeks used the tower as a prison.[15] The effect on Anglo-Greek relations if Lord Elgin's Tower had been built on the Acropolis can be imagined.

The argument about Lord Elgin's clock was perhaps only a symptom of a more profound change that was gradually occurring in Greece. This incident and the episodes of the Aegina and Phigaleian marbles seem to indicate that the Greeks had begun to claim a say in the disposal of their antiquities. A Greek view as distinct from a Turkish view peeps through.

For the Greeks to hold an opinion on any public matter was considered presumptuous by the Turks although some minor forms of Greek political organization still survived. To the Turks, the Greeks were *rayahs*, infidels little better than slaves. The foreign travellers tended to agree with them. The rich Westerners coming to visit the birth-place of civilization invariably drew melancholy comparisons between the glories of ancient Greece and her modern degradation. It was a pleasing antithesis especially as they and their readers were in no doubt that their own countries now represented the acme of modern civilization.

* 'Thomas Earl of Elgin presented the clock to the people of Athens. The Senate and People of Athens erected it and sited it here.' The marble slab with this inscription is preserved in the National and Historical Museum, Athens. It probably came originally from the Parthenon.

And lo! he comes, the modern son of Greece,
The shame of Athens: mark him how he bears
A look o'eraw'd and moulded to the stamp
Of servitude.[16]

So wrote William Haygarth and most of the travellers agreed with him. That the Greeks were a thoroughly contemptible race was, it was said, the only point on which Fauvel and Lusieri were agreed.[17]

Byron alone was of a different opinion. In his notes to *Childe Harold* he declared

They are so unused to kindness that when they occasionally meet with it they look upon it with suspicion, as a dog often beaten snaps at your fingers if you attempt to caress him. 'They are ungrateful, notoriously, abominably ungrateful!'—this is the general cry. Now, in the name of Nemesis! for what are they to be grateful? Where is the human being that ever conferred a benefit on Greek or Greeks? They are to be grateful to the Turks for their fetters, and the Franks for their broken promises and lying counsels. They are to be grateful to the artist who engraves their ruins and to the antiquary who carries them away: to the traveller whose janissary flogs them, and to the scribbler whose journal abuses them! This is the amount of their obligations to foreigners.[18]

Byron was right. The Greeks were not as despicable as was so readily assumed. The ideas of liberty and national independence so fashionable in Europe did not stop at the borders of the Ottoman Empire. Within twenty years of Byron's first visit, the Greeks were to throw out the Turks in a desperate war of national liberation and take their place among the proudest nations of modern Europe. And from the earliest days of independence the Greeks devoted themselves to the restoration and preservation of their ancient heritage with a passion that has grown steadily ever since.

It is hardly surprising that in the last years before the Greek Revolution, some signs of concern for their ancient monuments began to appear among the Greeks. During those last thirty years they probably lost more antiquities than at any time since the Romans. But if such signs can be detected in 1811 and later, what of the earlier period? Surely some Greek must have raised his voice against the greatest antiquarian of all? Surely Lord Elgin's agents must also have met some opposition five or ten years earlier? Surely someone in Athens between 1801 and 1805 appreciated what was happening? One would have thought so. Yet the evidence is surprisingly sparse. The travellers, on whose reports we largely depend, were, for the most part, ignorant of the modern Greeks. Usually they were only too pleased to describe the superstition with which the Greeks regarded their monuments and the mercenary eagerness with which they disposed of them to the first buyer. As Byron said, the travellers condemned the Greeks as a nation on much the same grounds that a Turk in England would condemn the English because he was wronged by his lacquey and overcharged by his washerwoman.[19]

But, even allowing for the unreliability of most of the sources, the indications that the Greeks were disturbed in any way by the export of the Parthenon marbles are slight. Logotheti, it is true, had some initial qualms, but he seems to have overcome them soon enough. Philip Hunt, who knew more about the first removals than anyone else and who could speak Greek, declared later, that no opposition to the scheme was made by any class of the natives of Athens.[20] Hamilton, who also spoke Greek, went further in answer to a similar question. Not only, he said, did the removals create 'no unpleasant sensation' among the Athenians but 'they seemed rather to feel it as a means of bringing foreigners into the country and of having money spent amongst them'.[21]

Even those travellers who wished to support their case against Lord Elgin by showing that his activities were disliked by the Greeks found it difficult to do so. One story, constantly repeated, was that when the Caryatid was removed from the Erechtheum the whole town was filled with doleful sighs and lamentations as the remaining Caryatids mourned 'their ravished sister'.[22] It was also said that some Greeks, who were conveying a chest of Lord Elgin's marbles to the Piraeus, suddenly threw it down and could not be prevailed upon to touch it for some time, protesting that they could hear the enchanted spirit within the sculpture 'crying out and groaning for his fellow-spirits detained in bondage in the Acropolis'. Hobhouse, who tells this story, says the Greeks regarded the statues as real bodies enchanted by evil spirits, but admits that they also supposed that the condition of the enchanted marbles would be bettered by removal from the country of the tyrant Turks.[23] These two stories suggest that any Athenian regard for the Parthenon marbles was every bit as superstitious as the Sigeans' wish to keep the Boustrophedon Inscription or the Eleusinians' worship of their Ceres.

Such, no doubt, were the opinions of the great majority of the Greeks. Nevertheless, despite the long years of subjugation and oppression, there were still a very few Greeks who maintained the ancient tradition, who still preserved a knowledge of the classical Greek language and who knew the history of their country. In Athens the old tradition was very nearly extinguished but not quite. In Lord Elgin's time there remained one very old man, Ioannes Benizelos, a teacher who wrote a history of Athens under the Turks.* Despite poverty and exile, Benizelos survived just long enough to see the revival of Greek which began in Athens, with the assistance of Western Philhellenes, at the beginning of the nineteenth century. In January 1803, shortly before Elgin's Embassy sailed for home, Benizelos wrote to his friend Philip Hunt. His letter was very friendly; it described how Athens was prospering under a benevolent voivode; and how prices were going down. In conclusion he wrote, in impeccable Greek:

I am sure if you saw Athens today you would be very happy. One thing only would make you sad as it does all those who have some understanding of these things—the last deplorable stripping of the Temple of Athena on the Acropolis and of the other relics of antiquity. The temple is like a noble and wealthy lady who has lost all her diamonds and jewellery. Oh, how we Athenians must take this event to heart, and how we must praise and admire those ancient heroes of Rome, Pompey and Hadrian, when we look on these things.[24]

Pompey and Hadrian had used their power to preserve Athens: the English, the modern Romans, had stripped her. It was a gentle

* Benizelos was the master of a school at Athens maintained by funds invested in Venice. When Venice fell to the French, Benizelos' school had to close for lack of money.

rebuke but a rebuke nevertheless. Benizelos' letter seems to be the
first sign of Greek protest. In his *History of Athens Under the Turks*
Benizelos recorded briefly the activities of Elgin's agents on the
Acropolis. The removal of the statues from the Parthenon, he
said, caused 'shock and consternation among all the travellers'.[25]
Significantly, he makes no mention of any reaction among the
Greeks or Turks.

In 1813, only eight years before the outbreak of the Greek
Revolution, Hobhouse, Byron's companion, wrote,

I have said nothing of the possiblity of the ruins of Athens being, in
the event of a revolution in favour of the Greeks, restored and put into
a condition capable of resisting the ravages of decay; for an event of
that nature cannot, it strikes me, have ever entered into the head of
anyone who has seen Athens, and the modern Athenians. Yet I cannot
forbear mentioning a singular speech of a learned Greek of Ioannina
who said to me 'You English are carrying off the works of the Greeks,
our forefathers—preserve them well—we Greeks will come and
redemand them.'[26]

Lusieri, contemptuous as always of the Greeks, failed to recognize the signs of change. It probably never occurred to him that
the time was not far off when the Greeks could want to preserve
every relic of antiquity as a precious heirloom and have the
ability to do so. But even if he had recognized the signs, Lusieri
would not have acted any differently. For the reasons which had
prompted the first removals—the desire to preserve the marbles
from destruction—were as powerful as ever.

There was great destruction of the monuments of Athens before
Lord Elgin took a hand: after he was obliged to stop, the
destruction became even greater. Not only was Athens thronged
with foreign travellers and artists, most of whom were willing
to buy choice pieces of sculpture, but, as a result of the war,
more and more casual visitors began to appear from ships that
put in to the Piraeus. They were even more unscrupulous in
souvenir-hunting than the travellers.

Between 1805 when Lusieri had to cease his operations on the
Acropolis and 1821 when the Greek Revolution broke out, every
monument in Athens suffered more or less severely. The destruc-

tion of the Erechtheum was appalling and has been closely documented. Most of the pieces known to have been taken have disappeared: others have turned up from unknown sources.[27] A glance at the drawings of the monument of Philopappos made at different times[28] during this period shows a steady attrition of arms and legs, to say nothing of a general destruction of the sculptured surface.

In 1813, Thomas Hughes, an English traveller, was a witness of this destruction. One day he noticed that Lusieri had a shivering fit. This was not, he recounted, due to ill health

but, as he observed to us, he is always thus attacked whenever an English or a French frigate anchors in the Piraeus. The young midshipmen are then let loose upon the venerable monuments of Athens, and are seldom deterred by the religion of the place from indulging in the most wanton devastation of statues, cornices and capitals, from which they carry off mementoes of their Athenian travels.[29]

A later traveller, Laurent, actually saw this happen and wrote,

The last time I visited the citadel . . . I was much displeased at seeing an English traveller, an officer of the navy (for such his uniform bespoke him to be) standing upon the base of one of the Caryatids, clinging with his left arm round the column, while his right hand, provided with a hard and heavy pebble, was endeavouring to knock off the only remaining nose of those six beautifully sculptured statues. I exerted my eloquence in vain to preserve this monument of art.[30]

As usual, it was the Parthenon itself which suffered worst. Two heads from the west pediment, those wrongly believed to represent Hadrian and Sabina, disappeared entirely, one going to Dodwell, the other to Fauvel.[31] Two slabs of the frieze fell in the few weeks between Byron's two visits to Athens.[32] The Turks, anxious as always to profit from the ready market resumed their old practice (virtually suspended during the supremacy of Fauvel and Lusieri) of chopping off small pieces, such as heads of the frieze.

The plaster casts of the west frieze which Lord Elgin's moulders made in 1801 and 1802 reveal many features including whole heads which were broken off or defaced from the originals shortly afterwards. In some cases the originals were almost entirely obliterated and Elgin's casts are our best record of what they once looked like.*³³ It was during this period that Fauvel, to his discredit, abandoned his principles. Despairing at last of sending any more sculptures to the Louvre while the war and British naval power lasted, he too joined the Turks. He began to sell off to passing travellers some of the antiquities from the enormous collection he had amassed during his long stay at Athens. Thus he too began to encourage the dispersal he had earlier done so much to prevent.³⁴ Four fragments which he sold were later obtained by the British Museum.³⁵ But, as in the earlier period, no doubt many others are now permanently lost somewhere in Europe.

For the most part the pieces sold were small, and easily lost. To obtain these small pieces the Turks destroyed the remaining slabs. Few travellers could afford the enormous bribes now demanded for larger pieces or the cost of carriage; and it is doubtful if they could have obtained firmans to remove openly from the Acropolis. The largest piece removed during this period was half a slab, obtained by Cockerell in a very extraordinary way. When he went to make a farewell call on his friend the Disdar of Athens in 1814, the Disdar said he wished to give him a present. He told Cockerell to bring a cart—no doubt the one that Lusieri had used to move the Elgin Marbles—to the foot of the Acropolis at night (to avoid offending the Greeks). When Cockerell appeared he heard a shout from above and without further warning a large piece of marble was bowled down the cliff, breaking into several fragments on the way. It turned out to be a part of the south frieze. Cockerell put it on the cart, took it straight down to the Piraeus and shipped it at once.³⁶ He later presented it to the British Museum. Needless to say, its appearance was not improved by its passage down the precipices of the Acropolis.

Helpless to prevent the continuing destruction, Lusieri remained at Athens increasingly debilitated by rheumatism and old age.

---

* This damage is independent of the severe erosion from atmospheric pollution which began in more recent times.

His own excavations and researches became more and more desultory and latterly he abandoned even his pencil. Hamilton, who had once told a traveller that 'he had never met anyone to whom he felt really attached to as a friend except Lusieri the Italian artist',[37] now advised Lord Elgin to read his latest letters only on a very fine day. Lusieri, he said, was 'an arrant Jew. . . . His excuses for his idleness are abominable and he evidently has finished nothing—nor indeed *done* anything *to the purpose* in any way whatever for the last four or five years.'[38]

Lusieri's presence at Athens now merely served as a constant reminder to travellers to moralize about the spoliation of the Parthenon. Fauvel, who was almost as lazy as Lusieri, was ever ready to talk of the great destruction of many years before, and the indignation at the barbarian Elgin spread to the Greeks.[39] When the Princess of Wales visited Athens she stayed with Fauvel in preference to any of the English colony and indulged in the usual sneers against Elgin.[40] Even the Turks remembered. In 1816, far from Athens at Askalon in Palestine, Lady Hester Stanhope led an expedition of Turks to look for hidden gold among the ruins of Astarte's Temple. When they discovered not gold but an exquisite marble statue, Lady Hester ordered it to be broken up and thrown into the sea to emphasize how much she differed from her countrymen who dug only for stones.[41]

Chapter 19

Lord Elgin Tries Again

THE second collection of Lord Elgin's marbles arrived in England in May 1812 just as the world's enthusiasm for *Childe Harold* was at its height. His promise to give the British Museum any marbles brought home by the king's ships was conveniently forgotten and the whole collection was taken to Burlington House. Under Flaxman's superintendence the new marbles were unpacked and arranged and were available for inspection at the end of the year. The museum at Burlington House was hardly a suitable home. It consisted of a small, irregular, half timbered outhouse which stood in the yard at the back of the house. There were no windows and the marbles could hardly be seen. What was worse, for lack of room in the shed, some of the marbles had to be left outside in the open air. The large architectural fragments, the pieces of Parthenon columns and architraves and miscellaneous pieces from the other buildings of Athens, were piled higgledy-piggledy on top of one another rather like the ruins on the Acropolis. Even some of the slabs of the frieze were left outside to the mercies of the English weather and soon grass began to grow round them.* Compared with this, the draughty museum at Park Lane had been a palace.[1]

Lord Elgin remained at Broomhall waiting patiently for his luck to change. But meanwhile the old aim of improving the arts in Great Britain was not forgotten. Nollekens, West, Flaxman, and Haydon continued to spend long hours sketching in the new museum, and West arranged for the medallists of the Royal Academy school to go there as part of their studies. The sculptor John Henning began work on a miniature restoration of the

---

* See Plate VI (*a*) and (*b*).

frieze which was later to become very well known.* Elgin also lent his drawings of the Theseum to the architect of the new Royal Observatory which was to be built at Edinburgh.

But the enmity of the Dilettanti Society continued—exacerbated by an unfortunate misunderstanding in 1814. After many years the last volume of the great *Antiquities of Athens* begun by Stuart and Revett in the 1750's was ready for publication. This was to contain engravings of some of the sculptures of the Parthenon taken from drawings made in Athens many years before Elgin's Embassy. The editor, naturally enough, wrote to Elgin to ask if he could be given the opportunity of comparing the engravings with the originals at Burlington House. Unfortunately his letter was not clear[3] and Elgin completely misunderstood it. He thought that the Dilettanti had somehow made engravings of his marbles without his permission and were about to forestall him in his long-cherished scheme of publishing them. He was affronted and gave the Dilettanti a curt refusal: the fact was recorded in volume IV of the *Antiquities of Athens* published shortly afterwards.[4]

At last in April 1814 came the news that Elgin had been waiting for. Napoleon abdicated from the throne of France and the long war came to an end. After eight years Elgin was freed from the crippling parole which he had given to Talleyrand in 1806 as the price of his freedom. If he could but restore his finances—in other words dispose of his marbles for a good price—there might still be hope of saving his ruined public career. He had made his plans well. He realized that the only hope of persuading British official opinion to take a different view of his collection than that represented by Payne Knight was to obtain an authoritative foreign opinion. In 1811 he had greatly strengthened his case by pointing to the great esteem in which the French held the

---

* In describing his first sight of the Elgin Marbles Henning wrote:
'It struck me forcibly that from the superior excellence they might some time or other become such an object of public curiosity that models of them, while they might be very improving to myself, might become objects of pecuniary advantage.' Henning was not to be disappointed in the latter hope. Besides selling numerous copies of his miniature restorations Henning prepared a full-scale restoration for the Hyde Park Corner Arch, the Athenaeum, the Royal College of Surgeons, Terling Place, Essex and elsewhere.[2]

Choiseul-Gouffier piece of the frieze. Now that the war was over he hoped to do even better.

As soon as peace was declared he set off for Paris. His object was to see the greatest antiquarian of the day, Ennio Quirino Visconti. Visconti had been director of the Capitoline Museum at Rome and had followed the masterpieces of Italy to Paris. He was now Director of the Louvre. It was he who, at Napoleon's instigation, had brought the Choiseul-Gouffier fragment into prominence there, and he now presided over the greatest accumulation of works of art that the world is ever likely to see. His reputation as the greatest connoisseur in Europe was well deserved. After some negotiation Elgin struck a bargain with him. Visconti would come to London to see the Elgin Marbles for a fee of £120. He would stay for a fortnight, and on his return, prepare a memoir on the marbles, the fee for which was to be settled later.

Elgin also took the opportunity of his visit to Paris to try to settle some other unfinished business. This was the affair of Choiseul-Gouffier's metope which he had bought at a Customs House sale in 1806. A misunderstanding had arisen between Elgin and Choiseul-Gouffier about this metope and Elgin now paid a call on on his old friend and rival to try to sort it out.

Soon after he had bought the metope (and other lesser antiquities) at the sale in 1806, Elgin realized that this was one of the antiquities that Choiseul-Gouffier had told him about at Barèges in 1803. It was the metope that Nelson had captured from l'Arabe and sent to England as prize. With his usual magnanimity, and in gratitude for Choiseul-Gouffier's help to him while he had been a prisoner in France, Elgin at once wrote to him offering to give it back. This was a pure act of kindness since his own legal title to the metope was indisputable. Choiseul-Gouffier, however, did not respond with the same generosity. He had somehow heard a story that Nelson himself had not sent the antiquities from l'Arabe to England but had directed that they should be kept at Malta to be returned to Choiseul-Gouffier after the war. Nelson, of course, had no power to do this even if he had wanted to. Nevertheless, despite Elgin's letter giving him the true story,

Choiseul-Gouffier remained convinced that his lost collection still lay at Malta.

On his visit to Paris in 1814 Elgin was able to convince his old friend that the metope was indeed his, but Choiseul-Gouffier was not satisfied. He just could not believe that there was no collection waiting for him at Malta. When inquiries on the spot there showed finally that this was so, he turned on Lord Elgin. Elgin's agents at Malta, he wrote shortly after Elgin's visit, must have stolen his cases there in an excess of zeal; and Elgin's agents in Athens had stolen some antiquities which Fauvel had hidden in a warehouse in the Piraeus.* He did, however, add a more characteristic touch.† The agents had also taken a cart and some other tackle which belonged to him. 'They did well,' he wrote magnanimously, 'I would have been delighted to lend them to you.'6

After his visit to Paris, therefore, Elgin's misunderstanding with Choiseul-Gouffier was not yet resolved. The affair of the cart had been settled, but that of the metope remained. This was certainly not Elgin's fault. He had gone to great trouble to discover the truth and explain it, and had offered to give back a valuable piece of his collection. Choiseul-Gouffier insisted on looking the gift horse in the mouth.

Visconti's visit to London took place in October 1814. On his return to Paris he wrote a letter to Hamilton as a first instalment

---

* It seems very unlikely that either of these accusations was true. Fauvel and Lusieri had made several attempts to steal one another's collections, but (apart from one useless piece of plain marble taken by Lusieri in 1803, cf. p.127) there is no evidence that either ever succeeded. It is just possible that in the glorious days of 1801 when Fauvel was off the scene, Lusieri may have obtained some French antiquities from the Turks at the same time as he obtained the cart, but there is no evidence of this.

† In the second volume of *Voyage Pittoresque de la Grèce* published in 1809, Choiseul-Gouffier wrote of a marble throne which he had seen on his travels in Greece.

'I saw this monument in front of the door of the bishop who put it there on certain festivals and had thus consecrated it to religion. This dedication thwarted all my attempts to aquire it. Lord Elgin, more fortunate than I, knew how to profit from the influence given him by the presence of a victorious fleet, the conquest of Egypt, and the restitution of that important possession. He thus obtained from the Porte an acquiescence which at other times even the most easy-going and benevolent ministers would never have dared to allow themselves. Lord Elgin has collected all over Greece a rich crop of precious monuments which I had long and vainly desired. It is difficult for me to see them in his hands without a touch of envy; but it must be a source of satisfaction for all who love the arts, to know that these masterpieces have been rescued from the barbarity of the Turks and are preserved by an enlightened connoisseur, who will give the public an opportunity of enjoying them.'5

of his promised memoir. It surpassed all Elgin's expectations. Neither Stuart's drawings, nor Choiseul-Gouffier's fragment and casts, had, Visconti wrote, been able to give him the idea of the works of Phidias that the sight of the actual objects had done. The frieze, the metopes, the pediments, all showed every perfection and were every bit as excellent as the famous statues of Italy. There could be no doubt, that the Parthenon marbles had been executed under the superintendence of Phidias himself. And, he went on, if the classical statues of Italy had been an inspiration to the Michelangelos and Raphaels of the sixteenth century, would not the Elgin Marbles inaugurate a new era for the progress of sculpture of England.[7]

Visconti's letter was just what Elgin needed to start a new campaign to sell his collection. He at once ordered a printed edition of the letter to be prepared. His own *Memorandum on the Subject of the Earl of Elgin's Pursuits in Greece* was revised and sent to the press with yet more appendices. Hamilton began to take soundings among the Government about how a new offer to sell the marbles would be received and he heard a hint that £80,000 might be forthcoming. All in all, for the first time since 1811, Elgin's prospects, nursed by careful public relations, began to look promising. Then suddenly once more everything seemed to be thrown back into the melting pot. On 1 March Napoleon landed at Antibes and the Hundred Days had begun. With a desperate war once more on their hands the Government could hardly be expected to have much time to consider the claims of Greek art for a share of public funds. It seemed as if, yet again, Elgin was to be a helpless victim of political upheaval.

But just before he heard of Napoleon's landing, bad news affecting him more personally reached Elgin. While looking over the newspapers at Broomhall on 4 March he read a report that the Duke of Devonshire had sold Burlington House; the new owner, Lord George Cavendish, intended to rebuild the whole structure, beginning work within a few weeks. It was now imperative that the Elgin Marbles should be moved at once. But where? Could a fifth London home be found at a few days' notice for several hundred tons of marbles? The situation was desperate. It would cost about £1,000 to move the marbles, even if a site could be found, and then probably another £1,000 to move them to the British Museum if a bargain could be concluded. The obvious solution was to seek to move them to the British Museum with the option to move them out again if the sale fell through. Such a move would obviously weaken Elgin's negotiating position, but he had little alternative. Despite the preoccupation of the Government with the war he set to work.

Hamilton pressed Lord George Cavendish to delay the rebuilding of Burlington House as long as possible to give time to manœuvre, and at once opened formal negotiations with the Speaker of the House of Commons and the Trustees of the British Museum. The first results were not hopeful. The Speaker (one of the principal trustees) said he did not believe the Government would have the courage to offer more than the £30,000 proposed in 1811 by Spencer Perceval. And Elgin's inevitable suggestion that a British peerage should be bestowed on him as part of the transaction was firmly discouraged.

On 8 April a meeting of the Trustees of the British Museum was held to consider Lord Elgin's overtures. To his consternation they decided to set up a committee consisting of Charles Long, Lord Aberdeen, and Richard Payne Knight to conduct the Museum's negotiations with Elgin and the Government. From Elgin's point of view there could hardly have been a worse choice. Payne Knight had never made any secret of his hostility and Aberdeen was widely regarded as his obedient disciple; Charles Long had been closely associated with the abortive negotiations of 1811.

Soon afterwards Hamilton heard from Lord Aberdeen what had occurred at the first committee meeting. They had agreed to recommend accepting the marbles on approval as it were, but could not spend money on building a shelter. As for a price, Long had talked of £35,000 at the very outside; Payne Knight, on the other hand, wished to draw the line at £15,000 or £20,000. Payne Knight had also declared that if Elgin tried to sell his collection abroad, an Act of Parliament should be passed to keep it in England. In the course of this conversation with

Aberdeen, Hamilton mentioned that Visconti's letter had been printed and was ready for publication. Aberdeen's reply was deflating. There could be no doubt, he observed, 'that Visconti was the best practical Antiquary in the world and that his independent unbiassed opinion would be of great weight everywhere, but that it was equally well known that he would write anything he was asked for £10.'⁸

Elgin was bitterly disappointed. After all his patience it seemed as if he might receive less for his total collection than he had refused for the first part of it four years before. But there could be no going back. By April the building operations at Burlington House had begun and Elgin's agent had to rearrange the marbles within the yard: Cavendish began to press him hard to remove them altogether. Yet while Payne Knight remained on the committee no improvement on the offer could be expected, especially as it had come to light that Payne Knight had made his pronouncement without even having seen the second collection.

At the end of May Elgin came to London to confer with Hamilton about the next move. The only way of averting Payne Knight's hostility that they could think of was to sell him Elgin's collection of ancient coins which he and Lord Aberdeen had long wanted: but Elgin was determined not to appease his enemies.⁹ It was probably at Hamilton's suggestion that he decided on a new approach. He wrote a formal letter to the Chancellor of the Exchequer suggesting that the direct negotiations with the Government and the British Museum should be discontinued. Instead, he proposed, consideration of the whole affair should be referred to a Select Committee of the House of Commons who could then investigate the circumstances in which the collection had been obtained and advise on whether, and at what price, the nation should acquire them. Elgin was, by this move, virtually throwing himself on the mercy of Parliament. The Government, relieved perhaps at not having to make up their own minds, accepted Elgin's suggestion with eagerness. Even Payne Knight made a point of calling personally on Elgin to say that he welcomed the move although at the same time, Elgin recorded, 'he exposed all his plan of hostility'.

The Petition of the Earl of Elgin Respecting his Collection of Marbles was presented to the House of Commons on 15 June.[10] It described briefly the circumstances in which the petitioner had acquired his collection and begged that the House should institute an inquiry on the advisability of transferring it to the nation. The *Petition* was the subject of a short debate. The Chancellor of the Exchequer accepted the proposal on behalf of the Government and made some remarks on the excellence of the collection. Others also praised it but some clearly took their brief from *Childe Harold*. 'It seemed to have been reserved for an ambassador of this country,' said Sir John Newport, 'to take away what Turks and other barbarians had always held sacred. It was the duty of the House to ascertain the truth of these matters; for otherwise in case they should consent to purchase the collection they would evidently sanction acts of public robbery.' Several members felt that the matter should be deferred until the next session so that Lord Elgin's right to the collection could be fully investigated. The Chancellor, knowing Elgin's difficulties, urged speed. Lord George Cavendish intervened in the debate to say that he would allow the marbles to stay at Burlington House for a short time. At the end of the debate the matter had not been settled: Elgin's *Petition* was to lie on the table.

Three days after the House of Commons debated the Elgin Marbles Napoleon was finally defeated at the Battle of Waterloo. Lord Elgin rejoiced with the rest, but it soon became clear that time to discuss his case would not be found before 1816. The session ended in the middle of July: the next session would not begin until February. The marbles would have to spend another winter in the yard of Burlington House. Even in his defeat Napoleon seemed to have interfered successfully in the affair of the Elgin Marbles. There was, however, an unexpected bonus— perhaps the biggest encouragement that Elgin ever received. Somewhat surprisingly one of the first questions which the victorious allies decided to settle was what should become of the numerous works of art that Napoleon had assembled in the Louvre. By the abdication agreement of 1814 France had been allowed to keep her looted treasures: the powers were determined

that she should not do so now. On one thing they were all agreed
—the Musée Napoléon must be broken up.

Statesmen and connoisseurs of the different countries gathered
in Paris in August to discuss the question. Visconti, of course,
was there as director of the Louvre. Canova represented the Pope
many of whose statues, including the Apollo Belvedere, the Torso
and the Laocoon, had been removed from Rome. Hamilton
himself and Charles Long represented the British Government.
The Prince Regent, realizing late in the day that Britain was poor
in these modern status symbols, let it be known that he favoured
splitting the collection among the victorious allies or at least
buying some of them from their former owners. The Prussians
too cast covetous eyes on this unique collection of masterpieces.

In the end the question virtually settled itself. The Prussians,
the Austrians, and the Belgians rescued their own works of art
and those of the other German States. It was then agreed that
the fairest solution would be for all the stolen art treasures to be
restored to the owners from whom Napoleon had taken them.
This solution meant, of course, that England got nothing. With
the conversation of Europe all about art it was inevitable that the
Elgin Marbles should be discussed. And it so happened that
Visconti's *Memoir* which Elgin had commissioned on his visit
to Paris the previous year was ready just at that time. Visconti
delivered it to a meeting of the French Institute on 18 August and
it was quickly printed.[11] Visconti's assessment, which was long
and scholarly, surpassed even his letter in its enthusiasm. He even
took trouble to disprove in detail Payne Knight's assertions that
the Parthenon sculptures could not be by Phidias and that they
were Hadrianic. He concluded one section

In their new situation in the midst of an enlightened nation particularly disposed to afford encouragement to sculpture, they will rouse the
talents of the young artist to exertion and will direct him in the road
which leads to perfection in his art. We have only to regret that the
noble idea which induced Lord Elgin to rescue them from the daily
ravages of a barbarous nation was not entertained a century and a half
earlier by some rich and powerful amateur.[12]

Visconti was also heard to declare that until he had been to London he had seen nothing. The English in Paris began to conclude that they need not be too disappointed at having failed to secure any trophies from the Louvre.

That was not all. Canova too was delighted at Hamilton's diplomacy in restoring the Papal collection to Rome. He became a close personal friend and considered himself under a strong obligation to him for the rest of his life. Canova, the other connoisseur with a European reputation, agreed to come to England in the autumn to see the Elgin Marbles of which he had seen only a small part in 1803. There was every prospect that he would endorse Visconti's judgement. In his quarrel with Payne Knight Elgin had made a diplomatic coup.

Canova's visit to London took place in November 1815. He was treated as an honoured guest by the Government and invited to all the great houses. Everywhere he went he spoke admiringly of the Elgin Marbles. They were the finest collection in Europe, he said (with the exception of course of the Apollo, the Venus, the Torso and the Laocoon); they were worth coming all the way from Rome to see; they had opened his eyes to the real principles of ancient art; they should create a new era in the art of sculpture.[13] Haydon followed Canova around gleefully, prompting him to confirm what he himself said about the Elgin Marbles and exulting in the discomfiture of the Payne Knight party.[14] Canova's enthusiastic letter of thanks to Lord Elgin when he left was yet another valuable piece of ammunition for the battle to be fought in the next session.[15]

Shortly before Canova's visit the Phigaleian Marbles which the Government had bought from Cockerell arrived at the British Museum.[16] The Payne Knight party, who had done much to secure their purchase, seized the opportunity of disparaging the Elgin collection yet again. The Phigaleian Marbles, said an article in the *Morning Chronicle*, 'are believed to be the only examples extant of entire subjects of the admirable school of Phidias and exhibit the sublimity of poetic imagination united to the boldness and power of execution resulting from extensive practice in the greatest school of antiquity.[17] Haydon was quick to respond to the implied slur and wrote in another newspaper:

This is written, I suspect, by the same hand who said the Elgin Marbles were the work of journeymen not worthy the name of artists in a less fastidious age.* Now so far from these Phygaleian Marbles being the only works of Phidias, they have not the slightest pretensions to be considered by his hand at all . . . As to the taste of those who hesitated to acknowledge the beauty of the Elgin Marbles and decided at once without hesitation on the Phygaleian ones, nothing need be said . . . There are one or two groups very fine in these Phygaleian Marbles but still approaching to manner; and in most instances they are entirely mannered. United with the Elgin collection their errors will do no injury to the student and both together will form the finest museum in Europe.[18]

Canova, invited by the Government to give his opinion, left the issue in no doubt. The Phigaleian Marbles were very good, he said, but if they were worth £15,000 (the price paid by the Government), then the Elgin Marbles were worth £100,000.[19]

Yet another foreign admirer of the Elgin Marbles, who had visited England some months before, was Ludwig the Crown Prince of Bavaria. It was he who had bought the Aegina Marbles in 1812 as a result of the muddle over the sale and he was eager to increase his collection. He showed his admiration in a very practical way. He deposited a large sum of money in a London bank and it soon became known that if the British Government declined to buy Lord Elgin's collection he was eager to step into the breach.[20] What with Visconti, Canova, and Prince Ludwig, Elgin's plan of obtaining authoritative foreign advice to pit against the prejudice of Payne Knight and his followers was succeeding beyond his most hopeful expectations.[21]

Meanwhile the Elgin Marbles themselves still lay at Burlington House, covered with dust and dripping with damp.[22] The building operations had begun and it was necessary to move them from place to place within the courtyard to give the builders room. It was during this period that one or two smaller pieces were stolen from the collection.[23] They included two votive reliefs which had been catalogued by Visconti and, perhaps, for

* I.e. by Payne Knight in *Specimens of Antient Sculpture*. See p. 177.

all we know, some fragments of the Parthenon: none has ever been found. There was also another casualty. Lord Elgin's agent, who was engaged in packing the collection into boxes for transportation, failed to recognize the small pieces of the moulds of the Theseum frieze and inadvertently destroyed them: fortunately the casts themselves were preserved.[24]

Lord Elgin now commissioned a full catalogue to be prepared of all his collection using Visconti's memoir as a basis. A further consignment of miscellaneous marbles arrived at Burlington House from Lusieri after Visconti's visit. They were not included in the main collection and were shipped to Broomhall where (with a few exceptions) they still remain. All was now ready for the Select Committee's investigation due to begin in February 1816.

Chapter 20

Tweddell J. and Tweddell R.

To Lord Elgin, therefore, 1815 was more than the year of Waterloo. As a result of careful planning and patient negotiation great advances had been made in the campaign to establish the artistic excellence of his collection. The Payne Knight view was now definitely on the defensive. Elgin's judicious republication of his *Memorandum* had redressed the balance somewhat against the Byronic interpretation of his activities. The sale, on which depended all his hopes of resuming his public career seemed at last to be near. For the first time for many years the outlook was distinctly promising.

It was at this very delicate juncture in his affairs that Elgin's reputation once more came under fire. He was struck a cruel and premeditated blow on a front that had so far not been attacked. His enemies chose their hour well. Their attack had nothing to do with the Elgin Marbles. In 1815 appeared a stout quarto volume, price three guineas, by the Reverend R. Tweddell, A.M., under the innocuous title of *Remains of John Tweddell late fellow of Trinity College Cambridge, being a Selection of his Correspondence, a republication of his Prolusiones Juveniles, An Appendix containing some account of the Author's Collections, Mss, Drawings etc. and of their Extraordinary Disappearance, preceded by a Biographical Memoir of the Deceased, and illustrated with Portraits, Picturesque Views and Maps*. On the face of it this was just a work of piety to a dead brother—yet another of the travel books for which the Regency public seemed to have such an insatiable appetite.

Tweddell's *Remains* was not all its title suggested. It contained an appendix of no less than 255 pages (over half the book) devoted entirely to accusations against the Earl of Elgin. The main charge was quite simple. It was that Lord Elgin had made use of his position of Ambassador at Constantinople to steal a large and valuable collection of drawings and journals which had belonged to John Tweddell. Other charges were thrown in—that Elgin had neglected his ambassadorial duties and behaved in an arrogant and irresponsible way to the British residents at Constantinople and to travellers; that he had allowed his staff, in particular Philip Hunt, to plagiarize Tweddell's papers; that he himself intended to pass off Tweddell's drawings as the work of his own artists; and that he had so far met all inquiries with a prevarication of lies and contradictions to avoid having to give up the stolen property. For good measure it claimed that Elgin's Embassy had been quite unnecessary in any case since the treaty of alliance with Turkey and the opening of the Black Sea to the British flag had been agreed before he arrived.

An extract from the index of the *Remains* gives a clear idea of the tenor of the argument.

So it goes on. The entry under Elgin alone in the Index runs
to nearly four columns. Philip Hunt is treated equally severely.
Tweddell's *Remains* caused a first-class scandal. Almost every
review (and this was the golden age of reviews) related Tweddell's
story at great length, calling on Elgin to give an explanation.
Most were openly hostile, making no secret of their belief in all
that Tweddell claimed. 'The case is a strong one,' wrote the
Edinburgh Review, 'In performing this . . . task, the Editor deserves
almost unmingled praise.'[1] The *Christian Observer* concluded that
'if the impression which will be felt by all the readers of this work
be unjust and unfounded, seldom has it fallen to the lot of a
human being to be placed in a more cruel situation than the
noble lord'.[2] The *New Monthly Magazine* went further. 'Most men
of simple judgement and honest hearts will be apt to think that
the spoliation of Athens and the loss of the Tweddell papers must
be considered as a lamentable drawback on the national
character.'[3] With one stroke Elgin's reputation fell deeper than
it had ever been even in the first days of *Childe Harold*.

The story of John Tweddell's papers was a complex one. John
Tweddell, a young man of quite exceptional academic promise,
had set out alone in 1795 on the grandest of grand tours, intending
to visit Switzerland, Germany, Russia, Turkey, the Holy Land,
Egypt, and Greece. In the course of his tour he composed and

collected a prodigious quantity of material—in the East alone 5 books of journals, 4 notebooks, 4 volumes of Greek inscriptions, 7 portfolios containing 364 drawings, 8 other books of drawings and much more besides. He had engaged Preaux, a painter who had once worked for Choiseul-Gouffier and later for Clarke, and kept him busy from dawn to dusk for many months. He had also bought some drawings from Fauvel. Without doubt he would in due course have produced the biggest and most learned of travel books, matching even Clarke in the mass of miscellaneous information he would have incorporated. And without doubt he would have made a great deal of money out of it.

In 1799 after four years' steady work he died of a fever in Athens. His friend Fauvel buried him in the Theseum hoping in the course of the digging to uncover the tomb of Theseus. Part of Tweddell's papers had been left at Constantinople in the possession of Thomas Thornton, a banker of the Levant Company, but they were largely destroyed in a fire that ravaged the city soon afterwards. The other part which was at Athens was sent by Logotheti to John Spencer Smith, the British Minister, to be forwarded to Tweddell's heirs. Unfortunately the ship in which they were sent was wrecked in the Sea of Marmara. Some boxes were recovered but reached the chancery in a wet and damaged condition.

Shortly after Tweddell's papers arrived, Lord Elgin reached Constantinople to supersede Spencer Smith as British Minister and the long period of bitterness between the two men began. Spencer Smith, as we have seen, refused absolutely to recognize Elgin's authority and continued to behave exactly as if he were still British Minister. Elgin struggled vainly to impose his authority until Spencer Smith had eventually to be dismissed. When he heard of the death of Tweddell (whom he had known at Berlin) Elgin ordered his papers to be laid out in his cellar in an attempt to dry them out, and Hunt and Carlyle were given the opportunity of sorting them and salvaging what was still useful. Elgin then gave orders that the recovered papers should be packed up and sent home (at his own expense) to Tweddell's family in England.

Unfortunately here some mistake was made. The papers seem never to have been properly packed or despatched although both Elgin and Hunt later recollected that they were sent in some merchant ship, whose name they could not remember. Some drawings were certainly sent home by hand of Mr. Nisbet, the father of Mary Elgin, when he returned from his visit to Turkey in 1801.

Spencer Smith as part of his feud with Elgin wrote to Tweddell's family complaining of Elgin's interference but making no more serious allegations. As a result of this letter Edward Daniel Clarke ('Eleusinian' Clarke) undertook to make some inquiries on behalf of the family when he started on his journey to the East. When he mentioned the subject to Elgin in 1801, Elgin told him that the papers had been sent home. When Clarke persisted with his questions, Elgin seems to have told him to mind his own business.

Here the matter of Tweddell's papers rested for nearly ten years. But Tweddell himself was not forgotten. The romantic theme of the young scholar dying amongst the ruins of his beloved Athens attracted the poetasters of the time.

> Such the fair pile where shrin'd in holy cell
> The slumb'ring ashes of the mighty dwell;
> Where Tweddell, youthful shade, to classic rest
> Sinks, like a wearied child, in science' breast.

So ran an Oxford prize poem on the Theseum.[4] Haygarth, too, could not resist the thought, in some of his less happy verses:

> Pause on the tomb of him who sleeps within,
> Fancy's fond hope, and Learning's fav'rite child,
> Accomplish'd Tweddell—but weep not, his death
> Was kind although untimely, for he rests
> Upon the shores to Taste and Genius dear.[5]

Tweddell's grave in the Theseum became a place of pilgrimage for the English travellers to Athens. Elgin himself went there in 1802 on his visit to Greece and told Lusieri to erect a suitable tombstone. He sent Lusieri a long Latin inscription but Lusieri had not much confidence in his patron's Latin grammar and sent it to Italy to be checked. But in 1810 he had still done nothing about committing it to marble.

In that year a number of English travellers were in Athens, including Lord Byron, and the question of Tweddell's tombstone was raised again. Byron's party had come armed with an eight-line Greek epitaph composed in Cambridge—headed rather unconvincingly *ΤΥΕΔΔΕΛΛ*—but Lusieri was insistent that Lord Elgin's Latin version must have pride of place. He had obtained a suitable piece of marble from the Acropolis, sawn from the back of a slab of the frieze, and offered to allow Byron's party to carve their inscription on it under Lord Elgin's. But this offer was turned down and they decided to act independently of him. The Disdar offered to sell them a piece of marble from the Acropolis but Lusieri had the only cart capable of carrying it. After a search in the town they found a suitable piece and in two days' hard work dragged it to the Theseum. Lusieri had the only saws in the town capable of cutting the marble but, with Fauvel's help, they managed to hammer it smooth. After another week's work the inscription was cut and the completed tombstone installed in the Theseum. Lusieri had been beaten in the race but he persevered with his Latin inscription. Soon there were two rival epitaphs over the bones of the unfortunate Tweddell.[*6]

The affair of Tweddell's papers had lain dormant from the death of their author in 1799 until 1810. In that year appeared the second edition of a book of reminiscences by Thomas Thornton, the Levant Company banker at Constantinople, called *The Present State of Turkey*. It was a dull book, factious, quarrelsome, and inaccurate: its main claim to be remembered is the stinging attack on it included by Lord Byron in his notes to *Childe Harold's Pilgrimage*. In making the usual eulogy to the memory of the lamented Tweddell, Thornton remarked that, if his papers had been collected by the hand of Friendship, they might have formed a monument to rescue his memory from unmerited oblivion. Thornton's book was reviewed anonymously in a journal, the

---

* Parts of the tombstone set in the Theseum by Lusieri can still be seen (wrongly restored) in the wall of the English Church in Athens. Others were found in the excavations in the Agora. The Greek version seems to have disappeared in its entirety.[7]

Naval Chronicle, by John Spencer Smith, three years after it first appeared.[8] Smith, still nine years later smarting under the humiliation of his dismissal by Elgin, made some biting but mysterious observations about Elgin's part in the dispersal of Tweddell's papers—hinting that much more was known if only he and Thornton were prepared to speak out. In a footnote Smith gave away his identity and the source of his discontent by remarking on the scandal of replacing a Minister who had negotiated a treaty by an Ambassador-Extraordinary to ratify it.

Spencer Smith could hardly have guessed what he was unleashing. The article attracted the attention of Tweddell's brother, the Revd. Robert Tweddell, and he decided to reopen the whole matter. The energy of the Reverend Robert was equal to that of the lamented John. He began by writing a polite, almost servile letter to Lord Elgin asking him to relate the circumstances of the loss of his brother's papers: he claimed that this was to help with a biography he was writing. When Elgin wrote, recounting what he could remember of the incident, Tweddell promptly wrote again asking for elucidation of certain points arising. When Elgin replied he wrote again for more, and by this procedure obtained a number of letters from his unwary victim. After six months Elgin's suspicions were aroused by a hint in one of Tweddell's letters and he asked for copies of the letters he had previously written. This was refused and the correspondence came to an abrupt end.[9]

Robert Tweddell adopted the same tactics towards Thornton, towards Philip Hunt, and towards a friend of Carlyle who might have been expected to contribute something. By this persistence he extracted a large number of letters containing the recollections of the various actors in an event nearly fourteen years old. He set to work on this material as if he were editing an ancient text, comparing and contrasting the various accounts, checking any points that could be confirmed by outside evidence, and documenting every step with great care. Not unexpectedly, he uncovered numerous inconsistencies. He then engaged a lawyer to turn this mass of evidence into a memorandum to the Levant Company. As a result the Levant Company in 1813 conducted its own investigation on the spot in Constantinople. Another mass of documents was produced and put into Tweddell's hands, copies of correspondence, statements of witnesses, fragments of reminiscence, and titbits of gossip. This second corpus was subjected to the same tendentious scholarship.

The man who lay behind this unusual diligence on the part of the Levant Company was John Spencer Smith. Smith decided that here was the opportunity for taking his revenge on Elgin that he had long looked for. Through the instrument of the indefatigable Tweddell, Spencer Smith could clear his own name of the stigma of dismissal by disgracing Elgin. Tweddell's *Remains* bears unmistakable signs of his influence and direction. It is full of quite irrelevant panegyrics on Spencer Smith, long tedious dissertations about the laws and usages of the Levant Company clearly contributed by him, and gratuitous information about how he had been hated by Napoleon. In an anonymous review of the *Remains* in the *Naval Chronicle* Spencer Smith boasted openly that he had been responsible for its publication.[10] The whole affair was a full-scale conspiracy to defame Elgin concocted by Spencer Smith and Tweddell. And the great Levant Company connived more or less openly at this disgraceful and underhand attack, no doubt reckoning that its ancient monopolistic privileges could not survive many embassies like Elgin's.

Clarke soon joined the conspirators.* In a volume of his encyclopaedic *Travels* published in 1814 he wrote cryptically of John Tweddell

That the literary property of this gentleman after being in the undisputed possession of the British Ambassador at Constantinople should absolutely have disappeared *in toto* and eluded the most diligent inquiries of his family and friends presents a subject for the deepest regret, and is a circumstance of the most unaccountable nature. Upon this point, however, the author refrains from saying all that he might in the expectation of seeing this strange mystery unfolded by a kindred hand which may justly aspire to the best information.[11]

In his next volume, published almost simultaneously with the *Remains*, he went further.

* Clarke's brother was editor of the *Naval Chronicle*.

Thus every doubt is done away as to this mysterious transaction. It is to be feared that if any other part of Mr. J. Tweddell's observations upon Greece ever see the light, it will only be in the garbled form of extracts made from his writings by those who had the ransacking of his papers which will be published, as perhaps they have been already, without any acknowledgement being made of their real author.[12]

An attempt was also made to enlist Byron, and Tweddell was very nearly immortalized in the later editions of *Childe Harold's Pilgrimage*. Writing in 1813 about *The Parthenon*, an attack on Elgin in verse by James and Horace Smith,*[13] Byron suggested: 'I wish I had the pleasure of Mr. Smith's acquaintance as I could communicate the curious anecdote you read in Mr. T's letter. If he would like it, he can have the *substance* for his second edition; if not I shall add it to our next, although I think we already have enough of Lord Elgin.'[14] 'Mr. T.' is surely the Revd. Robert Tweddell. Rather oddly in this letter Byron makes no mention that the ideas of *The Parthenon* bear signs of being derived from his own *Curse of Minerva*.

While *Tweddell's Remains* was being prepared for the press the conspirators indulged in some sniping in the reviews. In 1815 the *New Monthly Magazine* published an article by Hamilton, under the pseudonym Philalethes, which praised Elgin's efforts in saving Greek marbles from destruction. This produced a long, rambling, and obscure reply from 'T.' which concluded, 'I feel there is not a nobleman in England and but one in Scotland who has accomplished so much in some respects as the Earl of ***** towards the depression of the arts "and I may add painting"† in particular as also towards the suppression of literature.' Philalethes responded at once. 'Philalethes would be very much obliged if T. would have the goodness to put his observations on Lord Elgin's collection of marbles which appeared in your paper of 29 last into English or any other intelligible language in order that his meaning may be known and that his notions upon that subject which appear to be very confused may be set right.' T. replied

* Not, as far as I know, related to Spencer Smith.
† I do not know the significance of this allusion.

with a quotation from Byron: 'The last the worst dull spoiler etc.'[15] It was not a very constructive discussion.

Neither Hamilton nor Elgin guessed the identity of T. and they thus knew nothing of what Tweddell and Spencer Smith were preparing.[16] The publication of *Tweddell's Remains* at the most delicate stage of Elgin's negotiations for the sale of his marbles came as a complete surprise to him. His first news of it came when he read a review of it, praising Tweddell and condemning himself, in the *Edinburgh Review*. His mortification can be imagined. Stung with indignation at the gross unfairness of the article he could not wait until he had seen the book itself before launching his defence. He hurriedly composed a *Letter to the Editor of the Edinburgh Review* and had it published in pamphlet form in Edinburgh and London. In the *Letter* Elgin denied all the allegations. He was able to show from his own records that Tweddell had suppressed a number of letters inconvenient to his side of the story; that the importance of Tweddell's papers had been exaggerated; and, so far from seizing them, he himself had acted properly and generously throughout.

The *Letter* did something to restore the situation. As soon as he had obtained a copy of *Tweddell's Remains* he followed it with a *Postscript to a Letter to the Editor of the Edinburgh Review* which he also published. This was a more formidable defence, demonstrating, with great restraint, that Spencer Smith's animosity lay behind the whole story and that it was largely through Spencer Smith's negligence and punctilio that the papers had been so badly damaged. Elgin finished with a great burst of indignation against the *Edinburgh Review* couched in his usual ponderous style.

If ever you shall again be tempted to trespass beyond your province and to arraign the moral conduct of a private individual who has not even, as an author, subjected himself to your jurisdiction; remember— and let the recollection restrain you—that your pages must go where no answer or refutation can follow them; and that, if you lend them to the gratification of revenge and malignity—nay, even if you scatter firebrands and call it sport,—your *Review* is the most intolerable nuisance that can exist in a civilized country.[17]

Meanwhile, at Bedford, Philip Hunt, long estranged from Elgin, was also stung to action. He began by writing to the *Christian Observer*,[18] but soon he too felt obliged by the mounting tide of criticism and abuse to publish his own pamphlet. *A Narrative of What is Known Respecting the Literary Remains of the Late John Tweddell* is also a convincing account. It did, however, have one great weakness. Hunt now admitted, for the first time, that he had copied some notes from Tweddell's journals, hoping they would be useful on his visit to Greece. There was obviously no improper intention in this and Hunt had made no secret of it at the time, but it did tend to support Tweddell's claims.

Within a few months of the first, a second edition of *Tweddell's Remains* appeared, greatly enlarged, in which the publications of Elgin and Hunt were subjected to the same pettifogging knitpicking as their earlier letters. The scandal grew and with it the rumours. By the middle of 1816 the claims and counterclaims in the argument had become so complex and numerous that hardly anyone could have had the energy to take an objective view. Those who did take the trouble, for example the *Quarterly Review*,[19] were inclined to acquit Elgin of all the main charges. But few men can afford to have their affairs paraded in such detail before the public and hope to escape unscathed. Public opinion works on the dangerous principle of no smoke without fire. Hunt's admissions caused great glee in the Tweddell camp,[20] and even Elgin's explanations had some curious features. Why, for example, had he not done more to exert his authority over Spencer Smith? Why was it that Elgin seemed to have aroused the hostility of everyone he came in contact with in the Tweddell affair? For, almost without exception, Elgin had to admit sadly that all the main actors were now on bad terms with him or had been when they died—Spencer Smith of course, and Thornton, and Mr. Nisbet his former father-in-law, but also Clarke, Philip Hunt and Carlyle. Surely a man who made so many enemies must have something unpleasant about him?

The impression against Elgin seemed to be confirmed by a discovery arising from the dispute. Mr. Nisbet uncovered a number of drawings in his home which he had brought back from

Constantinople. On examination some of them turned out to belong to Tweddell. Mr. Nisbet had brought them back but lacking instructions, or forgetting them, he had assumed they belonged to Elgin. When Elgin's marriage to his daughter broke up he forgot about them. The 'Elgin Box' containing the Tweddell drawings was opened in the presence of solicitors in November 1816 and the drawings delivered to Robert Tweddell. Needless to say the Tweddell-Spencer Smith party hailed this as a 'triumphant vindication' of all their claims and accusations.[21]

So this sterile and unsavoury affair came to an end. It had done untold harm to Elgin's reputation. Breaking out just at the crisis in his affairs when events at last seemed to be moving in his favour, it continued all through the negotiations for the sale of the Elgin Marbles to the Government. Just what the effect was it is almost impossible to say, but surely it ruled out for ever the possibility of a British peerage. No doubt the conspirators were very pleased with themselves.

Chapter 21

The Fate of the Manuscripts

WHILE the Tweddell controversy was raging, another criticism of Lord Elgin's Embassy began to break through. This concerned the collection of ancient manuscripts which Professor Carlyle had brought back from the East in 1801.

As always Clarke's nose for scandal led him early to the scene. In his 1816 volume of *Travels*, he wrote in his usual sneering style that

as he has reason to believe that the *theft* of a Greek Manuscript which was committed in one of the monasteries [of Mount Athos] by persons who had seen Mr. Tweddell's Journals was owing to intelligence therein contained, he will not remain altogether silent as to the *fact*. The subsequent death of one who was principally concerned in that transaction, precludes the possibility of his communicating more upon this subject.[1]

Philip Hunt in his *Narrative* about *Tweddell's Remains* retorted brusquely,

If Dr. Clarke means to insinuate that any manuscript was taken by me from Mount Athos or elsewhere, I explicitly deny the charge. If the observation be meant to apply to my deceased friend, I beg leave to refer Dr. Clarke to the Archbishop of Canterbury's Library at Lambeth, in which all the Greek manuscripts he had procured in Turkey were deposited by his executrix after his decease.[2]

Nevertheless in this case Clarke did seem to have a point. It was well known that it was almost impossible to obtain any manuscripts legally from Greek monasteries. All alienation of Church property was forbidden unless with the authority of the Patriarch himself, or in some cases, of the local bishop. All Greek monks were bound by an oath, administered to them when they were first admitted, to preserve the property of their monastery, and it was largely because this rule had been rigidly enforced for hundreds of years that any property remained to them at all. If any manuscripts had come from Greek monasteries as a result of Elgin's Embassy—and it was undeniable that some had—then they had been obtained irregularly. Clarke was well qualified to speak of these matters since, in direct competition with Carlyle, he had himself brought home a collection of manuscripts which he sold to the Bodleian Library for £1,000.[3] As always the consciousness of his own guilt did not hinder Clarke from condemning other people. He had, however, ferreted out only a small part of the story of the Carlyle manuscripts and a very unimportant one. Had he known more he would no doubt have made more accusations. The story, as usual, was a complex one.

Professor Carlyle had been attached to Lord Elgin's Embassy by the Government for the specific purpose of looking for ancient manuscripts. Although he was unsuccessful in his main aim—that of discovering manuscripts of unknown classical authors—he did bring home, besides many Arabic manuscripts bought in the bazaars, thirty-seven ancient manuscripts,[4] some of which were very valuable for the study of the text of the New Testament. They ranged in date from the tenth to the fifteenth century. Carlyle obtained them in various ways. Six he brought from the monastery of St. Saba near Jerusalem.[5] Four or five others came from the Library of the Patriarch of Jerusalem at Constantinople.[6] To none of these manuscripts did Carlyle have any title. They were lent to him, at his own insistent request, to allow them to be collated in England and to help with the production of a revised edition of the New Testament. Before he left Constantinople for the last time in March 1801 Carlyle signed a declaration prepared by the Patriarch promising to return the manuscripts to the Patriarch at Constantinople 'when the purposes for which they were borrowed were completed or whenever the Patriarch should demand them'.[7] Philip Hunt as a secretary to the Embassy also signed the declaration thus making the British Government a party to the promise.

The remainder of the manuscripts which Carlyle brought home were bought. Some were bought in the monasteries of the Princes Islands near Constantinople which Carlyle visited in the spring of 1800, sometimes with Hunt, sometimes by himself; the others were bought later that year when Carlyle and Hunt visited Mount Athos. Special techniques were found to circumvent the ecclesiastical rules. 'All *direct* offers of purchasing manuscripts', wrote Carlyle to the Bishop of Lincoln, 'must and will be rejected by these communities especially if they be made in too public a manner for, in this case, the rigid scruples of a few members will counteract the pliancy of the rest.' But there were other means.

It may not be difficult to procure cession of some of the old vellum books which lie neglected in an obscure chamber of the building, especially if the negotiation be conducted with that degree of secrecy and delicacy which is necessary to avoid the worldly consequences of such a measure and to furnish a casuistic argument for quieting the consciences of the more timid members of the community. The transaction, for instance, may be disguised under the form of an exchange of presents and the Manuscripts may be given and received as a trifling acknowledgement for a pecuniary donation to the *Panagia*. The above hints are applicable to most cases which will occur to a traveller who is in search of Greek Manuscripts, but they will occasionally prove superfluous for there are a few Monastic Communities in this country so sordidly immersed in ignorance and barbarity as to permit a traveller to pocket a Tetravangelion almost with as much indifference as if it were a bundle of waste paper.[8]

Techniques such as Carlyle found effective had been used by travellers for centuries before Carlyle and were to be used long afterwards. In the circumstances of the time we need not take too seriously the charge of theft which was occasionally made in later years.[9]

Carlyle returned home with his manuscripts in 1801 and resumed the quiet life of priest and scholar in which his adventures in the East had been a hard interlude. Although he had failed to make his fortune and had parted on bad terms with Elgin, his manuscripts turned out to be more useful than he had thought. 'I believe,' he wrote, 'they amount to near a tenth part of all mss of the new Testament that have yet been examined in Europe.'[10] It was, therefore, decided that, with their help, he should prepare a new edition of the New Testament. The Arabic version to help convert the heathens was to follow later. In addition he wanted to publish a book of verses and journals from the voluminous notes he had made in the East.

For the New Testament edition, he gathered round him a number of scholars and clergymen and set them to work on the huge task of collation. To help them he had printed a memorandum entitled *Hints and Observations which Mr. Carlyle takes the liberty of suggesting to the consideration of the gentlemen who have kindly promised their assistance in collating the Greek Mss of the New Testament.*[11] This was a rough catalogue of part of the collection with some notes on where they had come from. Five were marked 'S' as coming from Syria; four marked 'C' for Constantinople; and eighteen 'I' for Princes Islands. The provenance of the others, which were manuscripts of other than the New Testament, was not identified. Carlyle mentioned in the *Hints* that some of the manuscripts belonged to the Patriarch, but, unfortunately, he did not make clear precisely which.

In April 1804, before the work of collation had gone far, Carlyle died. His heirs received a great disappointment. The journey to the East had made severe inroads into the Carlyle fortune and all there was to show for it was the collection of manuscripts. Carlyle's sister, Miss Carlyle, his executrix, immediately put in hand a posthumous edition of his poems and this was published, with a public subscription of some of the great names of the land, (including Elgin and the Smiths) in 1805.[12] She also decided to sell his manuscripts.[13] The Arabic collection was sold to the East India Company and is still in the India Office Library. The others did not all belong entirely to Carlyle. Apart from those borrowed from the Patriarch, which Miss Carlyle identified as the four marked 'C', she knew that Philip Hunt had a claim on some of the others.

Miss Carlyle wrote to Hunt, who was still in captivity in France, about how they should be disposed of. Hunt suggested depositing them with the Archbishop of Canterbury in the Library at Lambeth. Miss Carlyle then replied,

As to the manuscripts I think that as the survivor you have an undoubted right to dispose of those brought from Constantinople in any way you please; nor could you have fixed upon any place more agreeable to me to deposit mine in than under the patronage of the Archbishop of Canterbury. . . . It would give me great pain to separate what has cost us so dear to collect together. At the same time I do not conceive myself authorised to refuse any compensation for them which the Archbishop, after inspection, may think proper to make me. My brother, the day before he died, said to me that, as his unfortunate journey had been attended with a great pecuniary loss to his family, I must make what I could of his manuscripts for the benefit of his daughter.[14]

Hunt thereupon resigned all claim he might have had to any of the manuscripts and the whole collection was sold to the Archbishop, with the exception of one, a manuscript of Eutropius, which Miss Carlyle kept as a memento. The four manuscripts marked 'C' were not entered in the library catalogue since it was considered that they belonged to the Patriarch. On his release from France, Hunt called on the Archbishop to tell him that he had given up his share and to remind him of his arrangement with the Patriarch. He did not specify which manuscripts were involved thinking that Miss Carlyle had been able to identify them. Shortly afterwards, he went to Ireland as secretary to the Duke of Bedford.

So the matter rested for nine years. The manuscripts lay at Lambeth admired by many although little work seems to have been done on them. Then in 1813 Hamilton at the Foreign Office received a letter from the British Ambassador at Constantinople saying that the Patriarch of Jerusalem had formally asked for his borrowed manuscripts to be returned. Hamilton, after some delay, referred the matter to Hunt, who immediately wrote to the Archbishop of Canterbury asking him to return the manuscripts to Constantinople. The Archbishop made no reply. Hunt wrote again, and also to Hamilton, but two years passed and still nothing was done.

Then in June 1816 when the question of the Elgin Marbles still lay in the balance, and when the Tweddell affair was at its height, another, stiffer letter arrived from the British Embassy at Constantinople. The Ambassador declared that the 'National character suffers by this neglect and that the Patriarch looks on the transaction as a breach of confidence.'[15] Another criticism—and this time a well justified one—was levelled at Lord Elgin's Embassy.

When he heard of the second letter from Constantinople Hunt immediately called on the Archbishop again to tell him that the manuscripts must be returned. At long last some action was taken. At once another difficulty arose. The Archbishop had thought that only the four manuscripts marked 'C' belonged to the Patriarch: but the Patriarch's request was for no less than eleven. Contrary to what Hunt had presumed—but not checked—in 1805 there was no sure way of telling which belonged to the Patriarch, and Miss Carlyle had made the assumption most favourable to herself. An attempt was now made to find the Patriarch's missing manuscripts.

The Patriarch asked for two copies of the Gospels, three copies of the Acts, and a Libanius—all from St. Saba; and two Gospels, two Psalters and a Eutropius from his library at Constantinople. The Libanius and the Eutropius were easily picked out, and there were only two Psalters in the whole collection so it was assumed they must be his: the four marked 'C' consisted of three Gospels and one Acts and they were also clearly his. This left one more Gospel and two more Acts to be found. Since the only Acts remaining were in the series marked 'I' meaning bought in the Princes Islands it was assumed that Carlyle must have made a mistake. One of the Acts and two of the Gospels were, therefore, taken from the 'I' series. So the numbers were made up to the eleven the Patriarch had asked for. In 1817, after Miss Carlyle had paid back the Archbishop for the manuscripts he was returning, these eleven manuscripts were delivered at the Foreign Office for sending on to Constantinople. This complicated incident at last came to an end with little credit to anybody.

It is difficult to avoid the conclusion that those concerned in the transactions were a little obtuse, especially as they had all the evidence that is now available and more. It seems certain that the wrong manuscripts were sent. Although he had been rather careless about marking the manuscripts not containing the New Testament, Carlyle in his *Hints* had been quite specific about those which did—the ones that were to be farmed out to scholars for collation. His cataloguing was as follows:

'S' for Syria: i.e. borrowed from St. Saba	⎧ 2 Gospels ⎨ 3 Acts and ⎩ Epistles
'C' for Constantinople	⎧ 3 Gospels ⎨ 1 Acts[16]

The Patriarch's request was for:

From St. Saba	⎧ 2 Gospels ⎨ 3 Acts ⎩ Libanius
From Constantinople	⎧ 2 Gospels ⎨ 2 Psalters ⎩ Eutropius[17]

If we exclude the non-New Testament manuscripts excluded from Carlyle's catalogue the two are remarkably similar. For the manuscripts from St. Saba we also have the evidence of one of Carlyle's letters to the Bishop of Durham of July 1800. 'I was permitted to bring away with me to Constantinople six of what I judged to be the most curious Mss—viz two of the oldest copies of the Gospels and only one of the Epistles and Acts; two copies of Apostolic letters, and a copy of Libanius.'[18] The lists for St. Saba thus coincide exactly. One would have thought that Hunt and the Archbishop would have seen that Carlyle intended all marked 'S' to be returned to St. Saba. As for the others Carlyle was more likely to be right than the Patriarch. He kept such detailed journals of every day's events as to be a joke among his friends[19] and it is easy to believe that he was permitted to borrow a few more manuscripts after the agreement with the Patriarch was drawn up.

The Archbishop ought to have returned (at least):

1. The five manuscripts marked 'S'
2. The four marked 'C'

3. The two Psalters
4. The Libanius
5. The Eutropius.

Instead he returned:

1. Three marked 'I'
2. The four marked 'C'
3. The two Psalters
4. The Libanius
5. The Eutropius.

The five manuscripts from St. Saba, all very valuable, are still at Lambeth. Perhaps if he could find the three from the Princes Islands which are not strictly his, the Patriarch of Jerusalem might still reclaim them. He would make a good bargain if he did.

Lord Elgin was only indirectly concerned with the affair of Carlyle's Greek manuscripts. Most of the blame for the carelessness which was undoubtedly shown throughout fell, rightly, on Carlyle and Hunt, Miss Carlyle, and the Archbishop of Canterbury. One would be surprised, nevertheless, if some members of the Government and others who knew the long sad story did not hold Elgin responsible for at least some of the muddle.

Chapter 22

The Marbles are Sold

As soon as the new Parliamentary session began in February 1816 Lord Elgin again presented his Petition asking the House of Commons to appoint a Select Committee. He asked again that the Committee should investigate the circumstances in which he had obtained the collection and advise on whether, and on what terms, it should be sold to the Government.[1]

Lord Elgin's Petition was debated on 23 February.[2] The Chancellor of the Exchequer proposed to accept it on behalf of the Government. 'It was certainly one of the most wonderful events of the day', he was reported as saying, 'that the works of Phidias should become the property of a native of Caledonia. The desire of conferring honour on the arts as well as on the arms of this country was the object of his notion; for, of all the arts, sculpture was at present the least flourishing in England.' Eleven other speakers took part in the debate. Several spoke of the value of the collection but the House was by no means inclined to accept the proposal without reservation. Several members queried whether Lord Elgin had been right to use his position of ambassador to acquire the collection, and one was concerned that 'if ambassadors were encouraged to make these speculations, many might return in the character of merchants'. The old cries of 'spoliation' deriving from Byron were repeated. Lord Brougham, a prominent contributor to the *Edinburgh Review*, attacked the proposal on grounds of economy. If there was money to be spent, he said, it should be spent on alleviating the distress of men discharged from the Navy; if the country could not afford that then 'if we could not give them bread, we ought not to indulge ourselves in the purchase of stones.'* After two

* This theme was repeated in the Cruikshank cartoon reproduced on Plate VIII (*a*).

divisions, Lord Elgin's Petition was agreed to, and a Select Committee was appointed. It consisted of eighteen M.P.s of all shades of opinion. Among the members were the Chancellor of the Exchequer and Charles Long who had played an important part in the earlier negotiations. There were at least two M.P.s who knew Greece well: F. S. N. Douglas, who had written a book which included an attack on Elgin,[3] and J. H. Fazakerley, who had been concerned with Cockerell in the affair of the Aegina Marbles.

The Select Committee[4] began its hearings on 29 February with a two day examination of Lord Elgin. On the first day, in answer to a series of questions, Elgin recounted in simple straightforward terms, the now familiar story of his collection; how, before he had left England, the idea had been suggested to him of helping the arts of his country; how the Government had refused to help and he had gone ahead at his own expense; and how, when he saw the great destruction being perpetrated at Athens, he had obtained a firman allowing him to rescue everything that he could. The committee pressed him about the exact legal authority for his operations, how far the French were involved in similar schemes, and how far his position as Ambassador had been responsible for his extraordinary privileges. The questioning was thorough and very fair. To every question Lord Elgin was able to give honest and convincing answers.

In the course of his examination about the activities of the Comte de Choiseul-Gouffier, Elgin told the story of how Choiseul-Gouffier's metope had come into his possession through an accident of war, and how he had recently offered to give back all antiquities that belonged once to Choiseul-Gouffier. He made it clear that he still wanted to give them back. 'He has never yet sent about them,' Elgin said, 'and I do not know what he means to do at all; but there they are, marked among my things as belonging to him.'[5]

The next day Elgin was asked about the expense of making his collection. He began by presenting several documents which he had prepared for the committee's consideration to help settle certain questions that had been raised. They included a memorandum which argued forcefully, from examples such as that of Sir William Hamilton and his collection, that the Elgin Marbles belonged exclusively to Lord Elgin despite his having been an ambassador at the time they were collected; a copy of the letter which had formed the basis for negotiations in 1811; and a letter explaining in mild terms the hostility he had endured from the Dilettanti Society ever since 1806. The most important of the papers presented was a long letter setting out his estimate of expenses. It was, of course, a prodigious sum of money.[6]

In the negotiations of 1811 Elgin has assessed his expenditure to date at £62,440. He now added the money that had been spent since that time, emphasizing that about eighty more cases of marbles had since arrived at Burlington House. For the later years in Greece Elgin was able to produce detailed accounts. They showed that, despite his precarious financial state, he had not skimped. Presents to the authorities in Athens, for example, between 1803 and 1815, amounted to over £6,000. Interest at Malta on the large sums borrowed there was 17¾ per cent. The grand total of expenditure was £74,240. In submitting this enormous figure to the committee, Elgin observed,

I beg once more to repeat, that I do not offer this view of my expenses as a criterion of the intrinsic value of my Collection. I ever have been persuaded that, in justice to the Public, that should be calculated on other grounds. But it is, I trust, sufficient to prove, that in amassing these remains of antiquity for the benefit of my Country, and in rescuing them from the imminent and unavoidable destruction with which they were threatened, had they been left many years longer the prey of mischievous Turks, who mutilated them for wanton amusement, or for the purpose of selling them piecemeal to occasional travellers; I have been actuated by no motives of private emolument; nor deterred from doing what I felt to be a substantial good, by considerations of personal risk, or the fear of calumnious misrepresentations.[7]

From one who had suffered so much, it was a dignified defence. If the test of a man's enthusiasm is the price he is willing to pay, then Lord Elgin had certainly established his *bona fides*.

The next major witness was Hamilton, loyal as always to Lord

Elgin's cause, but universally respected as a man of standing in his own right. He was able to confirm almost all of Elgin's story from his own experience and had checked other parts from the Foreign Office files. Since he had by now acquired a well-deserved reputation as a judge of antiquities he was asked his opinion about the value of the Elgin Marbles. He told the sad story of the Aegina Marbles which had been sold for £6,000 and the Phigaleia Marbles which had cost £19,000, and then made a comparative evaluation of the Elgin collection. The principal parts of the pediment he put at £4,000 each; the metopes at £10,000 altogether; and the frieze at £400 a piece. The total value of the collection according to Hamilton was £60,000.

At the beginning of the next week the committee took evidence on the artistic value of the collection. All the most eminent sculptors of the day were called in, the aged Nollekens, Flaxman, Westmacott, Chantry, and Rossi; and two famous painters, Sir Thomas Lawrence and Benjamin West. West was too ill to attend but sent his answers in writing. Haydon too had been suggested as a witness by Lord Elgin but he was not called for fear of offending Payne Knight.[8] The questions which the committee asked the artists are as interesting as the answers. To all they put the same general questions—in what class of art did they place the Elgin Marbles; were they as good as the Apollo Belvedere, the Laocoon, and the other masterpieces of Italy; did they have more 'Ideal Beauty'; did the close imitation of nature which the marbles showed detract from their excellence; were they less valuable for not having been restored. All these questions are exactly what one would expect from a body of men brought up in the eighteenth-century tradition. Behind them lay the aesthetic assumptions of the day, the view that 'classical' art should be 'idealized'; should not conform too closely to nature; and should be more graceful than grand. Their taste was that of the Dilettanti, of the great English collectors before Elgin, of Byron, and (until they had seen the marbles) of Canova and Visconti. It was the taste of men taught to regard the restored Greco-Roman statues of Italy as the finest remaining works of antiquity.

The answers of the artists, all of whom had been educated in the same tradition, showed that, in a few short years, the Elgin Marbles had already made their taste out of date. These large mutilated marbles with the intimate knowledge of anatomy that they revealed had set an entirely new standard in the appreciation of ancient art. The artists answered in their different characteristic ways and some made some reservations, but on the main points, they spoke with one voice. The Elgin Marbles, said Nollekens, were 'the finest things that ever came to this country'.[9] 'The finest works of art I have ever seen', said Flaxman.[10] 'Infinitely superior to the Apollo Belvedere',[11] said Westmacott, because they have 'all the essence of style with all the truth of nature; the Apollo is more an ideal figure'.[12] 'There is in them', said Lawrence, 'an union of fine composition and very grand form, with a more true and natural expression of the effect of action upon the human frame than there is in the Apollo or in any of the other most celebrated statues.'[13] All the artists agreed that it was right that the Elgin Marbles had not been restored and that their acquisition would lead to great improvement in the arts in Great Britain. A revolution in taste had occurred. Unfortunately for Elgin, none of the artists felt it was his place to put a monetary figure on the value of the collection: that was a job for the patrons, not for the artists they employed.

After the artists came the connoisseurs. Richard Payne Knight, still regarded as the foremost authority in England, was asked more questions than any other witness except for Elgin himself. His performance was a dismal one. Not only did he try, helplessly, to maintain the old-fashioned artistic criteria which the artists had so decisively rejected, but all his hostility to Elgin and his deep-seated prejudices shone through. From the beginning his answers were unenthusiastic and supercilious.

Are you acquainted with the Elgin Collection—Yes: I have looked them over, not only formerly, but I have looked them over on this occasion with reference to their value.

In what class of art do you place the finest works in this Collection?— I think of things extant, I should put them in the second rank—some of them; they are very unequal; the finest I should put in the second rank.

Do you think that none of them rank in the first class of art?—Not with the Laocoon and the Apollo and these which have been placed in the first class of art; at the same time I must observe, that their state of preservation is such I cannot form a very accurate notion; their surface is gone mostly.

Do you consider them to be of a very high antiquity?—We know from the authority of Plutarch that those of the Temple of Minerva, which are the principal, were executed by Callicrates and Ictinus, and their assistants and scholars; and I think some were added in the time of Hadrian, from the style of them. . . .

In what class do you rank the fragments of the draped female figures?—They are so mutilated I can hardly tell, but I should think most of them were added by Hadrian: they are so mutilated I cannot say much about them: they are but of little value except from their local interest, from having been part of the Temple.[14]

It was obvious from his answer to the very first question of the committee that Payne Knight was keen to pronounce on the value of the collection. When eventually he was asked, his answer was even more extraordinary than one would have supposed. He delivered a paper to the committee in which a figure was put against the main items of the collection. The two large recumbent figures from the pediment he put at £1,500 each. The total for the frieze £5,000; for the metopes £7,000. Elgin's casts from the Parthenon and other temples he put at £2,500—that is half the value of 250 feet of the original frieze! The Caryatid and the Horse's Head he put at £200 and £250 respectively, but suggested £300 for a granite Egyptian beetle that had somehow become mixed up with the Greek sculptures*, and £500 for a coarse and quite undistinguished sarcophagus. He went on to suggest more for the architectural fragments, and even for unadorned blocks of marble and porphyry, than for the sculptures themselves.

Three capitals and part of a column from the same Temple (i.e. the Parthenon)	£500
Various shafts and blocks of marble	£350
Do. of Porphyry	£350

* This beetle can be seen in Plate VI (a) among the marbles outside the museum at Burlington House.

Payne Knight's grand total was £25,000 for the whole collection, which, he said, was far more than twice what they would fetch on the open market. The topsy-turvy scale of values which this estimate revealed, insulting though it was to Lord Elgin, was allowed to pass by the committee. But he did not go completely unscathed. When the committee pressed him about the authority for his glib assertions that the sculptures were Hadrianic, he had to admit it was non-existent.

After Payne Knight came two more witnesses who were generally expected to support his line. William Wilkins, the architect, admitted that the marbles had some merit but was very unenthusiastic. The most he would say was that they helped to show off the architecture. Lord Aberdeen, however, to everyone's surprise, took a different line and admitted that the Elgin Marbles were 'extremely valuable' and almost certainly of the time of Phidias. He refused, however, to admit it was possible to judge the excellence of the work by examining the sculptures alone: like his friend Payne Knight he declared that the surface was too corroded to allow a judgement and he timidly based all his aesthetic appreciation on the testimony of the ancient authors. Apart from Hamilton and Payne Knight, Lord Aberdeen was the only witness who ventured to put a monetary value on the collection. He suggested £35,000 for the whole, refusing to break the figure down into individual items.

Besides taking evidence on the artistic merit of the marbles, the Select Committee made many inquiries into the conditions prevailing at Athens when they were collected. Wilkins and Lord Aberdeen, who had both been in Athens while the removals were taking place, were able to confirm that great destruction of all the monuments was being practised by the Turks, by the French, and by other travellers. Aberdeen said nothing about his own contribution to the dispersal of the Parthenon sculptures. Another witness, John Morritt admitted frankly that, when he had been in Athens in 1795, he had bribed the Disdar to allow him to take some pieces of the frieze and a metope but had been prevented by Fauvel. John Fazakerley, himself a member of the committee, told the story of the Aegina Marbles. Finally Philip

Hunt, who happened to be in London on other business, was called in unexpectedly and was able to confirm Elgin's story in all its main particulars and to add to it. He later produced a copy of the firman which he had kept in his possession after his break with Elgin and sent it to the committee.

After two weeks of examining witnesses, the sittings of the Select Committee came to an end. Throughout the hearings Benjamin Haydon had stood patiently by, waiting to be called. Elgin obtained a promise that he would be called but the day passed and he was not.[15] Then the sittings came to an end. Haydon, passionate as always, could not restrain himself. Three days after the Committee rose, a long letter signed by him appeared in the principal newspapers. It was called *On the Judgment of Connoisseurs being preferred to that of Professional Men.*[16] It was a savage indictment of the Select Committee's work, written, said Haydon, in the fear that they would be influenced by the opinion of Payne Knight and the connoisseurs rather than by artists.

In no other profession is the opinion of the man who has studied it for his amusement preferred to that of him who has devoted his soul to excel in it. No man will trust his limb to a connoisseur in surgery; no minister would ask a connoisseur in war how a campaign is to be conducted; no nobleman would be satisfied with the opinion of a connoisseur in law on disputed property; and why should a connoisseur of an art, more exclusively than any other without the reach of common acquirement be preferred to the professional man?

Haydon drew his own excited picture of the overwhelming excellence of the Elgin Marbles and of Payne Knight's earlier attempts to disparage them.

These are the productions which Mr. Payne Knight says may be original! May be! There are some men who have that hateful propensity of sneering at all which the world holds high, sacred or beautiful; not with the view of dissipating doubt, or giving the delightful comfort of conviction, but to excite mysterious belief of their own sagacity, to cloak their own envy, to chuckle if they can confuse, and revel if they can chill the feelings: according to them love is nothing but lust; religion is nothing but delusion; all high views and elevated notions, wild dreams and distempered fancies.

Haydon's article was a powerful attack: it hit the target squarely in the middle. A huge public sensation immediately broke out. Haydon's article was widely published as were numerous replies and rejoinders. It was translated into several European languages.[17] Haydon for a time enjoyed the reputation of a fiery rebel. The sculptors and artists who had modestly declined to value the Elgin Marbles were put to shame. Perhaps artists were more than tradesmen after all. Despite the sensation, however, it is doubtful if Haydon's outburst did Lord Elgin's case any good. Contrary to what Haydon and the rest of the world thought, the Select Committee had not been greatly biased towards the Payne Knight view: they had been scrupulously fair. Haydon did not know in detail what Payne Knight had said, nor did he know that Lord Aberdeen had spoken differently from what had been expected. The Select Committee were drafting their report when Haydon's article appeared. For all we know it may have had the opposite effect from what he intended.

The Select Committee's Report was soon prepared. Apart from a passage proving the authenticity of the marbles from ancient and modern authors, it was a short but comprehensive document. It examined Lord Elgin's claims in four parts, first, the authority by which the collection was acquired; secondly, the circumstances in which the authority was granted; thirdly, the merit of the marbles as works of art and their prospects of promoting the fine arts in Great Britain; and lastly, their value as objects of sale. With all parts except the last, Lord Elgin had every reason to be satisfied. The Report upheld all his claims and vindicated him completely from all the charges of spoliation, misuse of ambassador's powers, desire for profit, and so on, that had been so consistently levelled against him. Its narrative of the circumstances in which the collection was obtained could almost be a précis of Elgin's own *Memorandum on the Earl of Elgin's Pursuits in Greece*. The Report became almost lyrical about the improvements to the arts that could be expected if the marbles were bought. Elgin's only cause for complaint was the price recommended for the marbles. After considering recent sales of Greek sculpture, Elgin's expenses, and the likely market elsewhere, the Select Committee recommended £35,000 for the collection—the figure named by Lord Aberdeen. The Committee recognized that this represented less than half Elgin's expenses, and was only £5,000 above the figure refused in 1811 before the second collection arrived: they tried to soften these apparent illogicalities by pointing to the rise in the value of money since then. They made no reference to the moral claim which the Government had to part at least of the second collection.

The full version of the Select Committee's Report, including a verbatim report of the replies of witnesses, became available to the public early in April.[18] Payne Knight's reputation as a connoisseur was instantly and finally destroyed. He was severely attacked in the press, and although he attempted to defend himself by replies, he now stood convicted by his own evidence.[19] The *Examiner* composed a ditty on the evidence of the connoisseurs to the Select Committee:

> Nay some, unconscious of remorse,
> Prefer a Beetle to a Horse,
>   And worship Egypt's models,
> Composed throughout of granite rare
> In substance hard, in outline square,
>   The type of their own noddles.
> Envelop'd by the shades of *Knight*
> Still must Athenian genius bright,
>   Be doom'd to shine unseen;
> To shew the depth of Art's rich mines
> No northern light from Glasgow shines
>   Nor yet from *Aberdeen*.[20]

In a less playful comment the *Examiner* finally exposed the pettiness of the Dilettanti. 'The great cause of all the animosity against Lord Elgin arose chiefly from the mean passions of collectors. . . . their vanity was deeply wounded at the prospect of a new era being effected in Art by works too dirty for their drawing-rooms.'[21] At the Royal Academy the talk was all about Payne Knight's downfall. 'It was gratifying to us,' wrote Farington, 'to see that Mr. Payne Knight had so fully and publicly committed himself in the opinion he gave of the Elgin Marbles. . . . Thus will the judgement ignorance of this presumptious connoisseur be recorded.'[22] The Academy decided immediately to omit Payne Knight's name from its list of invitations that year.[23] Haydon, certain in his own mind that he had been responsible for the recognition of the Elgin Marbles, filled his diary with accusations against the Select Committee and contempt for their judgement.[24] His earlier prophecy was now to be soon fulfilled. 'Remember, Mr. Payne Knight, the fame of the Elgin Marbles will encrease with our knowledge and treble with time. Remember that, when all thy works are sunk into oblivion . . . thou wilt be only recollected by thy presumption in disbelieving their beauty.'[25]

Lord Elgin, severely disappointed at the price offered, decided after some hesitation that he had no alternative but to accept.[26] The Government accordingly applied to Parliament for the sum of £35,000 to be voted. The debate took place on 7 June 1816.[27] With the Select Committee's Report now available to the House the standard of debate was a good deal higher than in the earlier discussion, but still the old charges of spoliation and breach of ambassadorial duty were freely made. Lord Elgin's case was, however, ably put by the Government and by some other members and the money was duly voted. The most interesting contribution to the debate, in view of the later history of the Elgin Marbles controversy, was a proposal by a Mr. Hugh Hammersley. 'It was to be regretted,' he said, 'that the government had not restrained this act of spoliation; but, as it had been committed, we should exert ourselves to wipe off the stain, and not place in our museum a monument of our disgrace, but at once return the bribe which our ambassador had received, to his own dishonour and that of the country.' Hammersley proposed an amendment which, after a long preamble, read

This committee,* therefore, feels justified, under the particular circumstances of the case, in recommending that £25,000 be offered to the earl of Elgin for the collection in order to recover and keep it together for that government from which it has been improperly taken, and to which this committee is of opinion that a communication

* The House was sitting as a committee of supply.

should be immediately made, stating that Great Britain holds these marbles only in trust till they are demanded by the present, or any future, possessors of the city of Athens; and upon such demand, engages, without question or negociation, to restore them, as far as can be effected, to the places from whence they were taken, and that they shall be in the mean time carefully preserved in the British Museum.

No one took Hammersley's proposal seriously.

In due course an Act of Parliament was passed transferring the ownership of the Elgin Marbles to the nation.[28] By the terms of the Act, Lord Elgin and his heirs were to be trustees of the British Museum. Of the £35,000 the Government immediately claimed £18,000[29] in payment for a debt which one of Elgin's creditors had shrewdly succeeded in transferring to them. The remainder was quickly disbursed to other creditors. In August the Elgin Marbles were moved to the British Museum where a temporary structure had been built to receive them.* At long last Elgin was free of the fateful marbles which had hung round his neck for over ten years and had been the ruin of his life.

The relief was partial only. Elgin's honour had been vindicated but he still was deep in debt. He still had no prospect of renewing his public career. A few months after the controversy over the marbles had died down, Elgin reverted to a familiar theme. He wrote a long and detailed letter to the Prime Minister relating, blow by blow, the disasters that had fallen on his innocent head, and imploring him to grant him a British peerage.[30] The letter makes sorry reading. He was just about to return in triumph from Constantinople in 1803, he said, when suddenly he was seized in France and 'persecuted with the most vindictive animosity' by Bonaparte.

It was while suffering under these severities and separated from all but the most constrained communications from my family in England, that the foulest and most insidious intrigue was darkly at work here, preparing the ruin of my domestic peace, creating prepossessions in

---

* A view of the Temporary Elgin Room in 1819 is reproduced in Plate VII. The seated figure in the left foreground is Benjamin West. Charles Long, with his hand on his chest, stands directly behind him. The figure at the extreme left of the picture is Benjamin Robert Haydon.

regard to my official conduct, which however I had subsequently the good fortune to remove at least from Mr. Perceval's mind: nor were the true motives of this undefined, unavowed, yet most injurious, persecution brought home to its real source in disappointment and jealousy till Mr. Spencer Smith, finding a willing instrument in Mr. Tweddle to distort one of the most ordinary incidents in foreign stations, could not refrain from standing prominently forward in the publications that then appeared against me. And presuming upon the ill will against my operations in Greece in which some late travellers had indulged, he actually transmitted anonymous abuse against me to the newspapers at the moment when the House of Commons was entering upon the subject of my marbles; one of which attacks in Mr. Spencer Smith's handwriting is now in my possession.

The Prime Minister may have sympathized, but there was no peerage.

Chapter 23

Last Days

LORD Elgin's purpose from first to last had been to improve the arts of Great Britain, and this was the aspect of his activities which won him what little praise he obtained. It seems strange nowadays that the Elgin Marbles were valued less for their intrinsic worth as works of art than for their effect on the performance of contemporary artists. The Select Committee's Report had ended with the hope that the marbles would 'receive that admiration and homage to which they are entitled, and serve in return as models and examples to those, who by knowing how to revere and appreciate them, may learn first to imitate and ultimately to rival them'.¹ William Hazlitt wrote that the marbles might 'lift the Fine Arts out of the limbo of vanity and affectation . . . in which they have lain sprawling and fluttering, gasping for breath, wasting away, vapid and abortive'.²

The artists may not have liked these reflections on their recent efforts. Yet they were more willing to admit they could learn from their ancient predecessors than artists are now. The Elgin Marbles were universally praised and held up as a model to all. Within two years of their removal to the British Museum, a spate of engravings had been published for the instruction of artists,³ and the Museum itself soon embarked on a full and authoritative publication with detailed engravings beautiful as works of art in their own right.⁴ Students of all types thronged the Museum, sketching or merely admiring. Casts of the Elgin Marbles were sent to museums and art schools all over Europe. Princes and dignitaries visiting London made a point of visiting the Museum to see the new treasures where they could usually find Haydon ready to enthuse over them for their benefit. Goethe, his home at Weimar decorated with drawings of the

Elgin Marbles by Haydon, seemed to have all his opinions about the nature of art confirmed by the new discoveries. In 1816 he experienced a great revival in his interest in Greece, and even had full-scale drawings of the Elgin Marbles sent from London. In future, he declared, every German sculptor should go to London rather than to Italy or Greece—'Everything else one could, if need be, do without.'[5] In the British Museum a well-dressed riding master could sometimes be seen exhorting his pupils to examine the frieze of the Parthenon to learn how to sit elegantly on horseback.[6] Even Byron had to admit that the Marbles had some merit.[7]

The fashionable Mrs. Hemans, in her famous, if uninspired, poem *Modern Greece* published in 1816 echoed the popular wish:

> And who can tell how pure, how bright, a flame,
> Caught from these models, may illumine the west?
> What British Angelo may rise to fame,
> On the free isle what beams of art may rest?

On the last day of the same year Haydon wrote in his diary: 'This year the Elgin Marbles were bought and produced an Aera in public feeling.'[8]

Yet, notwithstanding these auguries, the effect of the Elgin Marbles on English art is difficult to assess. The works of the sculptors, despite their conversion from the theory of 'Ideal Beauty' are far more reminiscent of the neo-classicism of Canova than of the Elgin Marbles. In the field of painting West and Haydon both saw themselves as British Angelos and made specific claims that some of their pictures owed their inspiration and composition to the study of the Elgin Marbles; but their styles of painting were totally at variance with the restraint of the Greek tradition. No one would guess the influence of the marbles on their paintings if the fact had not been documented.[9] Direct copies of the Marbles were, of course, common. Henning's reconstructed Parthenon frieze appeared on the Athenaeum and the Hyde Park Arch. William Threed incorporated the head of Selene's horse in several of his monuments.* The vase in Buckingham

* Notably the Monument to Sir William Ponsonby in St. Paul's and the Pediment of the Royal Mews of Buckingham Palace.

Palace Gardens which commemorated Waterloo has the horse-
men of the frieze as has Pistrucci's medal for the same
battle.[10] The Parthenon frieze was a common motif of Regency
wallpaper.[11] One looks in vain, however, for practical examples
of the revolution in taste that everyone was certain was in
progress.

In architecture too the Grecian style thrived, although here
the original impulse had come from Stuart and Revett and was
already in full flower a generation before. The Elgin Marbles
undoubtedly contributed to the popularity of the style, and
possibly the standard of technical accomplishment was improved
by a study of the architectural fragments in the Elgin collection.*
Caryatids appeared early in the architecture of Sir John Soane,
and two replicas of the whole Caryatid porch still stand incon-
gruously outside Euston Station in Inwood's St. Pancras Church.
All over Britain there are buildings of the time reminiscent of the
Erechtheum, the Propylaea, the Theseum, and, perhaps most
common because smallest, the Monument of Lysicrates. Copies
of the Parthenon were, understandably, seldom attempted. At
Lord Elgin's suggestion, however, it was decided that the National
Monument of Scotland to the heroes of the wars should take the
form of a full-scale reproduction of the Parthenon to stand on
Calton Hill in Edinburgh.[12] The National Monument was never
completed owing to lack of funds; but its stark columns on the
eastern skyline of the Athens of the North are almost as romantic
as those of the Parthenon itself. In the 1830's, however, the
Grecian gusto ceased as suddenly as it had begun sixty years
before. Lord Elgin had the mortification—despite a vigorous
campaign by himself and Hamilton in favour of the Grecian
style[13]—of hearing that the new Houses of Parliament were to
be Gothic.

Yet the Elgin Marbles produced some unexpected results in
other fields. In March 1817 Haydon took his new friend John
Keats, then aged twenty-one, to see the marbles.[14] Keats's

---

* Another collection of architectural fragments from the Parthenon and Erechtheum was
removed by the architect Inwood in 1819; they were bought by the British Museum for
£40.

reaction was as dramatic as Haydon's had been nine years before. He immediately wrote two sonnets and sent them to Haydon. The first expressed his own experience.

On Seeing the Elgin Marbles

My spirit is too weak—mortality
  Weighs heavily on me like unwilling sleep,
  And each imagin'd pinnacle and steep
Of godlike hardship tells me I must die
Like a sick Eagle looking at the sky.
  Yet 'tis a gentle luxury to weep
  That I have not the cloudy winds to keep
Fresh for the opening of the morning's eye.
Such dim-conceived glories of the brain
  Bring round the heart an indescribable feud;
So do these wonders a most dizzy pain,
  That mingles Grecian grandeur with the rude
Wasting of old Time—with a billowy main—
  A sun—a shadow of a magnitude.

The second sonnet was full of extravagant praise for Haydon and contempt for the Payne Knight party.

To B. R. Haydon, with the Foregoing Sonnet on the Elgin Marbles.

Haydon, forgive me that I cannot speak
  Definitively on these mighty things;
  Forgive me that I have not Eagle's wings—
That what I want I know not where to seek:
And think that I would not be over meek
  In rolling out upfollow'd thunderings,
  Even to the steep of Heliconian springs,
Were I of ample strength for such a freak—
Think too, that all these numbers should be thine;
  Whose else? In this who touch thy vesture's hem?
For when men star'd at what was most divine
  With browless idiotism—o'erwise phlegm—
Thou hadst beheld the Hesperean shine
  Of their star in the East, and gone to worship them.

These are not Keats' best poems, yet the Elgin Marbles were

an inspiration to some of his best work. The *Ode on a Grecian Urn* and *Hyperion* each show the strong influence they exerted. 'He went again and again to see the Elgin Marbles,' wrote the biographer of his friend Severn the painter, 'and would sit for an hour or more at a time beside them rapt in revery. On one such occasion Severn came upon the young poet with eyes shining so brightly and face so lit up by some visionary rapture, that he stole quietly away.'[15] For the young poet who knew no Greek, the Elgin Marbles opened a vision of the classical world.

While the praises of the Elgin Marbles were being sung all over Europe Lord Elgin himself returned once more to the quiet life of Broomhall and his ever growing family. He devoted himself patiently to the development of his estates in an attempt to relieve the huge debts which still encumbered them. His claim for expenses for his Embassy Extraordinary to Constantinople was not finally brought to account until 1818. Instead of the expected substantial addition to the £10,000 granted in 1806, the Government, to Elgin's consternation, calculated that he had been overpaid and successfully reclaimed £38. 11s. 11d.[16] His army half-pay went entirely to paying arrears of the Elgin Fencibles long since disbanded. All Elgin had to live on was a Foreign Office pension. Oblivious to the irony he even wrote and published a treatise *On the Present State of Pauperism in Scotland*.

In 1817 news came from France that his old friend and rival, the Comte de Choiseul-Gouffier, had died. For the final time the question arose of the ownership of the metope which Elgin had accidentally obtained at the Customs House sale in 1806. Elgin had deposited it with the rest of the collection in the British Museum but it was accepted on all sides that Choiseul-Gouffier could have it back for the asking. He had not reclaimed it before he died. In 1818 it was claimed by his heirs but the Trustees of the British Museum decided, rightly, that Elgin's offer to Choiseul-Gouffier had rested on personal friendship alone and did not extend to his heirs. The claim was rejected.[17]

Choiseul-Gouffier's heirs decided to sell his collection of Greek antiquities including the other metope which Choiseul-Gouffier had obtained from Fauvel in 1788. The British Museum bought several pieces but were unable to secure the metope: it was bought by the Louvre for 25,000 francs and, with the piece of frieze that Bonaparte had confiscated from Choiseul-Gouffier, it is still one of their most treasured possessions. Unfortunately the generosity towards Lord Elgin which had characterized Choiseul-Gouffier despite their rivalry did not descend to his heirs. They filled their published account of his collection with lies and accusations against Elgin which Choiseul-Gouffier would never have allowed.[18] Yet a curious accident turned this incident to Elgin's advantage. The British Museum Catalogue of the Elgin metopes, published in 1835,* confused the history of the two metopes and invented the following pretty story.

The fourteenth [metope] had been previously removed by Monsieur le Comte de Choiseul Gouffier, and having been captured on its way to France, was purchased at a Custom House sale in London by Lord Elgin, and with a liberality, of which it is to be lamented there are so few examples, was restored to its former owner. After the death of M. Choiseul, it was purchased by the French Museum against a strong competition from the British Government for the sum of twenty-five thousand francs or about one thousand guineas.[19]

This fictitious tale with the seeming authority of the British Museum behind it, entered the Elgin story and was repeated in several accounts[20] until exposed by A. H. Smith in 1916.[21] By this curious accident the memory of Elgin's generosity to Choiseul-Gouffier, which was indeed great, was preserved.

Meanwhile Lusieri continued in Athens at Lord Elgin's expense. His work had long since been virtually abandoned not only because of his natural laziness but also because he was increasingly afflicted by rheumatism. Perhaps because he knew the effects of this disease so well himself, Elgin was unwilling to terminate Lusieri's contract although reports from travellers were far from encouraging. He himself planned to go again to Greece but never carried out his intention. In 1817 the British Ambassador at Constantinople told Elgin that the ugly pillar which had been

* Elgin was then a trustee but he refused to take any part in the publication of his former collection. This magnificent catalogue, still unamended, is still on sale at the British Museum at the original price.

built to replace the Caryatid of the Erechtheum was still causing offence and suggested that a plaster copy of the original should be sent to replace the pillar. Elgin readily agreed,[22] but a copy of artificial stone had already been sent by Lord Guilford. When it arrived in Athens the Turks declared that it was the original Caryatid returned to its place because it could not be made to stand erect in England.[23] It was never put on the building. Travellers went to see its broken pieces lying abandoned in a yard and deduced, against all the evidence, that the Turks and the Greeks cared so much for their monuments that they were too proud to accept mere substitutes.[24]

Although a few more antiquities continued to arrive from Lusieri—including a case of 610 Greek vases—Elgin decided in the middle of 1819 that he could not afford to support Lusieri any longer. He wrote him a sad letter asking him to put his accounts in order and to arrange the drawings he had made. Yet, what with the delays in correspondence and difficulties in reconciling accounts, Lusieri managed to put off the evil day. Hamilton, who had followed his more famous namesake as Minister to Naples, attempted to arrange a personal meeting with him to discuss the final winding-up of the artistic mission, but nearly two years passed and nothing was achieved. Lord Elgin, despite his own poverty, could not bring himself to cast off the old man who had once served him so well. Then suddenly on 1 March 1821 Lusieri was found dead in his house, surrounded by his unfinished drawings.*[25] He had been in Lord Elgin's service for nearly twenty-two years.

Lusieri was buried in the grounds of the Capuchin Convent and the English colony at Athens subscribed to erect a marble monument to him. It can still be seen alongside the tombstone he

---

* Within a few years Greek indignation against Lord Elgin's activities had grown so great that the following tale was recorded by a credulous English traveller:

Signor Lusieri . . . died by the breaking of a blood-vessel. The feeling of the people ran so high against him that he thought it necessary to barricade his home at night, particularly as he lived quite alone. The day of his death, the neighbourhood, surprised at his non-appearance, forced the door, and found him extended on the floor, his blood about him, and a huge black cat seated on his breast, which the people to this day believe to have been the avenging spirit, the punisher of his crimes, or else the form assumed by his own black soul; according to this latter notion, the animal was instantly killed.[26]

had carved for John Tweddell, in the wall of the English Church at Athens. In the contract signed with Elgin in Sicily in 1799 Lusieri had agreed that all his drawings and sketches should be the property of his patron. When he died he had completed only two drawings—one of the Parthenon and one of the Monument of Philopappos: innumerable others were in various stages of completion. The picture of the Monument of Philopappos eventually reached Lord Elgin and is still in the possession of the Elgin family. The others, ironically, suffered a similar fate to those of John Tweddell over twenty years before. Sealed by the British Consul in Athens in March 1821, they were moved first to Cerigo and then to Constantinople. Seven years passed before the persistent efforts of Elgin and Hamilton caused them to be sent home, but the ship that was bringing them to England sank in the Mediterranean and they were lost. All Elgin had to show from Lusieri's twenty-one years' drawing at Athens was a single water-colour of the least distinguished of the antiquities of Athens.

In 1820 Elgin returned to the House of Lords as one of the representative peers for Scotland and held the seat for the remainder of his life. In 1821 he was, with the long-hated Byron, one of the first to subscribe to the Philhellenic Committee to support the Revolutionary Forces in Greece.[27] But he was never able to resume his public career. From time to time he renewed, despairingly, his request for a British peerage, begging to be allowed to bequeath something to his family besides his debts.[28] But it was never granted. Despite his efforts his debts still pursued him, his assets were put into trust, and eventually he was obliged to live in France to escape his creditors. He died in Paris on 4 November 1841. Broomhall was put under care and maintenance, the eighth earl was obliged to spend most of his life abroad, and the debts were not finally paid off by his family until another thirty years had passed. The affair of the marbles had left a bitter legacy.

Yet in his last years Lord Elgin was granted a grain of comfort. Payne Knight was dead and the Dilettanti at last recognized their fateful mistake in condemning his collection.[29] In July 1831 the ever loyal Hamilton, now the Secretary of the Society, wrote to Elgin to say he had been elected a Member of the Dilettanti. His letter reached Lord Elgin at Leamington where he had gone—as to so many spas—in an attempt to relieve his rheumatism. Lord Elgin's reply to Hamilton, in his familiar involved style, dignified and without bitterness, expressing yet again the honest aims that had caused his downfall, is a fitting end to his story.

No-one knows more intimately than you do, that the impulses which led me to the exertions I made in Greece were wholly for the purpose of securing to Great Britain, and through it to Europe in general, the most effectual possible knowledge, and means of improving, by the excellence of Grecian art in sculpture and architecture. My success, to the vast extent it was effected, will never cease to be a matter of the utmost gratification to me. If, when it was made known to the public, twenty-five years ago, or at any reasonable time afterwards, it had been thought that the same energy would be considered useful to the Dilettanti Society, most happy should I have been to have contributed every aid in my power. But as such expectation has long since past, I really do not apprehend that I shall be thought fastidious if I decline the honour now proposed to me at this my eleventh hour.[30]

Chapter 24

Epilogue

SINCE the outbreak of the Greek Revolution in 1821, Greeks have never doubted—officially at least—that they are the descendants and heirs of Classical Hellas. Whether ruled by Bavarian kings, Western-orientated republicans, uncomprehending colonels, or Panhellenic socialists, they have consistently asserted their cultural identity with the architects and sculptors of the age of Pericles. Disowning or downgrading the thousand years of Byzantium when the Greek Church sought to extirpate 'pagan' ideals, and preferring to forget the three Ottoman centuries altogether, they have come to regard the Parthenon as the 'soul of Greece'. The fact that much of the sculpture is held in a foreign city is widely felt as a national humiliation.

In Britain there have always been people to share the Greek view even amongst those who are familiar with the discontinuities of Greek history and who claim a substantial share of the classical tradition for their own country. British Philhellenes have been proud that Lord Byron, a European poet, gave impetus to the modern Greek national myth both in his poetry and in his life, and like him, they are not unduly troubled by the numerous transformations in the Parthenon's reputation. If Pericles intended the building to celebrate the dominance of Athenians over other Hellenes, contemporary Greeks and their friends abroad see it with different eyes. Symbolic significance is not easily susceptible to factual contradiction, and unsympathetic outsiders are liable to find themselves accused of ignorance, interference, paternalism, neo-imperialism, or worse.

Ever since Mr. Hugh Hammersley's motion in the House of Commons in 1816 suggesting that the Parthenon Marbles should be held in trust for the Greeks, the question of their possible return has been a political issue. Shortly after King Otho arrived in his newly independent kingdom in 1833, one of his soldiers declared in an open letter to the British Parliament that he had heard the ghost of Lord Byron on the Acropolis calling on his countrymen to restore the exiled sculptures, and the demand has been repeated many times since. The centenary in 1924 of the death of Byron at Missolonghi seemed a propitious moment in Anglo-Hellenic relations, and there was further talk in 1941 at a time when British and Greek troops were fighting together against the German invasion. During the Cyprus emergency in the 1950s the British Government hinted—without response—that the Greeks might have the Elgin Marbles if they would call off support for EOKA; but in 1961 when friendly relations had been restored, Mr. Harold Macmillan was fiercely warned by *The Times* to dismiss from his mind any suggestion of returning them, the newspaper declaring with more feeling than knowledge that the Marbles had been bought and paid for.*

In 1965 Mr. Harold Wilson diplomatically assured the House of Commons 'there is no automatic principle which we should follow that there should be a redeployment of works of art in accordance with their origin'—the stress being on 'automatic' since a number of other antiquities had been returned willingly to their country of origin. In the early seventies a few British idealists hoped that a return of the Marbles might feature in an international political package aimed at securing the voluntary departure of the Colonels. In 1983, Greece having assumed the presidency of the European Community, Ms Melina Mercouri, the Minister of Culture, has declared her intention to pursue the issue vigorously, and a British Committee for the Restitution of the Parthenon Marbles has been formed to assist the campaign.

The arguments used on either side have altered considerably over the years. In the nineteenth and early twentieth century, it was often claimed that the Marbles were safer in London than they would be in Greece. Only good luck and bad shooting had saved the surviving monuments of the Acropolis from irreparable damage during the fighting of 1821-7, and the Greek Govern-

* This was the occasion of the cartoon reproduced as Plate VIII (*b*).

ment long lacked the resources to give the remaining antiquities proper protection from tourists. During and after the Second World War the Acropolis was again endangered by the fighting, but the Marbles in London, sheltered in the British Museum vaults and in a disused section of the London underground, were also fortunate to survive the bombs, one of which fell on the Duveen Gallery in 1940. Whether comparative security considerations have any relevance in an age of international terrorism and nuclear balance may however now be doubted. Also obsolete in the world of mass travel is the former claim that the sculptures can be seen and appreciated by more people if they remain in London than if they were to be reunited in Athens. Nor for many years has been heard the suggestion that Greece lacks the technical expertise to preserve and exhibit her antiquities properly in modern museums, even if it is unlikely that she would match the proud record of the British Museum where every fragment is on view without restriction and free of charge seven days a week.

But as somebody once said of the Irish problem, as soon as an answer is discovered, it turns out that the question has been changed. Relations between Britain and Greece are either good—and, if so, why rock the boat?—or less than good, in which case the British public would not stand for any feeble concessions to external pressure.

In hopes of easing the path if a British Government should ever need an excuse, the Greeks have promoted international efforts aimed at producing a general return from foreign museums of artifacts deemed to be of uniquely special importance to the prospective recipient countries. UNESCO, a body in which the preponderant governments have their own more intractable problems in establishing national identity, has in recent years attempted to draft guidelines incorporating such novel legal concepts as diminution of cultural dignity. However, these are at present so widely drawn that, if they were adopted and implemented, the world's great museums would be stripped and many scientific collections wastefully dispersed.

Greek Governments once tried to appeal to British sense of fair play by suggesting that the Marbles should be reunited with the other surviving sculptures on the building for which they were designed. Mr. Ioannes Gennadios, for many years Greek Minister in London (and a noted anglophile), suggested in 1890 that the architectural fragments at least might be returned, and many people who were not necessarily sympathetic to a general restoration have felt a particular twinge of guilt that the Caryatid was separated from her three colleagues who still unconcernedly carried the weight of the Erechtheum porch on their proud heads. How could Greek sculpture be properly appreciated, it was often suggested, except in the piercingly bright Greek daylight for which it was originally intended? Was not the air of Athens so clear that you could count the columns of the Parthenon from the Piraeus with the naked eye?

But nobody now suggests putting the sculptures back on the building. On the contrary, the last remaining pedimental figures and the three Caryatids have had to be brought indoors to escape the air pollution which has done more damage to the monuments of Athens in twenty years than two millennia of natural weathering. Sulphur from petrol and central heating— combining with moisture to make sulphuric acid—is eroding the surface of the marble at an alarming rate, and no satisfactory solution is at present in sight. Furthermore, the iron clamps used to join the columns which were re-erected in 1926 are now rusting, causing the marble drums to burst, and an extensive programme of emergency works, internationally financed, is under way to try to slow the inexorable deterioration.

The story of how Lord Elgin acquired his collection and eventually sold it to the British Museum is of course largely irrelevant to the question of what should happen in the changed conditions of the 1980s. A respect for the autonomy of the past is however also part of the European classical tradition which we owe to the contemporaries of Pericles, and those who distort the historical record for contemporary purposes do not strengthen their case. It is evident that Lord Elgin's aims were, from the beginning, honourable; that he obtained as much legal authority for his operations as it was possible to do in the disordered circumstances of the time; and that the Parthenon sculptures would be in a far worse state today if he, or someone else, had not removed them.

Note on the Principal Sources

By far the most important source is a long article by Arthur Hamilton Smith in the *Journal of Hellenic Studies* of 1916, 'Lord Elgin and His Collection'. Smith was Keeper of Greek and Roman Antiquities in the British Museum and had written the authoritative work on the sculpture of the Parthenon; he was also related to the Elgin family. His article, written to mark the centenary of the transfer of the Elgin Marbles to the British Museum, was intended to be part of a full-scale biography of Lord Elgin to be written by Sir Harry Wilson: but this was never completed. Smith had full access to the large collection of papers at Broomhall relating to the Elgin Marbles and gave full transcriptions of many of them. His work was extremely thorough and accurate and I have relied very heavily on it. I have used his translations of letters between Elgin and Lusieri, the originals of which are in French. Where no authority is given for any statement of mine it usually derives from Smith. His article is an indispensable guide to the material relating to the marbles in the possession of the Elgin family at Broomhall. Through the kindness of Lord Bruce I have been allowed to examine the original documents and have made a few references to Elgin Papers not used by Smith. The Elgin Papers contain copies of much diplomatic and official correspondence published elsewhere and preserved in the Public Record Office.

The other main published source is *The Letters of Mary Nisbet, Countess of Elgin*, published by John Murray in 1926. These delightful letters of Lord Elgin's first wife were known only in part to Smith. They add many illuminating details to the early part of the story.

The work (in Greek) of Ioannes Gennadios, *Lord Elgin and the Previous Archaeological Invasions of Greece especially Athens*, 1930, is the first which examines the reaction of the travellers in any detail; it does not, however, take account of the Nisbet letters.

The Farington Diary, published in 1922, provides much information on the opinions of English artists about Lord Elgin's expedition and the marbles. A typescript of the whole diary, which was not published in full, is in the Print Room of the British Museum. I have referred to the Farington Diary by the date of the entries only, noting which parts have been published.

For the history of the French and British expeditions to Egypt I have relied on the late J. Christopher Herold's *Bonaparte in Egypt*, 1962. Lord Elgin's part in these events is related in the FO 78 series of records in the Public Record Office, London, and in the *Historical Manuscripts Commission's Report on the Manuscripts of J. B. Fortescue Esq. preserved at Dropmore*.

The Hunt Papers, which were very kindly given to me by Mrs. A. C. Longland, consist of a miscellaneous collection of documents which belonged to her great-grand uncle, the Reverend Philip Hunt. They are the rump of a much larger collection which was lost in the 1930's. Among the most interesting items are a series of letters by Hunt describing the voyage out, letters to Hunt from Elgin, Morier, Thomas Lacy and others, and drafts of letters from Hunt to Elgin describing his diplomatic missions to Greece.

Select Bibliography

Abbot, Charles, Lord Colchester, *Diary and Correspondence*, 1861.

Barrow, John, *Life and Correspondence of Admiral Sir William Sidney Smith GCB*, 1848.

Byron, Lord, *English Bards and Scotch Reviewers*, 1809.

— *Childe Harold's Pilgrimage*, Cantos I and II, 1812.

— *The Curse of Minerva*, 1812.

Lord Byron's Correspondence chiefly with Lady Melbourne, Mr. Hobhouse, the Hon. Douglas Kinnaird and P. B. Shelley, edited by John Murray, 1922.

Byron, A Self-Portrait, Letters and Diaries 1798 to 1824, edited by P. Quennell, 1950.

Carlyle, J. D., *Poems*, 1805.

Choiseul-Gouffier, Comte de, *Voyage Pittoresque de la Grèce*, 1782–1809.

Clarke, E. D., *The Tomb of Alexander*, 1805.

— *Greek Marbles*, 1809.

— *Travels in Various Countries of Europe, Asia and Africa*, 1811–1823.

Cockerell, C. R., *Travels in Southern Europe and the Levant 1810–1817*, 1903.

Cust, Lionel, and Colvin, Sidney, *History of the Society of Dilettanti*, 1898.

A Description of the Collection of Ancient Marbles in the British Museum, 1812–1861.

Dodwell, Edward, *A Classical and Topographical Tour through Greece*, 1819.

Douglas, Hon. F. S. N., *An Essay on Certain Points of Resemblance between the Ancient and Modern Greeks*, 1813.

Memorandum on the Subject of the Earl of Elgin's Pursuits in Greece, Editions of 1810, 1811, 1815.

Elgin, Lord, *Letter to the Editor of the Edinburgh Review on the subject of an article in No. L of that journal on 'The Remains of John Tweddell'*, 1815.

— *Postscript to a Letter to the Editor of the Edinburgh Review*, 1815.

The Farington Diary, edited by James Grieg, 1922.

The Trial of R. Fergusson, Esq., 1807.

The Trial of R. J. Fergusson, Esquire, c. 1808.

Forbin, Comte de, *Voyage dans le Levant*, 1819.

Fuller, John, *Narrative of a Tour through some parts of the Turkish Empire*, 1830.

Galt, John, *Letters from the Levant*, 1813.

— *Life and Studies of Benjamin West, Esq.*, 1816.

— *Life of Byron*, 1830.

— *Autobiography*, 1833.

Γεννάδιος, Ἰωάννης, Ὁ Λορδος Ἐλγιν και οἱ προ αὐτου ἀνα την Ἑλλαδα και τας Ἀθηνας ἰδιως ἀρχαιολογησαντες ἐπιδρομεις 1440–1837, 1930.
[Gennadios, Ioannes, *Lord Elgin and the Previous Archaeological Invasions of Greece especially Athens 1440–1837*.]

Haydon, B. R., *Autobiography and Memoirs*, new edition edited by Aldous Huxley, 1926.

— *Correspondence and Table Talk*, 1876.

— *The Diary of Benjamin Robert Haydon*, edited by Willard Bissell Pope, 1960–1963.

Herold, J. Christopher, *Bonaparte in Egypt*, 1962.

Historical Manuscripts Commission, *Report on the Mss of J. B. Fortescue Esq. preserved at Dropmore*, 1892–1927.

Hobhouse, J. C., *A Journey through Albania and other provinces of Turkey in Europe and Asia to Constantinople*, 1813.

Hughes, Rev. T. S., *Travels in Sicily, Greece and Albania*, 1820.

Hunt, Rev. Philip, *A Narrative of What is Known Respecting the Literary Remains of the Late John Tweddell*, 1816.

The Keith Papers, selected from the letters and papers of Admiral Viscount Keith. Navy Records Society, 1927–1955.

Larrabee, S. A., *English Bards and Grecian Marbles*, 1943.

Legrand, Ph.-E., 'Biographie de Louis-François-Sébastien Fauvel'. *Revue Archéologique* 3rd series XXX and XXXI, 1897.

— 'Contribution à l'Histoire des Marbres du Parthénon.' *Revue Archéologique* 3rd series XXV, 1894.

— 'Encore les Marbres du Parthénon,' *Revue Archéologique* 3rd series XXVI, 1895.

Lewis, Michael, *Napoleon and his British Captives*, 1962.

Marchand, Leslie A., *Byron, a Biography*, 1957.

Michaelis, A., *Ancient Marbles in Great Britain*, 1882.

— 'Supplement on Marbles at Broomhall', *Journal of Hellenic Studies*, 1884.

— *Der Parthenon*, 1871.

Michon, E., 'Les Fragments du Parthénon Conservés au Musée du Louvre', *Revue Archéologique*, 3rd series, XXIV, 1894.

Moore, T., *Letters and Journals of Lord Byron with Notices of his Life*, 1830/31.

Morritt of Rokeby, J. B. S., *Letters descriptive of a Journey in Europe and Asia Minor in the years 1794–1796*, 1914.

The Letters of Mary Nisbet, Countess of Elgin, 1926.

Otter, W., *The Life and Remains of the Rev. Edward Daniel Clarke*, 1824.

Report from the Select Committee of the House of Commons on the Earl of Elgin's Collection of Sculptured Marbles, 1816

Sicilianos, D., *Old and New Athens*, translated by Robert Liddell, 1960.

Smith, A. H., 'Lord Elgin and his Collection', *Journal of Hellenic Studies*, 1916.

— *The Sculptures of the Parthenon*, 1910.

— *Catalogue of Sculpture in the Department of Greek and Roman Antiquities, British Museum*, 1892.

Specimens of Antient Sculpture. Dilettanti Society, 1809 and 1835.

Spencer, Terence, *Fair Greece, Sad Relic*, 1954.

Stevens, G. P., and Others, *The Erechtheum*, 1927.

Stuart, James, and Revett, Nicholas, etc., *The Antiquities of Athens*, 1762–1816.

Todd, H. J., *Catalogue of the Archepiscopal Manuscripts in the Library at Lambeth Palace*, 1812.

— *An Account of the Greek Mss chiefly Biblical which had been in the possession of the late Professor Carlyle, the greater part of which are now deposited in the Archepiscopal Library at Lambeth Palace, c. 1820*.

Tweddell, Rev. Robert, *The Remains of John Tweddell*, Editions of 1815 and 1816.

Walpole, Rev. Robert, *Memoirs relating to European and Asiatic Turkey*, 1817.

— *Travels in Various Countries of the East*, 1820.

Walsh, Rev. Robert, *A Residence at Constantinople*, 1836.

Williams, H. W., *Travels in Italy, Greece and the Ionian Islands*, 1820.

Wittman, William, *Travels in Turkey, Asia Minor and Syria*, 1803.

Abbreviations used in the Notes

BM: British Museum.

BM Add.: British Museum Additional Mss.

BM Egerton: British Museum Egerton Mss.

Clarke, Travels: Clarke, E. D., *Travels in Various Countries of Europe, Asia and Africa.*

Cockerell: Cockerell, C. R., *Travels in Southern Europe and the Levant.*

Dodwell: Dodwell, Edward, *A Classical and Topographical Tour through Greece.*

Elgin, Letter: Elgin, Earl of, *Letter to the Editor of the Edinburgh Review on the subject of an article in No. L of that journal on 'The Remains of John Tweddell'.*

Elgin, Postscript: Elgin, Earl of, *Postscript to a Letter to the Editor of the Edinburgh Review.*

Farington: [see Note on the Principal Sources].

FO: Foreign Office Papers in the Public Record Office, London.

Fortescue: Historical Manuscripts Commission Report on the Mss of J. B. Fortescue, Esq., preserved at Dropmore.

Gennadios: Gennadios, Ioannes, *Lord Elgin and the Previous Archaeological Invasions of Greece especially Athens.*

Haydon, Autobiography: Haydon, B. R., *Autobiography and Memoirs,* new edition edited by Aldous Huxley, 1926.

Haydon, Diary: Pope, W. B., ed., *The Diary of Benjamin Robert Haydon.*

Herold: Herold, J. Christopher, *Bonaparte in Egypt.*

HMC: Historical Manuscripts Commission.

Hobhouse: Hobhouse, J. C., *A Journey through Albania and other provinces of Turkey in Europe and Asia to Constantinople.*

Hughes: Hughes, Rev. T. S., *Travels in Sicily, Greece and Albania.*

Memorandum: [Elgin, Earl of] *Memorandum on the Subject of the Earl of Elgin's Pursuits in Greece.*

NLS: National Library of Scotland Mss.

Nisbet: The Letters of Mary Nisbet, Countess of Elgin.

Select Committee Report: Report from the Select Committee of the House of Commons on the Earl of Elgin's Collection of Sculptured Marbles.

Smith: Smith, A. H., 'Lord Elgin and his Collection'.

Todd, Account: [Todd, H. J.], *An Account of the Greek Mss chiefly Biblical which had been in the possession of the late Professor Carlyle, the greater part of which are now deposited in the Archepiscopal Library at Lambeth Palace.*

Todd, Catalogue: Catalogue of the Archepiscopal Manuscripts in the Library at Lambeth Palace.

Tweddell, Remains: Tweddell, Rev. Robert, *The Remains of John Tweddell.*

Walpole, Memoirs: Walpole, Rev. Robert, *Memoirs Relating to European and Asiatic Turkey.*

Walpole, Travels: Walpole, Rev. Robert, *Travels in Various Countries of the East.*

Walsh: Walsh, Rev. Robert, *A Residence at Constantinople.*

Notes

Chapter 1. An Embassy is Arranged

1. *HMC, Fortescue,* IV, p. 359, Elgin to Grenville, 4 November 1798. Another copy is in *FO* 78/20.
2. *HMC, Fortescue,* IV p. 380.
3. Grenville informed Spencer Smith at Constantinople of Elgin's appointment on 18 December 1798 (*FO* 78/20). William Gartshore told Arthur Paget of the appointment as early as 4 December 1798. *The Paget Papers, diplomatic and other correspondence of Rt. Hon. Sir Arthur Paget, 1896,* I, p. 140.
4. *NLS,* 1055 f. 120. Elgin also alludes to his discussions with the King at Weymouth in *BM Add.,* 38266 f. 5.
5. For the Elgin Fencibles see the collection of letters in *NLS* 5085 and 5087. Much more material is among the Elgin Papers.
6. *HMC, Fortescue,* I, p. 603.
7. Earl Stanhope, *Life of Pitt,* 1861–2, IV, p. 400. For Elgin's early diplomatic career see *HMC, Fortescue,* I, II, III; *BM Add.,* 38266 f 5; *Cambridge History of British Foreign Policy,* I, pp. 206, 274.
8. *HMC, Fortescue,* II, p. 184.
9. *Ibid.,* IV, p. 276.
10. *Ibid.,* IV, p. 95.
11. E.g. *The Journal of Elizabeth Lady Holland 1791–1811,* edited by the Earl of Ilchester, 1908, I, pp. 86, 146.
12. *Tweddell, Remains,* pp. 49 ff.
13. *HMC, Fortescue,* IV, p. 425.
14. Lord Granville Leveson Gower, *Private Correspondence 1781–1821,* 1916, I, p. 262.
15. Elgin told Grenville of his engagement on 21 January 1799. *HMC, Fortescue,* IV, p. 446.
16. The information about the Nisbet fortune is contained in a short contemporary biography of Elgin in the periodical *Public Characters,* volume for

1807. Much of the other information—except where it relies on Wittman's *Travels in Turkey*—is inaccurate.

17. *The Trial of R. Fergusson Esq.*, 1807, p. 2.

18. *HMC, Fortescue*, IV, p. 446.

19. The letters between Elgin and Lady Elgin among the Elgin Papers at Broomhall leave no doubt of this.

20. That Elgin borrowed money in 1797 is clear from *Select Committee Report*, p. xiv, where he asks in 1811 for interest for fourteen years. The Elgin Papers contain several letters from the Dowager Lady Elgin about Elgin's financial difficulties at this time.

21. Colonel Anstruther to Elgin. 19 March 1799. Elgin Papers.

22. Hunt to his father, 2 April 1799, Hunt Papers.

23. *Select Committee Report*, p. 31. *Memorandum*, pp. 1 f. Haydon, *Autobiography*, p. 206. Haydon, *Diary*, I, p. 86.

24. *Select Committee Report*, p. 2.

25. Elgin to Lord Hawkesbury, 7 July 1801, FO 78/32.

26. Elgin's Report on his Embassy, 27 July 1806, FO 78/54.

27. *HMC, Fortescue*, V, p. 91.

28. *Farington*, 22, 25, and 27 April and 23 May 1799 (all unpublished). The offer to Robert Smirke is confirmed by his Ms Notes on Journal in Greece, Library of the Royal Institute of British Architects, London. See also Jonathan Mayne, *Thomas Girtin*, 1949, p. 49, who quotes *Morning Herald* of 6 May 1799.

29. Quoted in Thomas Girtin and David Loshak, *The Art of Thomas Girtin*, 1954, p. 38.

30. *Farington*, 27 April 1799 (unpublished), and 27 November 1798 (published).

31. *Select Committee Report*, p. 32.

32. *Smith*, p. 166.

33. Lord Holland, *Further Memoirs of the Whig Party 1807–1821*, 1905, p. 336. Porson told Samuel Rogers that the offer had not been properly made. *Recollections of the Table-Talk of Samuel Rogers to which is added Porsoniana*, 1856, p. 319.

34. *Walpole, Memoirs*, pp. xv, 84.

35. *Gentleman's Magazine*, 69, p. 369.

36. This is clear from a number of letters of Carlyle in the Ipswich and East Suffolk Record Office. Reference HA 174: 1026/68.

37. Elgin, *Postscript*, p. 17.

38. This is clear from Elgin's letter to Lord Liverpool. *BM Add.*, 38266 f 5.

39. *HMC, Fortescue*, V, p. 72.

40. *BM Add.*, 38266 f 5.

41. Hunt to his father, 28 August 1799, Hunt Papers.

42. *HMC, Fortescue*, V, p. 250.

43. Elgin to Dowager Lady Elgin, 10 September 1800, Elgin Papers.

44. Hunt to his father, 17 July 1799, Hunt Papers.

Chapter 2. Great Events in the Levant

For the general history in this chapter I have relied to a great extent on J. Christopher Herold, *Bonaparte in Egypt*, 1962, an excellent and well documented account. Additional information comes from the FO 78 series in the Public Record Office, London.

1. FO 78/24.
2. Quoted by *Herold*, p. 133.
3. C. A. Wood, *A History of the Levant Company*, 1935.
4. FO 78/20.
5. The circumstances in which the Military Mission was sent are related in FO 78/25–27. Some details of its activities are in William Wittman, *Travels in Turkey, Asia Minor and Syria*, 1803.
6. John Barrow, *Life and Correspondence of Admiral Sir William Sidney Smith GCB*, 1848.

Chapter 3. The Voyage Out

1. *Nisbet*, p. 7.
2. Hunt to his father, 16 September 1799, Hunt Papers.
3. Rev. Philip Hunt, *A Narrative of What is Known Respecting the Literary Remains of the Late John Tweddell*, 1816, p. 11.
4. Hunt to his father, 16 September 1799, Hunt Papers.
5. From Morier's Journal published in *Courier de l'Egypte* No. 70, p. 1.
6. Hunt to his sister, 22 September 1799, Hunt Papers.
7. *Nisbet*, pp. 12 ff.
8. Ibid., p. 17.
9. Ibid., p. 19.
10. *Herold*, p. 332.
11. *Nisbet*, p. 22.
12. Ibid., p. 25.
13. A. Michaelis, *Ancient Marbles in Great Britain*, 1882, pp. 109 ff.
14. Ibid., p. 111. M. L. Clarke, *Greek Studies in England, 1700–1830*, 1945, p. 186.
15. *Smith*, p. 168.
16. *Smith*, p. 169 and Elgin to Dowager Lady Elgin, 5 October 1799, Elgin Papers.
17. *Nisbet*, pp. 30 ff.
18. Quoted in *Smith*, p. 171.
19. There is an account of Theodor's extraordinary career by Karl Obser in *Ekkhart-Jahrbuch*, 1930, p. 18. An engraved self-portrait of Theodor is in the Victoria and Albert Museum. For this information I am grateful to Frau Margrit E. Velte of Karlsruhe.

20. *Smith*, pp. 171 ff.
21. *Nisbet*, p. 75.

Chapter 4. Reception at Constantinople
1. *Tweddell, Remains*, p. 262. *HMC, Fortescue*, IV, p. 438. Smith to Nelson, 24 January 1799, quoted in John Barrow, *Life and Correspondence of Admiral Sir William Sidney Smith GCB*, 1848, I, p. 251.
2. Spencer Smith to Grenville, 30 October 1799, FO 78/22.
3. *HMC, Fortescue*, IV, pp. 476 ff.
4. Ibid., V, p. 316.
5. John Barrow, op. cit., I, p. 381.
6. *Nisbet*, pp. 34 ff. Hunt letters among Hunt Papers.
7. FO 78/26.
8. *Nisbet*, p. 39.
9. *Smith*, p. 182.
10. *Memorandum*, 1815 edition, p. 35.
11. William Wittman, *Travels in Turkey, Asia Minor and Syria*, 1803, p. 65.
12. *Walpole, Memoirs*, p. 98.
13. William Wittman, op. cit., p. 65.
14. *Walsh*, I, p. 206.
15. *Nisbet*, p. 48.
16. Carlyle to Dr. Paley, 10 December 1799, Ipswich and East Suffolk Record Office HA 174:1026/68/10.
17. *Nisbet*, p. 56.
18. My account of Elgin's reception is a compound of several sources:
    (a) Elgin's report and claim for expenses FO 78/24.
    (b) Lady Elgin's letters, *Nisbet*, pp. 40 ff.
    (c) A long and detailed letter from Carlyle to Dr. Paley in the Ipswich and East Suffolk Record Office. HA 174: 1026/68/10.
    (d) Letter from Hunt to his father, 9 December 1799, Hunt Papers.
19. FO 78/24.

Chapter 5. The Smith Brothers
My source for events in Egypt is again mainly Herold's *Bonaparte in Egypt*. Much information about the Smith brothers is in John Barrow's *Life and Correspondence of Admiral Sir William Sidney Smith*, 1848.
1. Spencer Smith to Grenville, 10 June 1799, FO 78/22.
2. For Elgin's initial difficulties with Spencer Smith see a series of letters in FO 78/24 and 28 and others in *HMC, Fortescue*, VI.
3. Navy Records Society, *Private Papers of George, Second Earl Spencer*, 1913–24, IV, p. 85. Sidney Smith was a godson of Lady Elgin's grandmother and 'always considered her a sort of relation'. Smith to Elgin, 17 December 1799, Elgin Papers.

4. Navy Records Society, op. cit., IV, p. 90.
5. Elgin to Sir Sidney Smith, 17 December 1799, FO 78/24.
6. *HMC, Fortescue*, VI, p. 89.
7. Elgin to Grenville, 16 February 1800, FO 78/28.
8. Elgin to Nelson, 18 February 1800, FO 78/28.
9. Elgin to Grenville, 25 February 1800, FO 78/28. The Admiralty's letter to Lord Keith is published in Navy Records Society, *The Keith Papers*, 1927–1955, II, p. 203.
10. Elgin to Grenville, 10 March 1800, FO 78/28.
11. Elgin to Grenville, 9 May 1800, FO 78/29.
12. Published by the French in *Courier de l'Egypte* No. 70, 73, 74.
13. Grenville to Elgin, 28 March 1800, FO 78/28.
14. This was the view of the French in Egypt after the capture of Morier's papers, *Courier de l'Egypte* No. 70, 73, 74, 79. See also John Barrow, op. cit., I, pp. 394, 400; II, pp. 50, 60.
15. *Correspondance de Napoléon Ier Publiée par ordre de l'Empereur Napoléon III*, 8, p. 315.
16. *Nisbet*, pp. 249, 278, 289.
17. *BM Add.* 38266 f. 5.
18. By J. G. Alger, *Napoleon's English Visitors and Captives*, 1904. I cannot find Alger's source.
19. *Le Jeu de Whist. Traité elementaire des lois . . . traduit de l'anglais et redigé par un Amateur Anglais*, 1819. Smith's name is given in the edition of 1838.
20. This section is taken mainly from *Nisbet*.
21. The damage to Elgin's nose is described in letters of Lady Elgin to her mother, 11 March 1802, and to the Dowager Lady Elgin, 25 March 1802, Elgin Papers.
22. There is a long series of letters of complaint about the Smith brothers in FO 78/28, 29, 30. Others are in *HMC, Fortescue*, VI.
23. *HMC, Fortescue*, VI, p. 347.
24. *Nisbet*, p. 147.
25. *Ibid.*, pp. 101, 141, 210.

Chapter 6. Work Begins at Athens

1. *Hobhouse*, p. 293. Forbin, *Voyage dans le Levant*, 1819, gives the population as 12,000, but, to judge from the numerous views of Athens, this seems most unlikely.
2. D. Sicilianos, *Old and New Athens*, translated by Robert Liddell, 1960, p. 137.
3. *Dodwell*, I, p. 358.
4. A list of Revenues of the Ottoman Empire is in *FO 78/29*.
5. Sicilianos, op. cit., p. 136. Most travellers in Elgin's time and later believed that Athens was still under the tutelage of the Chief of the Black Eunuchs.

6. Plutarch, *Pericles*, xii.
7. R. Chandler, *Travels in Greece*, 1776, p. 51.
8. The latest exhaustive list of fragments is in A. H. Smith, *The Parthenon*, 1910. Information on the earlier history of these and of several lost fragments is in A. Michaelis, *Der Parthenon*, 1871, and *Ancient Marbles in Great Britain*, 1882. An up-to-date list of pediment fragments is in Frank Brommer's *Die Skulpturen der Parthenon-Giebel*, 1963, pp. 62 ff; and of metope fragments in the same writer's 'Fragmente Der Parthenonmetopen', *Jahrbuch des Deutschen Archäologischen Instituts*, 1960, pp. 37 ff. For the Vatican fragments see *Journal of Hellenic Studies*, 58 (1938), p. 276 and *Fasti Archaeologici*, II, 1947, item 243. For the Würzburg fragment see G. Rodenwaldt, *Köpfe von den Südmetopen des Parthenon*, Berlin 1948, p. 13.
9. Fauvel's biography is contained in a series of articles by Ph.-E. Legrand in *Revue Archéologique*, 3rd series, XXX and XXXI (1897).
10. Ibid., XXX, p. 57.
11. For the detailed history of these pieces see ibid., XXIV, as corrected by XXV and XXVI.
12. J. B. S. Morritt, *Letters descriptive of a Journey in Europe and Asia Minor in the years 1794–1796*, 1914. Letter of 18 January 1795. *Select Committee Report*, p. 130.
13. John Fuller, *Narrative of a Tour through some parts of the Turkish Empire*, 1830, p. 545. H. W. Williams, *Travels in Italy, Greece and the Ionian Isles*, 1820, II, p. 331.

Chapter 7. In Search of Ancient Manuscripts

The chief source for Carlyle's activities in the East is *Walpole, Memoirs* and *Walpole, Travels*. The letters to the Bishop of Durham quoted by Walpole, with some others, are preserved in the Ipswich and East Suffolk Record Office under reference HA 174:1026/68. Some Ms journals of Carlyle are in the *BM*. Others are quoted in his (posthumous) *Poems*, 1805. A short sketch of Carlyle's earlier life is in *Public Characters*, 1802/3.

1. J. Dallaway, *Constantinople ancient and modern with excursions to the shores and islands of the Archipelago and to the Troad*, 1797, p. 23. It is clear from a letter of Carlyle to Dr. Paley in the Ipswich and East Suffolk Record Office that Carlyle was very familiar with Dallaway's work.
2. *BM Add.*, 27604 f 5.
3. J. H. Marsden, *Memoir of the Life and Writings of W. M. Leake*, 1864, p. 7, gives an account of the circumstances in which the journey was decided. The journey itself is described by Leake in *Walpole, Travels*, p. 185.
4. Hunt Papers.
5. J. D. Carlyle, *Poems*, 1805, p. 13.
6. Ibid., p. 16.
7. *Walpole, Memoirs*, p. 162.

8. Ibid., p. 172.

9. *Clarke, Travels.*

10. Clarke's antipathy to Carlyle is clearly demonstrated in letters quoted in W. Otter, *Life and Remains of the Rev. Edward Daniel Clarke*, 1824, pp. 485, 497, 505. The quarrel was the talk of Constantinople in January 1802 (see *Nisbet*, p. 165) and of Egypt in April 1802 (see *Life of General Sir Robert Wilson*, edited by H. Randolph, 1862, pp. 163, 233).

11. *Clarke, Travels*, Part II, Section 1, p. 82. 'Tomb of Ajax'; Part II, Section 3, p. 12. 'Marathon Village'. The view of the plain of Marathon (Part II, Section 3, p. 14) is said on the engraving to be from a sketch by Lusieri: in Clarke's list of contents it is described as 'by the author'. Clarke also incorporated a drawing by Theodor the Calmuck (*Travels*, II, 2, p. 598). Another—of the Voivode, may also be by him (*Travels*, II, 3, p. 2).

12. *Walpole, Memoirs*, p. 138.

13. Hunt's account of Athos is in *Walpole, Memoirs*, pp. 198 ff.; Carlyle's is in *BM Add.*, 27604.

14. *Elgin, Postscript*, p. 17.

Chapter 8. The Conquest of Egypt and its Results

For the general history in this chapter I have relied, as usual, mainly on *Herold*. Elgin's part is documented in the *FO* 78 series in the Public Record Office.

1. FO 78/30–31. FO 78/54.

2. Elgin to Hawkesbury, 16 July 1801. FO 78/32.

3. FO 78/33.

4. *Nisbet*, p. 116, f.

5. Ibid., p. 119.

6. Ibid., p. 119.

7. FO 78/33. *Nisbet*, pp. 117 ff.

8. Ibid., p. 249, 278. *BM Add.*, 38266 f 5.

9. FO 78/33. The Embassy was burnt down in 1831. An engraving appears in *Walsh*, II, Frontispiece.

10. FO 78/35. *Nisbet*, pp. 162 ff.

11. Ibid., p. 171.

12. *BM Add.*, 38571 f 19.

13. Navy Records Society, *The Keith Papers*, 1927–1955, II, p. 406.

Chapter 9. The Firman

1. *Nisbet*, p. 92.

2. Quoted in *Smith*, p. 190.

3. Pisani to Elgin, 6 July 1801, Elgin Papers.

4. An Italian version of the firman, in the handwriting of Pisani the British interpreter at Constantinople, is among the Hunt Papers. Clearly this is the

document from which Hunt provided the translation for the Select Committee (*Select Committee Report*, pp. 141, xxiv). A search among the Turkish archives at Istanbul made possible by the kindness of Dr. Ilhan Özdil, the Turkish Cultural Attaché in London and Mr. Mithat Sertioğlu, the Director General of Archives, has unfortunately failed to reveal a copy of the original Turkish version.

5. *Nisbet*, p. 97.
6. Elgin to Lusieri, 10 July 1801. Quoted in *Smith*, p. 191.
7. Elgin to Lord Hawkesbury, 7 July 1801. *FO* 78/32. Hunt's instructions are among the Hunt Papers.
8. *Select Committee Report*, pp. 143, 146 .
9. These details are from a letter of Hunt to Elgin, 31 July 1801, among the Elgin Papers. Smith, although quoting much of the letter, makes no mention of them.
10. *Select Committee Report*, p. 146.
11. Ibid., p. 142.
12. Hunt to Elgin, 31 July 1801, Elgin Papers.
13. *Nisbet*, p. 123. Hunt wrote a very similar letter on 21 August 1801 to Lord Upper Ossory, Hunt Papers.
14. *Nisbet*, p. 123.
15. *Smith*, p. 197.
16. Ibid., p. 201.
17. Hunt to Lord Upper Ossory, 21 August 1801. Hunt Papers.
18. Hunt to Elgin, 21 August 1801. Elgin Papers.
19. *Select Committee Report*, p. 41.
20. *Smith*, p. 346.
21. Ibid., p. 196.
22. Ibid., p. 357 referring to *Revue Archéologique*, XXIV and XXVI.
23. He had no reason to. A. L. Millin's *Description d'un Bas Relief du Parthénon actuellement au Musée Napoléon*, which was incorporated as an appendix in the 1811 and 1815 editions of the *Memorandum*, says that the slab was detached from the Parthenon, 'a été détaché'. After Choiseul-Gouffier's death in 1817 the sale catalogue of his collection emphasized that the metope was found on the ground, L. J. J. Dubois, *Catalogue d'Antiquités . . . formant la collection de . . . M. le Comte de Choiseul-Gouffier*, Paris, 1818. This catalogue contained so many errors that the British Museum did well to ignore it.
24. *Description of the Collection of Ancient Marbles in the British Museum*, VIII, 1839, p. 97.

Chapter 10. 'The Last Poor Plunder from a Bleeding Land'
1. *Memorandum*, 1815 edition, p. 15.
2. *Select Committee Report*, p. 144.

3. Quoted in *Smith*, p. 207.

4. Ms Notes on Journal in Greece by Sir Robert Smirke. Library of the Royal Institute of British Architects, London.

5. Quoted in *Smith*, p. 196.

6. Navy Records Society, *The Keith Papers*, 1927–1955, II, p. 405.

7. Quoted in *Smith*, p. 205.

8. Lacy to Hunt, 8 October 1801. Hunt Papers.

9. *Dodwell*, I, p. 322.

10. *Clarke, Travels*, Section II, Part 2, p. 483.

11. *Dodwell*, I, p. 325. Dodwell's remarks on this fragment seem to be confirmed by a letter of Fauvel quoted in *Bulletin de la Société Nationale des Antiquaires de la France*, sér 6, 1900, p. 245. Dodwell's collection is now dispersed. The *Notice sur le Musée Dodwell et Catalogue Raisonné des objets qu'il contient*, Rome 1837 lists seven architectural fragments from the Parthenon and a '*testa barbata prov d'Atene*'. A metope fragment from the Dodwell collection is in Munich. Frank Brommer, 'Fragmente Der Parthenon-metopen' *Jahrbuch Des Deutschen Archäologischen Instituts*, 1960, p. 68.

12. E. D. Clarke, *The Tomb of Alexander*, 1805.

13. W. Otter, *Life and Remains of Rev. Edward Daniel Clarke*, 1824, p. 505.

14. *Clarke, Travels*, Section, II, Part 2, p. 475.

15. See G. P. Stevens and others, *The Erechtheum*, 1927, p. 502.

16. R. Chandler, *Travels in Greece*, 1776, p. 191.

17. E. D. Clarke, *Greek Marbles*, 1809, p. 32.

18. W. Otter, op. cit., p. 505.

19. *Clarke, Travels*, Part II, Section 2, p. 784.

20. Quoted in *Smith*, p. 206.

21. W. Otter, op. cit., p. 516.

22. E. D. Clarke, *Greek Marbles*, 1809, pp. 34 ff.

23. D. Sicilianos, *Old and New Athens*, translated by Robert Liddell, 1960, p. 229.

24. Quoted in *Smith*, p. 230.

25. Ibid., p. 206. Hunt had also suggested seizing Fauvel's collection in letters to Elgin on 31 July 1801 and 8 August 1801. Elgin Papers.

26. *Smith*, p. 362. See also note 5 to Chapter 19.

27. *Nisbet*, p. 154.

28. Elgin to Grenville, 3 July 1800. FO 78/28.

29. Elgin to Hawkesbury, 7 July 1801. FO 78/32.

30. *Nisbet*, p. 140.

31. Quoted in *Smith*, p. 211.

32. Lady Elgin to Elgin, 19 May 1802. Elgin Papers.

33. Lady Elgin to Elgin, 22 May 1802. Elgin Papers.

34. *Nisbet*, p. 199.

35. Quoted in *Smith*, p. 214; *Nisbet*, p. 187.
36. Ibid., p. 207; *FO* 78/36.
37. *Nisbet*, pp. 210 ff.
38. Lusieri to Elgin, 16 September 1802. Quoted in *Smith*, p. 232. Smith connects this with the destruction of the cornice mentioned by Clarke and repeated by Byron (see p. 103). Clarke had however left Athens in December 1801.
39. Quoted in *Smith*, p. 209.
40. Ibid., p. 217, Cf. *Nisbet*, p. 195.
41. Quoted in *Smith*, p. 218. Cf. *Nisbet*, p. 196.
42. Sir E. A. Wallis Budge, *The Rosetta Stone*, 1929.
43. E. D. Clarke, *The Tomb of Alexander*, 1805, p. 38.
44. *Annual Register*, 1859, p. 430.
45. Quoted in *Smith*, p. 233.
46. Ibid., p. 237. A slightly different version is in the Hunt Papers.
47. *Smith*, p. 239.
48. Ibid., p. 240. Captain Clarke's own account of the incident is given in William Falconer, *The Shipwreck*, edited by J. S. Clarke, 1811, p. 207.
49. *Nisbet*, pp. 232, 334.
50. Elgin to Lord Hawkesbury, 13 January 1803. *FO* 78/38.
51. Quoted in *Smith*, p. 234.

Chapter 11. Prisoner of War

For the general story of the British Prisoners in France see Michael Lewis, *Napoleon and his British Captives*, 1962. Many details of the Elgins' life at this time are to be found in *Nisbet*.

1. Hunt to Elgin, 19 December 1802. Hunt Papers.
2. *Moniteur*, No. 130.
3. *Nisbet*, p. 286. The passport given by the French Ambassador in Naples to Lord Elgin and his party is among the Elgin Papers.
4. Elgin to King of Prussia, 24 May 1803. *FO* 27/68.
5. *Nisbet*, p. 239.
6. Ibid., pp. 238 ff., 248 ff.
7. *Correspondance de Napoléon 1er Publiée par ordre de l'Empereur Napoléon III*, 8, p. 387.
8. *Nisbet*, p. 263.
9. Ibid., p. 259.
10. Quoted in *Smith*, p. 360; *Nisbet*, p. 259.
11. *Revue Archéologique*, XXIV, p. 92, XXVI, p. 238.
12. Ibid., XXIV, p. 88.
13. Ibid., XXX, p. 389.
14. Quoted in full in Edward Smith, *Life of Sir Joseph Banks*, 1911, p. 209. The subsequent story is told in *Smith*, pp. 358 ff.
15. *Farington*, 5 December 1806 (published).

16. *Revue Archéologique*, XXVI, p. 238.
17. Quoted in *Bulletin de la Société Nationale des Antiquaires de la France*, Sér. 6, 1900, p. 245.
18. *Nisbet*, p. 278.
19. Ibid., p. 249.
20. *Correspondance de Napoléon 1ᵉʳ Publiée par ordre de l'Empereur Napoléon III*, 8, p. 315.
21. See *Nisbet* and a series of letters in *FO* 27/68.
22. The fullest account of this puzzling episode is Sir Walter Scott, *Life of Buonaparte*, chapter cxxix, which derived from Elgin himself (See *NLS* 3902 f 95). Other evidence is in *Nisbet* and *BM Add.*, 38266 f 5. The 'confession' of the prisoner called Rivoire is in Lewis Goldsmith, *Recueil de decrets, ordonnances etc de Napoléon Bonaparte*, 1813, I, p. 1054.
23. *Nisbet*, p. 296.
24. Ibid., p. 321.
25. Ibid., p. 351.
26. E. d'Hauterive, *La Police Secrète du Premier Empire, Bulletins Quotidiens adressés par Fouché a l'empereur*, 1908, I, p. 387.
27. Michael Lewis, *Napoleon and his British Captives*, 1962, p. 183. For Ferguson see two pamphlets, *The Trial of R. Fergusson Esq.* 1807, and *The Trial of R. J. Fergusson Esquire*, c. 1808. Also the record of the divorce trial, 11 March 1808, before the Commissary Court of Edinburgh in the Scottish Register Office in Edinburgh.
28. *Nisbet*, p. 240.
29. *Select Committee Report*, p. 43.
30. The truth about Elgin's imprisonment at Melun is very difficult to disentangle. Fouché's report to Napoleon of 26 September 1805 (d'Hauterive, op. cit., II, p. 101) reads: '*Lord Elgin, Macmahon, Henri Seymour, Lord Yarmouth, sont autorisés à vivre à Melun sur parole.*' Since Lady Elgin had not yet left Paris this squares with Elgin's statement to the Select Committee that he was living with his family. On the other hand two later reports, of the 10 February 1806 (d'Hauterive, op. cit., II, p. 257) and 26 February 1806 (ibid., p. 276) seem to bear on the incident. The first reports the arrival at the Turkish embassy in Paris of letters for Lord Elgin; the second reports that Elgin and others were publicly and ostentatiously giving help to Austrian and Russian prisoners. Lord Elgin might have been arrested for the activities reported in the second but, because the letters from Turkey arrived at the same time, he might have connected his arrest with them. This explanation does not, however, square with his statement to the Select Committee that the incident occurred in 1805 when he was with his family.
31. *Memorandum*, 1815 edition, p. 93, Elgin to Spencer Perceval, 6 May 1811, *BM Add.*, 38246 f 119; Elgin to Long, *Select Committee Report*, p. vii.

32. *The Times*, 16 December, 1805.
33. *NLS*, 1709 f 202.
34. *BM Add.*, 38266 f 5.

Chapter 12. Lusieri on His Own 1803–1806

1. *Smith*, p. 255. The Calmuck went to Paris in August 1805 '*pour suivre une affaire contre Lord Elgin*'. d'Hauterive, *La Police Secrète du Premier Empire*, 1908–, II, p. 45.
2. Elgin Drawings in BM Greek and Roman Department.
3. Hunt to Elgin, 29 December 1802. Hunt Papers.
4. Hunt to Hamilton, 13 December 1802. Hunt Papers. A copy of Gavallo's letter is also in existence.
5. W. Otter, *Life and Remains of Rev. Edward Daniel Clarke*, 1824, pp. 502, 505.
6. Quoted in *Smith*, p. 236.
7. Ms Notes on Journal in Greece. Library of the Royal Institute of British Architects, London.
8. In 1801 Morier published a *Memoir of a Campaign with the Ottoman Army in Egypt*. That this was unauthorized and caused a breach with Elgin is clear from a letter from Lady Elgin to Dowager Lady Elgin, 12 June 1802. Elgin Papers.
9. *Revue Archéologique* XXX, p. 389.
10. Quoted in *Smith*, p. 258.
11. Ibid., p. 257.
12. Lord Aberdeen's Ms Diary. BM Department of Greek and Roman Antiquities.
13. A list of antiquities shipped by Gropius on Lord Aberdeen's account is in *BM Add.*, 43256 f 6.
14. Quoted in *Smith*, p. 261.

Chapter 13. Homecoming

1. The sources for this passage are the two pamphlets *The Trial of R. Fergusson Esq.*, 1807, and *The Trial of R. J. Fergusson Esquire, c.* 1808, and the official records of Elgin's divorce suit before the Commissary Court of Edinburgh in March 1808 in the Scottish Record Office, Edinburgh.
2. Quoted in *The Trial of R. Fergusson Esq.*, p. 6.
3. Ibid., p. 10.
4. Quoted in the Commissary Court Record.
5. Quoted in *The Trial of R. Fergusson Esq.*, p. 32.
6. Ibid., p. 19.
7. The full titles of the pamphlets give an idea of their style: *The Trial of R. J. Fergusson Esquire for Adultery with the Countess of Elgin, wife of the Earl of Elgin, in the Sherriff's Court on December the 22nd 1807. Damages Ten Thousand Pounds!!!*; *The Trial of R. Fergusson Esq. for Crim. Con. with the*

Rt. Hon. Lady Elgin before R. Birchall Esq., Under Sherriff, in the Sherriff's Court Tuesday Dec 22 1807. £10,000 Damages. With a Biographical Sketch of the Life of Lady Elgin. See also Sir Walter Scott's letters to Lady Abercorn in *Familiar Letters of Sir Walter Scott*, 1894, I, pp. 92, 116.

8. *Nisbet*, p. 248.
9. Ibid., p. 306.
10. *BM Add.*, 38266 f 5.
11. *HMC, Fortescue*, II, p. 184.
12. *Nisbet*, p. 326.
13. Ibid., p. 161.
14. *FO* 78/54.
15. *Smith*, p. 312.
16. *BM Add.*, 38266 f 5.
17. *Smith*, p. 312.
18. Sir N. H. Nicholas, *Letters and Despatches of Nelson*, 1845–6, V, p. 478.
19. *Select Committee Report*, p. xi.
20. *BM Add.*, 38266 f 5.
21. Rev. Philip Hunt, *A Narrative of What is Known Respecting the Literary Remains of the Late John Tweddell*, 1816, p. 4; *NLS* 5645 f 210.
22. *Smith*, p. 295.
23. Ibid., p. 357. *Select Committee Report*, p. 44.
24. Some amusing stories of Italian restorations are in J. T. Smith, *Nollekens and his Times*, 1828, I, p. 10.
25. Quoted in *Smith*, p. 227.
26. *Memorandum*, 1815 edition, p. 39.
27. *Farington*, 5 December 1806 (published).
28. *Smith*, p. 297.
29. B. R. Haydon, *Correspondence and Table Talk*, 1876, I, p. 256. Elgin was still talking about restorations as late as 1814. *Smith*, p. 318.

Chapter 14. The Second Collection

1. *Smith*, pp. 266 ff., *Revue Archéologique*, XXX, p. 389.
2. *BM Add.*, 40096 f 21. Elgin to Mulgrave, 16 February 1808.
3. Quoted in *Smith*, p. 269.
4. Ibid., p. 269.
5. Ibid., p. 273.
6. Ibid., p. 276.
7. *FO* 78/67.
8. Quoted in *Smith*, p. 279.
9. This seems to be the meaning of the entry for 29 April 1811 in *Diary and Correspondence of Charles Abbott, Lord Colchester.* 1861. See also Sir Robert Adair, *The Negociations for the Peace of the Dardanelles in 1808–9*, 1845, I, p. 272. The original of this letter and the letter to which it is a reply are in *FO* 78/64.

10. *FO* 78/68.

11. *FO* 78/68. Adair to Wellesley, February 22 1810. A slightly different version dated 27 February is quoted in *Smith*, p. 279. The fact is recorded in Adair, op. cit., II, p. 6.

12. John Galt, *The Life and Studies of Benjamin West, Esq.*, 1816, II, p. 75.

13. Quoted in *Smith*, p. 280

14. John Galt, *Autobiography*, 1833, I, p. 159.

15. *Hobhouse*, p. 292.

16. Ibid., p. 346.

17. *Childe Harold's Pilgrimage*, Canto II, Note 2.

18. Ibid., Canto II, Note 6.

19. I do not know for certain whether Lusieri was legally married to Nicolo Giraud's sister. In *Lord Byron's Correspondence*, edited by John Murray, 1922, Nicolo is referred to once as 'Lusieri's wife's brother' (I, 13); and once as the 'brother of Lusieri's should-be wife' (I, 23); In *Byron, A Self-Portrait*, edited by Peter Quennell, 1950, he is referred to in another letter as the 'brother of Lusieri's spouse' (I, 83). An apparently official document (quoted in *Revue Archéologique*, XXX, p. 385) mentions among the French colony at Athens '*la veuve du sieur Giraud dont la fille a épousé un Italien sous protection anglais*'.

20. T. Moore, *Byron*, chapter XII.

21. *Lord Byron's Correspondence*, edited by John Murray, 1922, I, p. 43. See also Leslie A. Marchand, *Byron, a Biography*, 1957, I, p. 282.

22. *Smith*, p. 313.

Chapter 15. Artists and Dilettanti

1. Flaxman had, however, shown an interest in the fragment of the Parthenon frieze owned by the Dilettanti (Margaret Whinney, *Sculpture in Britain 1530–1830*, 1964, p. 185) and in Choiseul-Gouffier's casts (David Irwin, *English Neoclassical Art*, 1966, p. 73).

2. Quoted in *Smith*, p. 297.

3. *Haydon, Diary*, II, p. 15.

4. Henry Crabb Robertson, *Diary, Reminiscences and Correspondence*, 1869, I, p. 395.

5. *Farington*, 30 March 1808 (published).

6. Published as an Appendix to the *Memorandum*.

7. *Farington*, 2 March 1809 (unpublished).

8. Ibid., 27 February 1808 (published).

9. Ibid., 6 June 1807 (published).

10. Ibid., 27 February and 30 March 1808 (published).

11. Turner to Elgin, 7 August 1806. Elgin Papers.

12. W. T. Whitley, *Art in England 1800–1820*, 1928, p. 135.

13. *Farington*, 20 June 1808 (published).

14. Ibid., 29 July 1808 (published).
15. Quoted in *Smith*, p. 306.
16. *Memorandum*, 1811 edition, p. 42. The reference was removed from the 1815 edition, perhaps as a result of some scornful remarks in *Clarke, Travels*, Part II, Section 2, p. 485.
17. Haydon, *Autobiography*, p. 66.
18. Ibid., p. 68.
19. Ibid., p. 69.
20. Haydon, *Diary*, I, p. 15.
21. Ibid., I, p. 27.
22. Ibid., I, p. 28.
23. Ibid., I, p. 29.
24. *Quarterly Review*, XIV, p. 533.
25. Richard Payne Knight, *An Analytic Inquiry into the Principles of Taste*, 1805, p. 4.
26. Haydon, *Autobiography*, p. 207. *Select Committee Report*, p. v.
27. George Wheler and Dr. Spon, *A Journey into Greece*, 1682, p. 361.
28. E.g. letter from Hunt, February 1805, in *Nisbet*, p. 334. Fauvel who obtained and lost the head of one of these figures also believed this story. See *Revue Archéologique*, XXXI, p. 97, *Select Committee Report*, pp. 24, 118.
29. *Farington*, 30 March 1808 (published).
30. *Select Committee Report*, p. xxii.
31. *Specimens of Antient Sculpture*, 1809, I, p. xxxix.
32. William Wilkins, *Atheniensia*, 1816, pp. 119 f.
33. Lionel Cust and Sidney Colvin, *History of the Society of Dilettanti*, 1898, p. 133.
34. Leslie A. Marchand, *Byron, a Biography*, 1957, I, p. 221. Marchand obtained this information from Hobhouse's unpublished diary. See also *Don Juan Canto III* a spurious piece of Byroniana published in 1819. Notes. 'Lord Byron took many sketches of the ruins of Athens and its environs and, I understand, expressed his opinion that the Elgin Marbles were of a modern date.'

Chapter *16*. Elgin Offers his First Collection to the Government

1. Sir George Jackson, *The Bath Archives*, 1873, p. 409.
2. Quoted in *Smith*, p. 306.
3. *Farington*, 11 December 1802 (unpublished).
4. A copy is in *NLS* 1709 f 204. Most of it is published in *Nisbet*, p. 328.
5. Quoted in *Smith*, p. 308.
6. *Description d'un bas relief du Parthénon actuellement au Musée Napoléon* by A. L. Millin. *Memorandum*, 1811 edition, p. 72.
7. *Select Committee Report*, p. viii.
8. *BM Add.*, 38246 f 119.

9. *BM Add.*, 38191 f 197.
10. *Diary and Correspondence of Charles Abbott, Lord Colchester*, 1861, II, p. 330.
    Quoted in *Smith*, p. 311.
11. *Smith*, p. 313.

Chapter 17. Poets and Travellers
1. Byron to Hobhouse, 31 July 1811. Quoted in *Lord Byron's Correspondence*,
    edited by John Murray, 1922, I, p. 43.
2. T. Moore, *Byron*, chapter XI.
3. *Childe Harold's Pilgrimage*, II, xi ff.
4. *BM Egerton* 2869 f 7. Byron to Clarke, 19 January 1812.
5. *Childe Harold's Pilgrimage*, Canto II, Note 6. Byron says that Aberdeen
    completely disowned Gropius' collecting activities. It is clear, however,
    from a letter of Hamilton to Elgin (2 May 1809. Elgin Papers) that Aber-
    deen at that time was laying claim to the vases collected by Gropius. The
    occasion of Byron's apology to Aberdeen is described in *BM Add.*, 43230
    f 114.
6. *BM Egerton* 2027.
7. A. Michaelis, *Ancient Marbles in Great Britain*, 1882, p. 285.
8. *BM Egerton* 2027.
9. *Childe Harold's Pilgrimage*, Canto II, Note 7.
10. *BM Egerton* 2869. Byron to Clarke, 15 December 1813.
11. *Clarke, Travels*, Part II, Section 2, p. 484.
12. Ibid., Part II, Section 2, p. 485.
13. Hon. F. S. N. Douglas, *An Essay on Certain Points of Resemblance between the
    Ancient and Modern Greeks*, 1813, p. 89.
14. *Dodwell*, I, p. 324.
15. Ibid., I, p. 322.
16. *Hughes*, I, p. 261.
17. J. C. Eustace, *A Classical Tour through Italy*, 1813, II, p. 20.
18. Especially F. C. H. L. Pouqueville, *Voyage dans la Grèce*, 1820, IV, pp. 36, 74;
    J. L. S. Bartholdy, *Voyage en Grèce*, 1807, p. 45; and Forbin, *Voyage dans
    le Levant*, 1819, p. 11.
19. Chateaubriand, *Travels to Jerusalem*, 1835 edition, I, p. 187.
20. Hunt to Elgin, 22 May 1801. Elgin Papers.
21. William Black, *Narrative of Cruises in the Mediterranean*, 1900, p. 295.
    Black gives the date 1806 which is clearly impossible. Byron, *The Curse of
    Minerva*, 1812, Note 5.
22. Forbin, *Voyage dans le Levant*, 1819, p. 11. Compare *Dodwell*, I, p. 353,
    who read 'ΕΛΓΙΝΟΣ ΕΠΟΙΕΙ' and *Quarterly Review*, May 1820.
23. *Hobhouse*, p. 345. Many other references.
24. In Soane Notebooks, 13 August 1816, Sir John Soane Museum, London.
    Another version is quoted by *Gennadios*, p. 77. This couplet, said to have

been quoted by Byron, seems to have come from Archer Shee's *Rhymes On Art*. See *Medwin's Conversations of Lord Byron*, edited by Ernest J. Lovell Jr., 1966, p. 211.

25. *Smith*, p. 220, quoting W. Turner, *Tour in the Levant*, 1820, I, p. 347.
26. *BM Egerton* 2027.
27. T. Moore, *Byron*, chapter LXV.
28. Byron to Clarke, 27 May 1812. *BM Egerton* 2869 f 10.
29. Rogers' copy is in the British Museum.
30. *New Monthly Magazine*, April 1815, 'The Malediction of Minerva'.
31. [James and Horace Smith], *Horace in London*, 1813, Ode XV 'The Parthenon'.
32. A month after 'The Malediction of Minerva' was published in the *New Monthly Magazine* a correspondent had pointed out that the author was Byron, *New Monthly Magazine*, September 1815. Other versions of *The Curse* were published in London in 1816, 1818 and 1819. Full versions under Byron's name were published in the United States in 1815 and 1816.
33. John Galt, *Letters from the Levant*, 1813. Letter of 1 March 1810.
34. John Galt, *Autobiography*, 1833, chapter VII.
35. An edited version of the *Atheniad* is given in John Galt, *Autobiography*, 1833, chapter VII. Another version appeared in the *Monthly Magazine*, 49, 1820.
36. Elgin Papers.
37. John Galt, *Life of Byron*, 1830, p. 180.
38. For a discussion of this point see Terence Spencer, *Fair Greece, Sad Relic*, 1954, pp. 247 ff.
39. *A Letter from Athens addressed to a Friend in England*, 1812. T. Spencer, op. cit., p. 279, gives the author as Charles Kelsall.
40. William Haygarth, *Greece, a poem in three parts*, 1814.
41. Byron, *A Letter to **** ****** [John Murray] on the Rev. W. L. Bowles's Strictures on the Life and Writings of Pope*, 1821, p. 25.
42. Quoted in Byron, *A Self-Portrait*, edited by P. Quennell, 1950, I, p. 119.
43. This seems to have been Hamilton's explanation to Haydon. *Haydon, Diary*, IV, p. 594: 'October 27, 1839. Spent the greater part of the day with Hamilton—a delightful one. He let me into the secret of the opposition of Lord Elgin at the time. He said Lady Elgin's Friends who were Tories (the Manners) and Ferguson's friends who were Whigs were violent in the hatred of everything he did and made all that stir in opposition backed by the jealousy of connoisseurship.' Elgin's counsel accused Ferguson of deliberately attempting to misrepresent Elgin's public life in the trial of 1807. *Trial of R. J. Fergusson Esquire, c.* 1808, p. 9, and *Trial of R. Fergusson Esq.*, 1807, p. 8.
44. *BM Add.* 38266 f 5.

Chapter 18. Later Years in Greece

1. See *Cockerell*.
2. Ibid., p. 51.
3. *FO* 78/77. An edited version is in *Cockerell*, p. 56.
4. Quoted in *Smith*, p. 283.
5. See *Cockerell* and 'Papers on Aegina Marbles' in BM Greek and Roman Department.
6. *Smith*, pp. 284, 314. *HMC, Report on the Laing Mss preserved in the University of Edinburgh*, 1914–1925, II, p. 757.
7. 'Papers on Aegina Marbles' in BM Greek and Roman Department.
8. *Cockerell*, p. 219.
9. Apart from the usual sources, two more friendly accounts of Lusieri's last years are worthy of notice. John Bramsen, *Letters of a Prussian Traveller*, 1818; John Fuller, *Narrative of a Tour through some parts of the Turkish Empire*, 1830. See also the Ms journals of Byron's friend Hanson in *BM Add.*, 38591 and 38592, and of Rev. Robert Master in *BM Add.*, 51313.
10. *Walsh*, I, p. 126.
11. *Hughes*, I, p. 267.
12. H. W. Williams, *Travels in Italy, Greece and the Ionian Isles*, 1820, II, p. 361.
13. *Gennadios*, p. 40.
14. Ibid., p. 77.
15. Richard Monkton Milnes (Lord Houghton), *Memorials of a Tour in Some Parts of Greece*, 1834, p. 133. M. B. Poujoulat, *Voyages dans l'Asie Mineure*, 1840, p. 5.
16. William Haygarth, *Greece, a poem in three parts*, 1814, II, ll. 222 ff.
17. *Childe Harold's Pilgrimage*, Canto II. 'Papers referred to by Note 33'.
18. Ibid.
19. Ibid.
20. *Select Committee Report*, p. 144.
21. Ibid., p. 57.
22. For example Hon. F. S. N. Douglas, *An Essay on Certain Points of Resemblance between the Ancient and Modern Greeks*, 1813, p. 85; *Hughes*, I, p. 259; L. Dupré, *Voyage à Athènes*, 1825, p. 36; and H. W. Williams, *Travels in Italy, Greece and the Ionian Islands*, 1820, II, p. 307.
23. *Hobhouse*, p. 348.
24. Hunt Papers. Elsewhere Hunt describes Benizelos as 'the sole representative of all the ancient philosophers of his country'. 'Notes on Travelling in the Levant.' Hunt Papers.
25. *Gennadios*, p. 2.
26. *Hobhouse*, p. 347.
27. G. P. Stevens and others, *The Erechtheum*, 1927, pp. 536 ff.
28. For example, in Stuart and Revett, *Antiquities of Athens*, III; *Clarke, Travels*, Part II, Section 2, p. 544; Lusieri's drawing in *Smith*; Pomardi, *Viaggio*

Nella Grecia, 1820, p. 146; and Cassas et Bence, *Grandes Vues Pittoresques des Principaux Sites et Monumens de la Grèce*, 1813.

29. *Hughes*, I, p. 266.

30. Peter Edmund Laurent, *Recollections of a Classical Tour*, 1821, p. 110. H. W. Williams (op. cit., p. 316) also mentions the destruction of the Caryatids by British midshipmen.

31. *Select Committee Report*, pp. 24, 118. A. Michaelis, *Der Parthenon*, 1871, discusses the fate of these two heads. See also a letter of Fauvel in *Bulletin de la Société Nationale des Antiquaires de la France*, 1900, p. 245, and note 28 to Chapter 15.

32. J. C. Hobhouse, *Recollections of a Long Life*, 1909, I, p. 26.

33. This comparison is very well illustrated in the *Illustrated London News*, 18 May 1920. Further damage from air pollution has occurred since then.

34. *Revue Archéologique*, XXXI, p. 94. Forbin, *Voyage dans le Levant*, 1819, p. 14.

35. Two pieces of metope and one of frieze were presented by J. J. Dubois in 1840; a fragment of the frieze was bought at the sale of the Pourtales collection in 1865. Several pieces of the frieze from a private collection in Karlsruhe also came into the Museum's collection. A. H. Smith, *Catalogue of Sculpture in the Department of Greek and Roman Antiquities, British Museum*, I, 1892.

36. *Cockerell*, p. 262.

37. Sir Robert Smirke, Ms Notes of Journal in Greece, Library of Royal Institute of British Architects, London.

38. Quoted in *Smith*, p. 287.

39. *Walsh*, I, p. 125; *Adventures of a Greek Lady, the adopted daughter of the late Queen Caroline Written by Herself*, 1849, p. 111.

40. Ibid., p. 111; *Voyages and Travels of H.M. Caroline Queen of Great Britain by one of her suite*, 1823, pp. 436 ff.

41. Doctor Meryon, *Travels of Lady Hester Stanhope*, 1846, III, p. 168.

Chapter 19. Lord Elgin Tries Again

1. Three drawings showing the Elgin Marbles at Burlington House in 1816 are in the Print Collection of the Greater London Council. Two of them are reproduced in Plates VI (*a*) and (*b*). See also *Haydon, Diary*, I, p. 441.

2. See Rupert Gunnis, *Dictionary of British Sculptors 1660–1851*, n.d. Further information about Henning and the Elgin Marbles is in his evidence to the Select Committee on Arts and Manufactures. *Parliamentary Papers*, V, 1835.

3. *Smith*, p. 317.

4. Stuart and Revett, *Antiquities of Athens*, IV, p. 25.

5. See *Smith*, p. 362. For the reference to the 'negotiant Cairac' which Smith could not explain see the quotation in G. P. Stevens, *The Erechtheum*, 1927,

p. 593. Choiseul-Gouffier's fragment of the frieze was stored in his warehouse in 1789.

6. Choiseul-Gouffier, *Voyage Pittoresque de la Grèce*, II, p. 85.

7. *Memorandum*, 1815 edition, p. 78.

8. Quoted in *Smith*, p. 322.

9. Hamilton to Elgin, 13 February 1810; Elgin to Hamilton, 18 April 1815; and Aberdeen to Elgin, 16 April 1816. Elgin Papers.

10. Hansard, ccci, p. 828.

11. *Two Memoirs read to the Royal Institute of France on the Sculptures in the Collection of the Earl of Elgin by the Chevalier E. Q. Visconti.* Printed with the *Select Committee Report*, 1816.

12. Ibid., p. 46.

13. Quoted in *Smith*, p. 333.

14. *Haydon, Autobiography*, p. 224. See also *Farington*, 22 November 1815 (published).

15. *Select Committee Report*, p. xxiii.

16. In the *Autobiography* this incident is put in February 1816 during the Select Committee sittings. It is clear from the *Diary*, I, p. 488 that the marbles arrived in December 1815.

17. Quoted in *Haydon, Autobiography*, p. 231.

18. Ibid., p. 231.

19. *Diary and Correspondence of Charles Abbott, Lord Colchester*, 1861, II, p. 564.

20. *Library of Entertaining Knowledge: Elgin and Phigaleian Marbles*, 1833, I, p. 10.

21. *Haydon, Autobiography*, p.226.

22. *Haydon, Diary*, I, p. 439.

23. *Library of Entertaining Knowledge: Elgin and Phigaleian Marbles*, 1833, II, p. 107.

24. *Haydon, Autobiography*, p. 223.

Chapter 20. Tweddell J. and Tweddell R.

1. *Edinburgh Review*, no. 50. October 1815.

2. *Christian Observer*, June 1815.

3. *New Monthly Magazine*, November 1815.

4. Quoted in *Tweddell, Remains*, following title page.

5. William Haygarth: *Greece, a poem in three parts*, 1814, II, ll. 347 ff.

6. *Tweddell, Remains*, p. 15.

7. W. B. Dinsmoor, 'Observations on the Hephaisteion', *Hesperia, Supplement V*, 1941, p. 16. Dinsmoor notes that Tweddell's Greek epitaph is referred to by numerous travellers but the Latin version by none. He suggests that this reticence was due to the hostility of the travellers to anything connected with Lord Elgin. That the two versions did in fact exist side by side in the Theseum is, however, proved by a reference in the Ms Journal of Rev. Robert Master *BM Add.*, 51313.

8. *Naval Chronicle*, xxiii, quoted in *Tweddell, Remains*.
9. *Elgin, Letter*, pp. 21 ff.
10. *Naval Chronicle*, January–June 1816; also July–September 1816.
11. *Clarke, Travels*, Part II, Section 2, p. 533
12. Ibid., Part II, Section 3, p. 389.
13. [James and Horace Smith] *Horace in London*, 1813, Ode XV, 'The Parthenon'.
14. Quoted in T. Moore, *Byron*, chapter XVI.
15. *New Monthly Magazine*, January 1815.
16. That Philalethes was Hamilton and that he did not guess the identity of T. is clear from a letter of Hamilton to Elgin 14 February 1815. Elgin Papers.
17. *Elgin, Postscript*, p. 32.
18. *Christian Observer*, August 1815.
19. *Quarterly Review*, October 1816.
20. *Naval Chronicle*, July–September 1816.
21. Ibid.; Rev. Robert Tweddell, *Account of the Examination of the Elgin Box at the Foreign Office in Downing Street on 7 Nov. 1816*, 1816.

Chapter 21. The Fate of the Manuscripts

1. *Clarke, Travels*, Part II, Section 3, p. 389.
2. Rev. Philip Hunt, *A Narrative of What is Known Respecting the Literary Remains of the late John Tweddell*, 1816, p. 46.
3. W. Otter, *Life and Remains of Rev. Edward Daniel Clarke*, 1824, p. 562.
4. The figure is not certain. Miss Carlyle gave thirty-seven Mss to Lambeth excluding the Eutropius but at least one of these belonged to Carlyle before his journey.
5. *Walpole, Memoirs*, pp. 163, 183.
6. Ibid., p. 176.
7. Philip Hunt to Robert Liston giving a résumé of the whole story, 20 June 1817. NLS 5645 f 210. Some official correspondence, including a copy of Carlyle and Hunt's certificate to the Patriarch is in FO 78/83, 87 and 89.
8. Carlyle Mss. Ipswich and East Suffolk Record Office. Undated Memorandum by Carlyle HA 174:1026/68/10.
9. For example in *Quarterly Review*, April 1818.
10. *Todd, Catalogue*, p.v.
11. Ibid., p. iv.
12. J. D. Carlyle, *Poems*, 1805.
13. The Account of the sale of the Mss is mainly in *Todd, Account*. Further information is in NLS 5645 f 210.
14. *Todd, Account*, p. 38.
15. NLS 5645 f 210.
16. *Todd, Catalogue*, p. iv.

17. *Todd, Account*, p. 68.
18. *Walpole, Memoirs*, p. 183.
19. Rev. Philip Hunt, *A Narrative of What is Known Respecting the Literary Remains of the Late John Tweddell*, 1816, p. 36. Thomas Lacy to Hunt, 20 June 1800. Hunt Papers.

Chapter 22. The Marbles are Sold

1. Hansard, xxxii, p. 577, 15 February 1816.
2. Ibid., p. 824, 23 February 1816.
3. Hon. F. S. N. Douglas, *An Essay on Certain Points of Resemblance between the Ancient and Modern Greeks*, 1813.
4. *Select Committee Report*, p. 31.
5. Ibid., p. 45.
6. Ibid., pp. vii ff.
7. Ibid., p. xvii.
8. *Haydon, Autobiography*, p. 232.
9. *Select Committee Report*, p. 67.
10. Ibid., p. 70.
11. Ibid., p. 81.
12. Ibid., p. 83.
13. Ibid., p. 90.
14. Ibid., p. 92.
15. *Haydon, Autobiography*, p. 232.
16. Ibid., p. 233.
17. Ibid., p. 239. See also A. Michaelis, *Ancient Marbles in Great Britain*, 1882, p. 148.
18. *Farington*, 10 April 1816 (unpublished).
19. *Quarterly Review*, 28 May 1816; *Farington*, 6 June 1816 (unpublished). Payne Knight replied in an anonymous pamphlet reproduced largely in the *Examiner*, 7 April 1816, and *Classical Journal*, 1816, p. 98. Visconti's Ms reply is in the Gennadios Library, Athens.
20. *Examiner*, 28 April 1816
21. Ibid., 19 May 1816.
22. *Farington*, 10 April 1816 (unpublished).
23. Ibid.
24. *Haydon, Diary*, II, p. 12. Entry for 10 April 1816.
25. *Haydon, Diary*, I, p. 442. Entry for 13 May 1815.
26. *Smith*, p. 342.
27. Hansard, xxxiv, pp. 1027–40.
28. Cap. XCIX of 56th year of George III.
29. *Smith*, p. 332; W. T. Whitley, *Art in England 1800–1820*, 1928, p. 261.
30. Elgin to Lord Liverpool, 18 April 1817. *BM Add.*, 38266 f 5.

Chapter 23. Last Days

1. *Select Committee Report*, p. 27.
2. *Examiner*, 16 June 1816.
3. For example: *The Elgin Marbles . . . selected from Stuart's and Revett's Antiquities of Athens . . . with Report of Select Committee*, 1816; Rev. E. I. Burrow, *The Elgin Marbles*, 1817; J. L. Combe, *A Brief Account of the Marbles collected by Lord Elgin at Athens*, 1817; William Sharp, *Elgin Marbles, a series of outline drawings*, 1817; and Richard Lawrence, *Elgin Marbles*, 1818.
4. *Description of the Collection of Ancient Marbles in the British Museum*, 1812–1861.
5. See H. Trevelyan, *Goethe and the Greeks*, 1941.
6. J. T. Smith, *Nollekens and His Times*, I, p. 289.
7. Byron: *Letter to ***** ******* [John Murray] on Rev. W. L. Bowles's Strictures on the Life and Writings of Pope*, 1821, p. 27, where the Elgin Marbles are listed with the Apollo Belvedere, the Laocoon, Venus dei Medici etc.
8. *Haydon, Diary*. Entry for 31 December 1816.
9. For Haydon see his *Autobiography* and *Diary*; for West see Grose Evans, *Benjamin West and the Taste of his Times*, 1959.
10. For Pistrucci's Waterloo Medal see Cornelius Vermeule, *European Art and the Classical Past*, 1964.
11. *Report of the Select Committee on Arts and Manufactures*. Parliamentary Papers, V, 1835.
12. Elgin to Peel, 27 August 1822, *BM Add.*, 40350 ff 193, 195, 199.
13. *Letter from W. R. Hamilton to the Earl of Elgin in the New Houses of Parliament*, 1836; *Second Letter from W. R. H. Esq. to the Earl of Elgin on the propriety of adopting the Greek Style of Architecture in the Construction of the New Houses of Parliament*, 1836; *Third Letter from W. R. H. Esq. to the Earl of Elgin on the propriety of adopting the Greek Style of Architecture in preference to the Gothic etc.*, 1837.
14. See M. A. Goldberg, 'John Keats and the Elgin Marbles', *Apollo*, November 1965, and S. A. Larrabee, *English Bards and Grecian Marbles*, 1943.
15. William Sharp, *Life and Letters of Joseph Severn*, 1892, p. 32.
16. The account for Elgin's Embassy is among the Elgin Papers. Some details are in *FO* 78/89. A statement of the history of Elgin's finances dated 1 May 1835 is among the Elgin Papers.
17. *Smith*, p. 365. See also *The Banks Letters*, edited by Warren R. Dawson, 1958, p. 100.
18. L. J. J. Dubois, *Catalogue d'Antiquités . . . formant la collection de . . . M. le Comte de Choiseul-Gouffier*, Paris, 1818. Elgin is called '*un spéculateur anglais, [qui avait] entendu vanter le prix des sculptures*'.
19. *Description of the Collection of Ancient Marbles in the British Museum*, VII, 1835, p. 28.

20. For example, R. C. Lucas, *Remarks on the Parthenon*, 1845, p. 29; E. Edwards, *Lives of the Founders of the British Museum*, 1870, I, p. 384; and L. Pingaud, *Choiseul-Gouffier, la France en Orient sous Louis XVI*, 1887, p. 162.

21. *Smith*, p. 357.

22. *NLS* 45649 ff 127–8.

23. Ms Journal of a Tour in Egypt, Palestine and Greece in 1819, by Rev. Robert Master, *BM Add.*, 51313.

24. *Dodwell*, I, p. 353; *Hughes*, I, p. 260; and W. G. Black, *Narrative of Cruises in the Mediterranean*, 1900, p. 149.

25. *Walsh*, I, p. 122.

26. Richard Monkton Milnes (Lord Houghton), *Memorials of a Tour in Some Parts of Greece*, 1834, p. 130.

27. See Virginia Penn, 'Philhellenism in England', *Slavonic Review*, 14, p. 363.

28. E.g. *NLS* 1055 f 118 (1821); 1055 f 120 (1824).

29. *Specimens of Antient Sculpture*, II, 1835, p. liv.

30. Quoted in Cust and Colvin, *History of the Society of Dilettanti*, 1898, p. 173; in *Historical Notices of the Society of Dilettanti* (by Hamilton), 1855, p. 101; and *Smith*, p. 368. The *Historical Notices* quotes another letter from Elgin on the same occasion.

Chapter 24. Epilogue

1. [Frederick von Suckow], *The Shadow of Lord Byron or The Voice of the Akropolis to the British Nation*, 1835. A copy of this interesting pamphlet is in the Gennadios Library, Athens.

2. See George Karo, 'The Problem of the Elgin Marbles' in *Studies presented to D. M. Robinson*, 1951–53; *Gennadios*, pp. 211 ff; besides the occasions mentioned in these works the British newspapers discussed the matter on numerous occasions when Greece has been in the public eye—for example in the 1924 centenary of Byron's death; the 1926 rebuilding of the north colonnade of the Parthenon; the 1939 cleaning of the Elgin Marbles; and the 1941 war in Greece.

3. For example Sir Roger Casement, Harold Nicolson, Jacob Epstein, Robert Byron, Lord Esher, Compton Mackenzie, Lawrence Durrell, Lord Belhaven (great grandson of W. R. Hamilton), and Furneaux Jordan.

4. Winter Words 'Christmas in the Elgin Room'.

5. Hansard, (Commons), 23 January 1941.

6. Ibid., 9 May 1961.

7. *The Times* leader, 10 May 1961, 'Bought and Paid For'.

8. Hansard (Commons), 1 July 1965.

Index

OXFORD PAPERBACKS

The Greeks

Kenneth Dover

In this lively, authoritative and stimulating book one of our foremost Greek scholars shows what it meant and felt like to be Greek, and what the importance of the Greeks is to us today. He describes how they thought and lived, and examines their distinctive and rewarding approach to history, poetry, art and philosophy. He makes clear how radically new and different Greek civilisation was, and how, no matter how much we may have learned since their day, the way we think and organise our lives is still profoundly affected by Greek ideas.

OXFORD PAPERBACKS

Ancient Greek Literature

Kenneth Dover and others

Kenneth Dover and three other classical scholars have collaborated in writing this historical survey of Greek literature from 700 BC to AD 550. The book concentrates on the principal authors and quotes many passages from their work in translation to allow the reader to form his own impression of its quality. Attention is drawn to the elements in Greek literature and attitudes to life which are unfamiliar to us, and to those elements which have appealed most powerfully to succeeding generations. Poetry, tragedy, comedy, history, science, philosophy, and oratory are all examined through the available literature.

Homer

Jasper Griffin

The *Iliad* and the *Odyssey* stand at the very beginning of Greek literature. Much has been written about their origins and authorship, but Jasper Griffin, although he touches briefly on those questions, is here concerned with the ideas of the poems, which have had such an incalculable influence on the thought and literature of the West. He shows that each of the two epics has its own coherent and suggestive view of the world and of man's place within it.

'a brilliant little introduction' *The Times*

'Mr Griffin brings English scholarship up to date by bringing it firmly back to Homer.' *London Review of Books*

OXFORD PAPERBACKS

The Fire and the Sun
Why Plato Banished the Artists

Iris Murdoch

New Society described this book on its first publication in 1977 as 'a triumph of lucid and light-textured compression as well as of vividly illustrated relevance to our own world'. Based on the author's 1976 Romanes Lecture, *The Fire and the Sun* offers a coherent and fully argued account of Plato's theories of art and of beauty and of their metaphysical background, and also shows that Plato was aware of the dangers of his own artistry. The argument more widely concerns the place of art in life, and includes brief discussions of the ideas of many other thinkers, including Kant, Tolstoy, Freud, and Kierkegaard.

OXFORD PAPERBACKS

Praeterita
An Autobiography

John Ruskin

Praeterita is one of the most remarkable autobiographies of the nineteenth century. Written in the 1880s in the periods of calm between Ruskin's attacks of brain fever, it gives a fascinating account of his upbringing in a severely respectable Victorian household, his Continental travels, his friends and relations, and the development and refinement of his aesthetic tastes.

As Kenneth Clark remarks in his Introduction, '*Praeterita* is the only one of Ruskin's works intended to give pleasure'.

Vision & Design

Roger Fry

Roger Fry's trenchant rejection of nineteenth-century Academicians was part of his attempt to open the eyes of a whole generation to the special formal properties of art. The range of his interests was enormous: the twenty-five essays included in this collection cover topics from Negro art to Giotto and from William Blake to contemporary domestic architecture. Among the central themes explored by Fry are the relationships between ancient and modern art, and between art and life.

OXFORD PAPERBACKS

Eothen

or Traces of Travel Brought Home from the East

Alexander Kinglake

New introduction by Jan Morris

Eothen is among the most idiosyncratic and witty travel books ever written. Alexander Kinglake visited the Near East in the 1830s, making notes and sketches of all he saw. A highly unconventional traveller, he revelled in the exotic and dangerous atmosphere of the East. His book ran through six editions almost immediately and, as Jan Morris says in her introduction, it has cast 'a sort of spell over the genre from that day to this'.

A complete list of Oxford Paperbacks, including books in the World's Classics, Past Masters, and OPUS series, can be obtained from the General Publicity Department, Oxford University Press, Walton Street, Oxford OX2 6DP.